The Eighteenth Century Short Title Catalogue

And though it be vnperfect, as I know not what
first Booke either of Dictionarie, or Herball, or
such like was perfect at the first or second edition,
yet he that helpeth me to put in one Booke that
I haue not seene, I hope that I shall shew him ten
that he neuer heard of.

Andrew Maunsell
*The First Part of the Catalogue
of English Printed Bookes,* 1595.

BIBLIOGRAPHY
MACHINE READABLE CATALOGUING
AND
THE ESTC

A Summary History of the
Eighteenth Century Short Title Catalogue

Working Methods

Cataloguing Rules

A Catalogue of the Works of Alexander Pope
Printed between 1711 and 1800 in the
British Library

By

R. C. ALSTON & M. J. JANNETTA

THE BRITISH LIBRARY
1978

THE EIGHTEENTH CENTURY SHORT TITLE CATALOGUE

British Library Cataloguing in Publication Data

Alston, Robin Carfrae
Bibliography, machine-readable cataloguing and the ESTC.
1. Eighteenth Century Short Title Catalogue Project
2. Pope, Alexander—Bibliography—Catalogs
3. British Library. Department of Printed Books—Catalogs
I. Title II. Jannetta, M. J. III. British Library.
Reference Division
025.3'028'5442   Z699.4.E/

ISBN 0-904654-17-6

Set in Monophoto Baskerville.
Designed at The Janus Studio, Ilkley.

Printed at Grove Press Ltd., Ilkley, Yorkshire.

Published by The British Library
Great Russell Street London WC1B 3DG

Table of Contents

Acknowledgements

Many friends and colleagues have contributed, in one way or another, to this book and it is difficult here to do justice to their several contributions. Only those who are familiar with the ESTC can appreciate the debt I owe to the team of enthusiastic young scholars in the British Library who have given unselfishly their energy and enthusiasm to the project. Two of them, Michael Crump and Jane Douglas, have been associated with ESTC since the first pilot project; three, Patrick Vasey, Frances Harris and Susan Jeffs since the second; the remaining seven joined after October 1977—Helen Smith, Bridget Ikin, Christine Ferdinand, Johan Zeeman, Nicholas Savage, Alan Sterenberg, and Richard Goulden. It is difficult to estimate the contribution of Neil Dickinson who has carried out, with unfailing efficiency and good humour, the multitude of tasks heaped on him, and has been responsible for the maintenance of the files so vital to the project.

To three people in particular I owe a debt which no words are adequate to express. To Laurence Wood, who retired as Keeper of Printed Books in 1976 and has, from the beginning, made available to the project his intimate knowledge of the Library, and his skill as a cataloguer. On countless occasions his experience, knowledge and tact have helped to maintain the forward thrust of a project which necessarily, at times, conflicts with the day-to-day running of a large and complex institution. To Mervyn Jannetta who has, since the summer of 1977, thrown all his energies and skills into ESTC, and shares the burden of solving the daily problems associated with its development. In supervising and editing the catalogue of Pope's works printed in this book he has given us all an ideal to strive after, and if that specimen of ESTC's ultimate ambitions is judged worthy, then the credit is his. To Don Richnell, Director General of the Reference Division, who has bestowed upon this project innumerable blessings, and whose wisdom and experience has, from the beginning, been quite indispensable.

Only those who understand the workings of an institution as large and complex as the British Library will be able to comprehend the debt we all owe to the staff of virtually every department within its structure for their help and cooperation. Without exception they have accommodated cheerfully the extra demands which ESTC has placed upon them and their contribution has been a substantial one.

Since this book attempts, in part, to provide a summary of the ways in which ESTC has grown since June 1976 to become a significant contribution to retrospective union cataloguing, it is a pleasant duty to record here the encouraging support we have received from numerous individuals in libraries and universities throughout the British Isles. Some measure of the recognition that ESTC is now established as a national project may be gained from the contributions made to it by the three great research libraries at Oxford, Cambridge and Manchester; and their example is now being followed by a growing number of libraries of every type and size.

For permission to reproduce a number of items in this book, I am grateful to the Curators of the Bodleian Library.

June, 1978.   R. C. Alston.

Foreword

ESTC has already established itself as the accepted abbreviation for an Eighteenth Century English Short Title Catalogue, which is now in process of compilation. Although this process is still in its first phase, it is clear that even the longer title is, in some senses, a misnomer, since the Catalogue like previous STCs will include many works not in English, and has already moved far from the modest claim of 'Short Title'. These and other points are explained in the pages that follow.

The book here presented is not in any sense a definitive history of the ESTC project; it is more a field report. For although the project has been well-publicised in some quarters, it is still only in its early stages, and there is a need for continuing reports on progress, so that the historians, librarians and bibliographers who may be called on to participate at some stage and who will certainly all be the beneficiaries of its development, can support it with an understanding of what is being done.

The British Library has been fortunate in having been able to make the initial contribution the creation of a machine-readable 'base-file' of the largest single collection of eighteenth century English printed material in the world. When this idea was first mooted, there was a justifiable uncertainty as to whether the mammoth task could be accomplished except over a period of many years; now, however, with the task well under way, there are few who doubt that the base-file will be completed and available in the early 1980s. If this target can be achieved, the British Library record will provide an instrument by which the recording of the holdings of other libraries can be facilitated; thus providing not only a catalogue of all known eighteenth century English material, but a union list of libraries' holdings in all parts of the world.

This initial contribution has naturally involved experiment and trial and error. Because of the importance of the lessons that are being learned from the experience in the British Library, we have felt justified in producing this book, and in presenting it under a title that draws attention not only to the project itself, but to the implications it has for bibliographers dealing with the recording of other printed material in machine-readable form.

There is no attempt here to produce a blue-print for the future management of the whole project. It has been an Anglo-American project from its inception, and it is intended that it will continue to evolve as such. But it is more than that, since it has already engaged the interest and co-operation of many other countries with significant holdings of pre-1800 English-language material, and this active involvement will certainly be encouraged.

D. T. Richnell

Director-General, British Library Reference Division
Chairman, Anglo-American Organising Committee, ESTC

Glossary

The following abbreviations are used in the text of this book:

AACR: Anglo-American Cataloguing Rules.

AACR2: Anglo-American Cataloguing Rules (second revised edition in preparation).

AIPP: American Imprints Publication Project.

ASECS: American Society for Eighteenth-Century Studies.

BALLOTS: Bibliographic Automation of Large Library Operations Using Time-Sharing Systems. Based at Standford University.

BLAISE: British Library Automated Information Service.

GK: British Museum, *General Catalogue*.

GK1: The first printed version of the *General Catalogue* (1881-   ).

GK2: The revision of the printed *General Catalogue* A-DEZ.

GK3: The lithographic reprint of the *General Catalogue* (1955-   ) and *Supplements*.

LOC: London-Oxford-Cambridge Project LOC investigated means of compiling a machine-readable union catalogue of pre-1801 books in Oxford, Cambridge and the British Museum.

LOCAS: Local Cataloguing Service. The British Library.

MARC: Machine-Readable Cataloguing (UK and US versions).

NEH: The National Endowment for the Humanities, Washington.

NUC: *National Union Catalog Pre-1956 Imprints* (Mansell, 1968-   ).

NYPL: The New York Public Library.

OCLC: Ohio College Library Center (on-line cataloguing facility). Based at Columbus, Ohio.

STC: A. W. Pollard and F. R. Redgrave, *A Short-Title Catalogue of Books printed in England, Scotland and Ireland . . . 1475-1640*. London, 1926. Revised edition in progress.

Wing: D. Wing, *Short-Title Catalogue of Books printed in England, Scotland, Ireland, Wales and British America . . . 1641-1700*. New York, 1945-51. Revised edition in progress.

The Eighteenth-Century Short-Title Catalogue

Beginnings

The Eighteenth-Century Short-Title Catalogue (now generally referred to as ESTC), as it is at present being developed in the Reference Division of the British Library, was conceived as an Anglo-American project at a conference held at the British Library in June 1976.* The conference was sponsored jointly by the British Library and the National Endowment for the Humanities in Washington, and was attended by over forty distinguished librarians, bibliographers, and computer experts. The body chiefly responsible for bringing the conference into being was the American Society for Eighteenth Century Studies (ASECS), and in the submission to the National Endowment for the Humanities *(A Feasibility Study for an Eighteenth-Century British Short-Title Catalogue)* Paul Korshin wrote as follows:

> An Eighteenth-Century STC would be a large and complicated research tool in the following ways: (1) the funding necessary for its implementation would be substantial; (2) the project would involve the collective efforts of many researchers working in a number of countries; and (3) the work would take at least a decade to complete.
>
> In attempting to devise a feasible plan for this project, the ASECS has had the cooperation of numerous scholars and librarians, since June 1975, in the United States and Great Britain; much additional cooperation will be needed in the next eighteen months to two years. An Eighteenth-Century STC seems so important to the ASECS and to the humanistic and library communities in the United States and Great Britain that we believe it is desirable to give a proposal dealing with it the maximum possible preparation and the fullest possible consultation and discussion. For almost two decades, there has been much discussion in the United States and Great Britain about the value and feasibility of such a research tool; it appears clear that its use would be widespread.
>
> An Eighteenth-Century STC would be of immense value to scholars in many disciplines of the humanities, social sciences, and natural sciences, for it would provide a ready guide to and much bibliographical information concerning upwards of half a millon titles in all of these fields. Every scholar and student in every aspect of eighteenth-century studies, whether in language and literature, history, economics, and other aspects of the social sciences, would benefit from its existence. Librarians and rare-book cataloguers would benefit immeasurably: libraries would profit from having their 1701–1800 contents added to a national data base, and rare-book cataloguers would gain invaluable assistance for their work. . . The task of research into all aspects of the eighteenth century, and indeed in historical research generally, would be simplified by the existence of such a research tool . . .
>
> In any scholarly project of the magnitude of an Eighteenth-Century STC, it is inevitable that a feasibility study must face, and prepare solutions to, a number of critical questions concerning geographical and chronological scope, methodology, the use of computers, personnel, libraries, and funding. This proposal is not meant to answer those questions. Its purpose is to provide a rationale for a feasibility study only. That study, which will include an international STC Conference at London in June 1976, is intended to do two things: (1) to provide answers to the questions upon which a London conference can come to agreement within a five-day meeting; and (2) in the case of questions which are too complicated to be solved in such a conference, to exclude irrelevant approaches and to isolate the most important problems which an STC Project must face.

The *Feasibility Study* is, in the light of subsequent developments, an enlightening document to re-read, for it demonstrates convincingly the doubts and uncertainties

*Under the joint chairmanship of Sir Frank Francis, former Director of the British Museum, and Douglas Bryant, Director of Harvard University Library.

1

which were to be expressed repeatedly in the papers presented to the conference. Given even a collective determination to succeed supported by enthusiasm, intellectual commitment to a bibliographical ideal and the realisation that failure now, after so many previous failures,* would be final, it is clear that neither the planners of the June Conference nor its delegates possessed clear answers to a number of questions of crucial importance. No one present at the June Conference could estimate the magnitude of the project: its scope (what it would include and what exclude) was the subject of animated discussion; its methodology was undecided; the precise use to which computer technology might be put was largely unknown; and over all the debates hung the unanswered question as to the physical location of a project of such unprecedented proportions. The oracles remained mute.

The agenda for the conference, as distributed to delegates, was as follows: *Definitions, Scope and Coverage of the STC* (June 14); *Cataloguing Methodology* (June 15–16); *Libraries and their Problems with Respect to the STC* (June 16); *Organizing and Managing an STC Project with Special Reference to the Planning Phase* (June 17); *Appointment of the Provisional Organizing Committee, Approval of the Drafting Committee, Conference Review* (June 18). For reasons which are perfectly understandable the only day which conformed to the published agenda was the last: delegates were quick to perceive the fact that since every consideration about scope, methodology or management involved inter-reactive consequences, promiscuous debate was both inevitable and constructive. The formal minutes of the conference reflect clearly the apparent obscurity of purpose surrounding many of the daily discussions. The progress of events since June 1976 has, it is true, contributed answers to the many unresolved questions and reassuring solutions to the many expressed doubts and anxieties, but the conference fulfilled its objectives more than adequately by merely raising them: it was, after all, an elaborate exercise in exploring problems rather than an occasion during which definitive procedures would be formulated.

Although scheduled to occupy the first day of the conference, the scope and coverage of the ESTC presented opportunities for discussion throughout the week. Broadly speaking, debate focused on two principal aspects: geographical origin and type of material. While it was agreed by all that printing within the British Isles, in whatever language, should be included, there was much argument about the necessity to include printing in North America (since it was well documented) and other territories under British dominion during the eighteenth century. There were ample opportunities for those with a sound historical sense to engage in entertaining explorations of the difficulties which might have to be faced in deciding upon the inclusion or exclusion of material from such unstable territories as French India, Trinidad, Malta and Tranquebar. Would printing in English from any country be included, and how much of it was there? Inclusiveness, happily, seemed to be the only practicable principle to apply, and Nicolas Barker summed up the consensus as follows:

> I believe it will be simplest to try and include all books printed in "colonies" or "possessions", no matter when in the eighteenth century the territory became a British possession, or even if it was only partly a British possession. This would include printing in French and Spanish on the North American continent (well recorded already and therefore easy), and all printing in India. This latter would demand the inclusion of the Danish press at Tranquebar (well recorded and small) and also Portuguese and French printing in Southern India (less well recorded, but not on the face of it difficult). I am working on the assumption that the number of items involved is small, and that it is easier to tell some one who is combing a library or catalogue that all Trinidad or Madras imprints are in, than to say "only Trinidad after 1797", or "only books in English or from the English press at Madras".

*Discussed in some detail in the *Feasibility Study*

Scope, in terms of types of printed material, proved less easy to determine. There were those who argued forcibly for the exclusion of all material deemed "ephemeral", in spite of the self-evident fact that some very important literary texts first appeared in an "ephemeral" format. Was selection of material to be made on a subjective basis? The late Graham Pollard spoke eloquently about the importance of much material commonly regarded as the "ragged edge", and though aware of the necessity to exclude items of virtually negligible significance (blank forms, tickets, etc.) urged the conference not to adopt a too rigid definition of ephemera. Historians were, he said, increasingly aware of the value of much apparently trivial printed matter, and the inclusion of such material would constitute a significant proportion of previously unrecorded items.

Discussion about cataloguing methodology predictably focused on the use of the computer and the precise nature of the entry. Should the basic data be derived from library catalogues, or should at least one copy of every item be examined? Should the entries be, as have been those of previous short-title catalogues, brief, or should they approximate to the length and detail of a MARC record? In an exercise performed during the weeks prior to the conference R. C. Alston had attempted to compile a catalogue of the works of Addison printed before 1800, based on available printed catalogues and the answers to a questionnaire distributed to eighty libraries within the British Isles. The results of his survey demonstrated convincingly that nothing short of muddle would result from any such approach, especially since the process involved matching unknown quantities. Those who advocated the superficially appealing approach of starting with the holdings of the British Library (as represented in the General Catalogue), to which might be added titles and locations listed in the National Union Catalogue, ran the risk, he warned, of creating a bibliographic file which, however useful, would in any case require subsequent revision based on examination of the books. Such a procedure with over half a million entries involved, would be irresponsible. The official minutes record that: "Other members of the Conference, however, felt that this examination would involve an unacceptable amount of time and money; that the existing catalogues formed an adequate initial data base and that, once in machine-readable form, records could be amended and modified comparatively easily at any stage."

On the following day the conference considered the implications of a paper presented by Richard Christophers in which he commented:

It is reasonable for the British Library to consider how far the content parameters of the 18th century STC are relevant to its broader requirements, given that access to the Library's reference collections via a catalogue of the highest possible bibliographical standard is an objective of prime importance. It is conceivable that the Library would contribute to the construction of a bibliographical work which would have no impact, except indirectly, on the usefulness and use of its own catalogue and its own books, but an integration of the two aims would increase the yield from work done. It would be regrettable if this opportunity were missed because of an accidental dissociation between antiquarian bibliographers and the practitioners of modern catalogue production and maintenance. The necessary record for a short-title catalogue may be defined as the shortest possible meaningful title (taken from the opening words of the titlepage) together with author statement, imprint and format: beyond this "points" may have to be given in note form to distinguish otherwise identical works. An STC is traditionally concerned more with physical bibliographical identification than with establishing the corpus of an author's work and giving some indication of its intellectual content, which are two functions of a library catalogue. It follows that a catalogue such as that of the British Library would need more elaboration in the title, collation and descriptive notes fields, additional apparatus for collocation of editions, collections, etc., in a structured order, and means of clearly identifying authors not only for 18th century works individually but also in the context of the complete catalogue. Certain methodological points emerge here. Within the criteria stated above for STCs, it would seem that the eventual length of an STC record when it appears cannot be determined until all, or a representative number of copies, states, variants, etc., have been examined. Meanwhile, the library catalogue will require entries which carry an amount of bibliographical detail commensurate with the criteria for the whole catalogue, as well as those "points" required to distinguish differences among items held—or even to distinguish the library's copies from among all those in the STC. This means that the library would require more, and possibly more structured information than the STC would eventually show, but not so much more than should be recorded during the compilation of the STC.

As we shall see, a central point in Christophers' remarks (unheeded at the time) is the concept of a "structural order", based on "entries which carry an amount of bibliographical detail commensurate with the criteria for the whole catalogue." During the discussion which centred on Christophers' paper, and one given by William B. Todd, it became clear that the closer the project drifted in the direction of library cataloguing the more necessary became the need to compile records based on an examination of the original books. Todd's paper, though brief, raised crucial points:

> If there is to be an ESTC all the descriptive elements, I am convinced, must conform in style and order to those already prescribed for MARC, a system now being accepted internationally. Already various U.S. libraries are inputting 18C items in MARC form (generally into OCLC) and many more, I suspect, may be inclined to do so if it is recognized that such records—of immediate use to the libraries involved—may also eventually be of common use to all in ESTC. This shared cataloguing will accelerate in any event, largely in recognition of an inevitable circumstance: that on-line reader-catalogues will henceforth constitute the only efficient way of maintaining bibliographical control. It is therefore unreasonable to suppose that any library, now or later committed to go on-line, will assist us in compiling yet another record, requiring still other data, and sequestering that data in a "private" system to which it is denied instant access. The only reasonable course, at least in the U.S., is to participate in the national system and thereby secure, probably at no cost whatever, the rapidly accumulating results from diverse cataloguing now under way around the country.

As the conference neared its end two principles had emerged: that the ESTC should attempt to record as much material as possible within very broad definitions of scope and that the resulting record should, as far as possible, conform to the patterns established in America for large bibliographical data-bases such as OCLC and BALLOTS. No one could foresee the intricate problems which such a commitment would produce, both with regard to the harvesting of data and its organisation in a machine-readable file of considerable size.

The management of the project proved a topic for discussion of limited usefulness, since there were, it appeared, too many unknowns to permit practical resolutions to be adopted. The role of the British Library and that of its sister institution the Library of Congress had not yet emerged, and without the support of a large institution it was not at all clear how, or where, the ESTC could begin. Complicated management structures were proposed, with advisory boards, executive committees, and all the usual paraphernalia associated with international bureaucracy, but in the absence of any firm institutional support it all amounted to little more than idle speculation. The first note of optimism, in a day overshadowed by uncertainty and misgiving, was sounded when R. J. Fulford, Keeper of Printed Books in the Reference Division, publicly announced that the British Library would undertake to sponsor a limited pilot project for six weeks, in order to assess some of the problems which would have to be faced. The experiment would be constructed, monitored and evaluated by Richard Christophers. It was a profoundly significant gesture, and one which has determined the course of the ESTC ever since.

The final day of the conference was devoted to the election of an Organising Committee which would be responsible for the future development of the project on both sides of the Atlantic. The membership of that committee was as follows:

D. T. Richnell *(elected in his absence) Director General, Reference Division, British Library*
R. Shackleton *Bodley's Librarian*
E. B. Ceadel *Librarian, Cambridge University Library*

4

F. W. Ratcliffe *Librarian, John Rylands University Library, Manchester*
J. W. Jolliffe *Keeper of Catalogues, Bodleian Library*
N. J. Barker *British Library*
R. C. Alston *University of Leeds*
D. W. Bryant *Director of Libraries, Harvard University*
T. R. Adams *(Elected in his absence) Librarian, John Carter Brown Library*
W. B. Todd *University of Texas*
P. J. Korshin *University of Pennsylvania*
W. Matheson *Chief Rare Books Division, Library of Congress*
A. H. Epstein *BALLOTS Centre, Stanford University*

On his return from abroad D. T. Richnell accepted the position of Chairman of the Organising Committee.

On June 18 the conference addressed to the newly formed Organising Committee a memorandum summing up the views for which there seemed to be a measure of agreement:

> The STC should include categories which are readily definable including the ephemera falling within this definition; government documents should also be included. If feasible, a separate volume should be devoted to newspapers. The question of other kinds of serial publication, and part publications has been raised but not resolved. Maps and engraved music are to be excluded. The question of uncatalogued material is not fully resolved: there is a strong argument for including it to make it accessible, but there are reservations on grounds of the time and expense involved. The question of scope has been resolved: as a general principle all books printed in the eighteenth century in the English language and British vernaculars wherever printed and all books printed in the British Isles and in British North America in whatever language, should be included. Some special classes of material not covered by this definition might require further consideration. There is a strong persuasion that all pertinent information should be recorded in the data base, and abbreviated as necessary, perhaps in accordance with existing STC formula, at a later stage. Alternatively, in the interests of speed and economy, it has been suggested that the STC formula be defined at the outset, and only so much information be recorded as will comply with this. *Fingerprints:* it has been recommended that these be recorded when a book has to be examined for whatever reason . . . If, as has been suggested, all books are to be examined, then it is recommended that all be fingerprinted, as an alternative to complete recataloguing. The question of whether the fingerprint should be included in the STC printed entry has not been resolved. It has been proposed that the project start by converting the pertinent entries in the British Library catalogue to machine-readable form in accordance with MARC format; this would involve limited recataloguing but not the verification of every item in the file. It is argued that once the records are in machine-readable form they can be modified and amended with comparative ease at any stage . . . It is worth noting that if it is decided that the data base should contain the fullest possible descriptions from the outset, much of GK3 will need complete recataloguing since many requisite details are missing in the printed entries. Alternative suggestions were that NUC be taken as the base file, or some combination of the two. It has also been argued that once a file is in machine-readable form, it will be possible to check items as necessary by shelf-list order; in some libraries it may be convenient to do this in alphabetical sequence. A proposal has been made to set up a comparative sample study, to help clarify questions of this kind. It was suggested that for a large, inclusive catalogue, such as was envisaged, it would be essential to employ computer technology. The question of personnel was considered and it was suggested that a considerable amount of voluntary help might be expected, though the main brunt of the work would have to be carried out by specially employed staff. No estimates of the size of such staff could be formed until the nature and size of the operation were more fully investigated and better understood.

As a first step in the planning of ESTC the June Conference may be said to have been a success: it was certainly regarded as such by Nicolas Barker who wrote as follows, in a summary account in the *Times Literary Supplement* (July 2, 1976):

> Beyond these practical matters stretched the potentially vast questions of the staffing and financing of the STC, introduced by Professor P. J. Korshin of ASECS. The joint chairmen were careful to stress the need for caution here, before the intellectual and practical problems which the conference had raised were resolved. One of its chief functions was their identification. It is a measure of the success of the conference—and it certainly was a success—that there was a general determination to stick to bus-

iness, despite the temptations offered by the immensity of the undertaking. The small organizing committee was set up to consider further and resolve the questions identified by the conference. After this promising start, it is very much to be hoped that the great national libraries of Britain and the United States will be able to take the lead in bringing the project to fruition. Its value to a vast range of scholarship reflecting all areas of eighteenth-century English culture needs no stressing.

The proceedings of the conference were published in microfiche by the Lending Division of the British Library in July 1976: Ref. BAB 2001.

The First Pilot Project

The first practical step following the June Conference was a limited pilot project, authorised by R. J. Fulford, Keeper of Printed Books, and conducted by Richard Christophers. Its terms of reference were as follows: "To investigate the relative timings and efficiency of using the Reference Division's General Catalogue for a machine-readable base file for an STC, in view of the unchallenged position of the Reference Division's collections as the largest single holding of English books. The project also had as its remit a study of the feasibility of using the same file as a base for retrospective conversion of the General Catalogue to machine-readable form." With a staff of six specially recruited persons (four graduates, three with library training, and two non-graduates) the pilot study was set the following aims:

1. To compare relative timings and efficiency of various methods of cataloguing eighteenth century items entered in GK in the context of contributing a base for an STC, and providing suitable entries for use as part of the retrospective conversion of GK to machine-readable form.
2. To determine the level of staff required for the compilation of STC entries.
3. To determine the speed and quality of the operation using staff of different levels.
4. To determine the minimal number of characters required for machine-readable entries.
5. To determine the general value and validity of the results.

Four tasks were drawn up, all to be applied to the whole of the sample, but with each member of the project staff taking one-sixth of the sample in rotation. The four tasks were:

1. To construct the fullest possible catalogue entry from the GK entry alone.
2. To construct a catalogue entry from the books themselves (including a fingerprint).
3. To take very basic entries from GK and then enhance these records from the inspection of the books themselves.
4. To construct an entry adequate for an STC from the GK entry alone.

In methods 1 and 4, staff were instructed to look at the book only as a last resort, but none did so.

The data was recorded on a "bibslip" (reproduced on page 7) modified from that in use in the British Library and containing the numbers of the "tags" for each segment of the entry as well as short descriptions of their function. It was designed so that, folded from A4 to A5, essential information would remain visible when the slips were filed. Staff were issued with instructions for all four methods with basic definitions of what they were looking for, and how they should write it down according to the practices of AACR and the UK MARC format.

In a report submitted to the Reference Division, Christophers gave the following synopsis of the results achieved. From a sample of 461 items:

```
Author/heading/title_____00100_____

- - - - - - - - - - - - - - - - - - - - - - - - - - - - - - - - - - - - - - - - - - - - - - - - - - - - - -

100 0 00 author  $a                                              $h

100 0 10         $a                                              $h

110 0 10         $a

240 0 unif. title $a

245 0 title (main) $a




        (sub) $b

      (author) $e

250 0 00 edition (number) $a                      (author) $c

260 0 00 imprint (place) $a

     (publ) $b

     (date) $c              (col) $x

300 0 00 (pag/fol) $a                             (format) $c

500 0 00 (notes: general) $a

503 0 00 (notes: bibliog) $a

700 0 (pers. name add) $a                         $h

999 0 00 (locations) $a         $b
- - - - - - - - - - - - - - - - - - - - - - - - - - - - - - - - - - - - - - - - - - - - - - - - - - - - - -

008 0 00 $a              $b              $c              985 0 00 $a

955 0 00 (shelfmark) $a                            505 0 00 (fingerprint) $a
----------------------------------------------------------------------------------------------------------

GK3 heading

GK3 other copies:                                 NUC copies:

Bibl. refs:


Notes:




Cataloguer_____ date_____ checked before filing_____
```

The record sheet used in the First Pilot Project (reduced)

Heading: AACR heading or entry point differed from that of GK in 132 cases.

Uniform title: Required for collections, translations and changed titles in 21 cases. (Not always explicitly shown in GK).

Title and statement of authorship: GK adds square brackets to explain titles or give authorship in 91 cases. In AACR practice most of these would appear in a note. Most difficult is the 18c. tendency to use alternative titles frequently (26 cases) and to string together with conjunctions titles of other co-equal or subsidiary items in a book (42 cases) sometimes by the same author, sometimes not.

Edition statement: This presents no real problems: it is suggested that it should appear in full rather than in numerical and abbreviated form as recommended in AACR.

Imprint: When the books were examined 34 were found to bear no place of publication, 64 no publisher and 50 no date. The first and last of these could generally be supplied from GK. GK, however, omits place in 18 instances and publisher in 287 instances. In 87 cases more than one place or person was concerned with the production of the book: in 24 cases more than five firms were concerned.

Collation: This was not given by GK in 246 instances. In one case GK omitted the format.

Added entries: These were needed in 33 instances for additional statements of authorship. In 17 instances the main entry gave insufficient data to construct a heading.

Blocked entries: The titles of 59 items were supplied from the titles for entries above them in the GK column: in the test of 50 items they proved inadequate 7 times.

The characteristics of the four methods were summarised with indications of advantages and disadvantages:

Method 1: *Full transcription of GK entry*
Advantages: *a) Establishes a choice and form of heading*
            b) Establishes a uniform title
            c) Establishes, generally, sufficient title information, imprint, collation and notes for both GK and STC and MARC coding
            d) Generally suitable for untrained staff: few decisions needed
Disadvantages: *a) Choice and form of heading may not be in accord with AACR*
            b) Blocked entries may not reveal correct or full titles
            c) Difficulty of establishing correct form of added entries

Method 2: *Cataloguing directly from the book*
Advantages: *a) Much of the requisite data for the book in hand is present*
            b) Fingerprint, and other data not recorded in GK can be ascertained
Disadvantages: *a) Checking of GK is really necessary for missing data*
            b) In choice and form of heading, and in judging length of title, not susceptible to use by untrained staff

Method 3: *Short entry from GK, enhanced by consultation of the book*
Advantages: *a) Guidance is given from the start on many headings, dates and formats*
            b) Enables the preparation of a pressmark sequence to facilitate the fetching of books
            c) Other advantages of method 2
Disadvantages: *a) While MARC programs do not permit any amendment but of complete fields, considerable duplication of writing and keyboarding is necessary. In only 51 cases were the titles taken on the first round of this method found adequate for the second round*
            b) Information in the GK entry still needs to be sought, since the short entry does not give the data missing from the book itself

Method 4: *Short-title entry from GK*
Advantages: *a) Establishes a choice and form of heading*
            b) Establishes a uniform title
            c) Establishes quickly enough for an STC entry for work items
Disadvantages: *a) Does not produce a suitable entry for GK conversion*
            b) Requires an element of discretion in abbreviating and, at times, supplying data
            c) GK does not always give enough imprint information for an STC

Christophers' report concluded that a suggested method of establishing a data base should be as follows:

Every book must be inspected in association with its GK entry; no keyboarding should be done at first; no more than an average time of 10 minutes per book should be allowed; some hard copy of the entries should be made and retained; the hard copy must be legible to a keyboarder; the input conventions must be acceptable to both British Library systems and whatever system is to be adopted for the ESTC; the catalogue data must be acceptable to both the British Library and the STC editor. Cataloguers would compile records in one of the following ways:

The new scheme consider'd. - London : J. Baker, 1710.
    8o.
        R2144620   8132.bb.29

A new scheme for reducing the laws relating to the poor into
one Act of Parliament. - second edition. - London, 1737.
    8o.
        R2144621   518.h.10 (4)

News from the country : or the ploughman's lamentation. -
    Bristol, 1747.
    12o.
        R1712640   T.469(5)

News from the dead. - London : J. Thompson, (1725).
    8o.
        R1712641   12331.ee.31(8)

NICHOLSON, Henry
    The falsehood of the new prophets manifested. - London,
    1708.
        R1716290   695.c.6(2)

NICHOLSON, Henry
    Methodus plantarum in horto medico Collegii Dublinensis jam
    jam disponendarum. Dublini, 1712.
    4o.
        R1716291   B.70(2)

NIETO, David ben Phinehasu
    Sermon (on Ps. lxviii.6). - Londres, 5463 (1703).
    4o.
        R1720320   4033.h.31(8)

NIETO, David ben Phinehas
    Los triumfos de la Pobreza, panegirico (on Levit. xxii.28
    etc.). - Londres, 5469(1709).
    4o.
        R1720321   4033.h.31(5)

NIXON, John
    An essay on a sleeping cupid. - London, 1755.
    4o.
        R1724010   604.f.22(1)

NIXON, John
    Marmor estonianum, seu dissertatio de sella marmorea ootiva
    estoniae. - Londini, 1744.
    4o.
        R1724011   603.d.24(5)

Notes on two reports, by a Jamaica planter. - London, 1789.
    8o.
        R1144481   8156.aaa.43

NOYES, Robert
    Distress. A poem.. - Canterbury, 1783.
    4o.
        R1736430   1465.k.12

Short title catalogue print-out based on records compiled from the General Catalogue in the First Pilot Project (reduced)

NICHOLSON, Henry
The falshood of the new prophets manifested with their
corrupt doctrines and conversations / by one who hath had
intimate conversation with them, whilst he had an opinion of
their integrity : but now he thinks himself obliged to
discover their enormities, for the publick benefit. – London
: Joseph Downing, 1708.
31 p. ; 8o.
tcinerh,orasTiMu.
R1716290   695.c.6(2)

NICHOLSON, Henry
Methodus Plantarum in horto medico Collegu Dublinensis jam
jam disponendarum. : in duas partes divisar, quarum prima de
Plentis, altera de fructibus & artoribus agit. – Dublin : A.
Rhames, 1712.
viii, 35 p. ; 4o.
thatr.n.t.b.meli.
R1716291   B.70(2)

NIETO, David Ben Phineas
Los triumfos de la pobreza, paregrico : predicado dela
solemnidad dela fundacion de la pia y Santa Hebra de Bikw
Halen. – Londres, (1709).
32 p. ; 4o.
l-n,e-a-i-talopu.
R1720321   4033.h.31(5)

NIETO, David Ben Phinehas
Sermon, anacien, y problematico dialogo : que se hizieron
enla celebridad dela fundacion dela Santa y pia Hermerdad de
Sa nere ora, vaavi ceronun. – Londres, (1703).
32 p. ; 4o.
uen-asn-quo-Teln.
R1720320   4033.h.31(8)

NIXON, J.
Marmor Estoniarum : seu dissertatio de sella marmorea votwa
estonial in agro Northamptoniensi conservata. – Londini : J.
Bettenham : R. Marby & H. S. Cox, 1744.
36 p. ; 4o.
d.7.9.s.sital.op.
R1724011   603.d.24(5)

NIXON, John
An essay on a sleeping cupid, being one of the Arundelian
marbles in the collection of the (late) Right Honourable the
Earl of Pomfret. – London : R. Marby, 1755.
37 p. ; 4o.
seheT.5.C.6.p.8rL.
R1724010   604.f.22(1)

*Full title catalogue print-out based on examination of the original books (with fingerprints added) in the First Pilot
Project (reduced)*

   i) MS bibslips from book and GK in conjunction
  ii) MS bibslips from GK, amended on inspection of book
 iii) Marking GK with tags and writing bibslips for amendments from the book
 iv) Typing bibslips (with an OCR type-face machine) from book and GK in conjunction
  v) Typing bibslips from GK and retyping or making amendment slips on inspection of book
 vi) As method iv but using a Singer terminal
vii) As method v but using a Singer terminal

The statistics which emerged from the pilot test were as follows:
Method 1: *Full transcription of GK entry:*   *7.25 m.p.r.**
Method 2: *Cataloguing directly from book:*   *16.11 m.p.r.*
Method 3: *Short GK entry enhanced from the book:*   *16.69 m.p.r.*
Method 4: *Short title entry from GK:*   *16.06 m.p.r.*
*Minutes per record

Though it must be admitted that the first pilot test was carried out somewhat hurriedly, with insufficient training of the project staff in either AACR-MARC or GK cataloguing principles, and without the necessary supervision, it nevertheless did yield some valuable statistics and furthermore made it clear that a workable strategy for compiling the ESTC was still uncertain, though it was becoming clear that an ESTC could not satisfactorily be completed without examining the books themselves. Much would depend on the degree to which the British Library could be persuaded to become involved; and if it were to commit itself to a recataloguing operation (the extent of which would be determined by the resources available) would there be a similar commitment from a major institution in the United States? What relationship would there be between the British Library and the editorial staff of the ESTC as approved by the newly-formed Organising Committee? While no one at the June Conference doubted that the support, in some as yet undefined way, of the British Library was an indispensable prerequisite for the success of ESTC, the answers to these, and other questions of equal substance, were difficult to anticipate. The Organising Committee, only too well aware that they had to be resolved before progress could be made, and anxious not to dissipate the enthusiasm for the project which the conference had engendered, decided that a full meeting of the Committee should be held at the earliest possible opportunity. It was held at the Library of Congress over three days during November 1976.

The Washington Meeting

The meeting of the Organising Committee in Washington set for itself the following topics for discussion:

(1) The inclusiveness of an ESTC;
(2) A quantification of the size and scatter of ESTC material;
(3) The overlap of material in GK3 and NUC;
(4) A comparison of the cataloguing standards of GK3, NUC, and other major catalogues;
(5) The elements required in an ESTC entry;
(6) Computing and technology standards;
(7) The relationship of the project to organisations and other projects.

Working papers (with the exception of 3) were circulated in advance, and the entire proceedings were recorded on tape in order to facilitate the production of a comprehensive set of minutes.

It is, in retrospect, perhaps not altogether surprising that the Washington meeting re-rehearsed much of what had been discussed during the June Conference. Even those who had spent much time preparing documents for discussion since June were still unable to answer with confidence questions of critical importance. How many items would ESTC seek to record during its first phase? How many items were there in the British Library? Where would the project be based? What order of funding would be required for work to proceed on both sides of the Atlantic? How would the project be administered, and who would actually be editorially responsible for the intellectual content? Should the project have its own computer facilities, or should one of the various on-line data bases (OCLC or BALLOTS) be used? What form should the first publication of ESTC take—a series of printed volumes? Microfiche? How was enrichment from other libraries to be effected? What procedures would be adopted to ensure accurate matching? How could the proposed Drafting Committee (which the meeting was later to appoint) construct a detailed plan for the execution of the ESTC which could serve as the basis for raising the necessary funds from foundations with so many fundamental questions unanswered? Rhetoric would clearly be insufficient to secure these funds: what was needed were facts, and these seemed as elusive now as they had been in June.

It was becoming increasingly clear to all that finding an institution in the United States which would support and administer the ESTC was going to be difficult. For various reasons, the Library of Congress, while wishing the project well and prepared to bestow on it the necessary moral support, could not consider acting as a host institution. Numerous other major institutions had adopted a similar posture. However, any possibility that the project might collapse had already been averted by the announcement of the Chairman, D. T. Richnell, that he proposed to appoint R. C. Alston as a consultant to the Reference Division of the British Library to undertake a more ambitious pilot project, which might well provide answers to some of the questions which were causing such concern. Given a wide range of specific problems to explore, the second pilot project should, it was argued, yield much of the data needed to enable a Drafting Committee to carry out its work of preparing a proposal for funding further stages of the project.

The Washington meeting concluded with a short session in which the Drafting Committee was appointed and its brief summarised. The members of the committee were:

T. R. Adams *Librarian, John Carter Brown Library (Chairman)*
P. J. Korshin *University of Pennsylvania, Executive Secretary ASECS*
R. C. Alston *Consultant to the British Library*
R. J. Roberts *Keeper of Printed Books, Bodleian Library*

The tasks of the committee were: to propose a strategy for the ESTC both in Britain and the United States, to indicate in detail how it was to be executed, and to prepare a document which would form the basis for securing adequate funds to carry out that strategy. The committee has met on several occasion and its activities are summarised in Appendix I.

The Second Pilot Project

R. C. Alston was appointed as Consultant to the British Library in January 1977, and steps were taken to recruit a team of graduates. This proved to be simpler than expected: four permanent members of the British Library staff asked to be transferred to the project, and two of the staff from the earlier pilot project (Summer 1976) were available to be hired on a temporary basis. By a happy coincidence the recently retired Keeper of Printed Books, J. L. Wood, offered to help the project—and has remained with it ever since. Work began in February.

The project was given a complex variety of tasks to perform and a number of questions to answer. One important directive given by the Director General was that the project should be so framed as to provide the beginnings of a base-file of British Library holdings. A manual of cataloguing rules had to be written in which the needs of an STC could be provided for as well as those of a national data base (the British Library's BLAISE); a routine for identifying and cataloguing relevant items had to be devised; a system of manual files which would enable proper bibliographical control to be exercised had to be evolved; the number of eighteenth-century items, both catalogued and uncatalogued, had to be accurately estimated; AACR and MARC had to be applied to the widest possible variety of printed materials in order to ascertain the extent to which they are hospitable to different items; limited keyboarding had to be undertaken in order to satisfy the Library that cataloguing methods were not incompatible with BLAISE records; cataloguing rates had to be established; above all, it had to be demonstrated that a major recataloguing project could be sustained within the Reference Division without adverse consequences upon the routine functioning of the Library.

During the months which had elapsed since the June Conference the problems which cataloguing eighteenth-century material would present had been given much thought: a rudimentary record card (which was to evolve through successive stages of refinement) had been designed; hundreds of "difficult" items (mostly single sheet) had been identified in the collections (whether catalogued or not) and were studied with a view to devising rules for their incorporation in the ESTC in such a way that access was simplified; and a manual system of files was developed which would permit editorial control over the data prior to its conversion into machine-readable form. Broadly speaking, the cataloguing methods and the various files begun during the early stages of the pilot project have proved themselves to be suitable, and the methods now regarded by the project as routine have remained little changed since February 1977.

There are, doubtless, many possible approaches to the cataloguing of material within defined chronological limits in a large library. Approaching the material in main-heading order (the procedure adopted in the revision of the General Catalogue in this century for the alphabet from A to DEZ-) would have been attractive, for it would have enabled the project to issue the ESTC in parts: such a procedure had to be rejected, however, since the British Library now subscribes to AACR, and AACR headings for anonymous books and pamphlets cannot be ascertained until the entire General Catalogue has been scanned. The "old" rules did not enter anonymous books under the title, and since over fifty percent of the eighteenth-century material in the collections is anonymous it would have necessitated much additional work just to identify and catalogue items the headings for which are comprehended in the letter A. The main heading UNITED STATES OF AMERICA—APPENDIX: History and Politics—II. *Chronological Series* contains the following anonymous items (the AACR heading is italicised):

Considerations on the American war. 1776.
A *Dialogue* on the principles of the Constitution. 1776.
Arguments in favour of recognizing the independence of the United States. [1777].
Reflections on the present state of the American war. [By John *Hampson*.] 1776.
American resistance indefensible. By a *Country Curate.*
Historical anecdotes, civil and military. 1779.
The *Detail* and conduct of the American war. 1780.

There was another reason, of perhaps even greater importance, why such an approach had to be rejected. It would have had disastrous consequences upon the books themselves, and would have involved the staff of the library and the project in thousands of unnecessary book-movements. A guard-book containing two hundred single sheets would have to be fetched and returned to the shelves two hundred times!

Since such a large proportion of the library's eighteenth century collections are bound in tract-volumes or guard-books it was immediately clear that once a volume was in hand all relevant items in it would have to be catalogued at that time. The time saved in book-fetching which such an approach determines is significant: it is estimated that to catalogue the 350,000 odd items in the library only some 75,000 book-movements will be required.

It was determined, at an early stage, that all copies of an item would be examined simultaneously in order to ensure that the bibliographical record could be made as authoritative as possible. It will come as no surprise to anyone familiar with the General Catalogue that numerous items referred to as [Another copy] are, in fact, different editions or re-settings, and that [Another edition] frequently signals a reissue. The decision to undertake bibliographical examination of all copies, and sequences of suspicious editions, has, of course, consequences: it can, and frequently does, trap a cataloguer in a situation from which there is no apparent escape. Thus, one stray sermon bound in a tract-volume inexorably led one member of the staff into the library's vast collections of eighteenth century sermons: six months later he is still fighting his way through the Lettsom collection, with up to sixty volumes at a time under continuous scrutiny! Other categories of material which produce a similar situation are: political pamphlets, medical and botanical tracts, single sheet ballads, garlands, Parliamentary papers, pamphlet verse, and sale catalogues. On balance, the decision to approach the material in this way has proved beneficial, since it provides cataloguers with opportunities to develop their knowledge of a genre or period, and the project has already made a substantial contribution to the improvement of the *General Catalogue* entries.

The procedure established at the beginning of the pilot project for cataloguing books and duplicating the master record a number of times in order to maintain subsidiary files required for the exercise of editorial control has remained unchanged. In addition to the main sequence, which is arranged strictly in title order, five manual files are kept: personal authors; corporate authors; imprints; certain limited genres; and chronological. In addition to these the project has a file of all items not separately catalogued in the *General Catalogue.*

At an early stage in the pilot project it was realised that since little was known about the book trade in the eighteenth century, particularly the provincial trade, it would greatly facilitate cataloguing if the project could begin to compile a comprehensive book trade index. Initially this index was based on imprint information, but now incorporates information from a wide variety of sources, including directories, poll books, newspapers, advertisements, and studies of printing in particular localities.

The problem of ascertaining the extent and range of uncatalogued items in the

Library led the project into its most ambitious undertaking: a volume-by-volume search of those volumes in the Department of Manuscripts which might contain eighteenth-century printed material. The search lasted for six weeks, and from a total of over seventy thousand volumes and parcels searched some ten thousand eighteenth-century printed items, many of them unrecorded, were identified. A separate index was kept of all manuscripts containing printed matter in any language up to the year 1800.

It has been stressed at the outset that the pilot project should explore ways of gathering records from other libraries, since ESTC is, after all, a union catalogue operation. With the help of the staff in Cambridge University Library a representative sample of eighteenth century titlepages was xeroxed, marked for format and pagination, and sent to the project. These titlepages were identified, where possible, in the General Catalogue. The British Library copies were then catalogued on record cards. At this stage a match between the xerox titlepage and the record was attempted. The British Library copies were then compared with the xerox titlepages. Matching failed in one percent of the cases. It is perhaps worth observing that while different titlepages frequently conceal identical text, the reverse is quite rare.

Since many libraries will not be able to supply ESTC with xerox titlepages of their holdings, a slightly modified version of the record card (printed with blue shading, together with a severely abridged set of rules) was tested with a number of libraries. The principle underlying the use of this record card is that the cataloguer does not have to establish a heading, need not be concerned with the MARC tags and transcribes exactly what is in hand. It has proved a remarkably successful technique and is now being used by over forty libraries in Britain.

By the beginning of March 1977 the pilot project had undoubtedly been established as a viable operation: much had been achieved; the library had a firmer grasp of the extent of its holdings, both catalogued and uncatalogued; and the benefits which would be derived if it continued understood. With the support of the Director General of the Reference Division, the British Library Board was requested to consider the funding of an operation to recatalogue the entire eighteenth century English holdings, now estimated at over 360,000 items. With the cataloguing rates that had been established in the pilot project, and taking into account all the various tasks involved in maintaining editorial control over the material, it was estimated that, given a team of fifteen, the task could be completed in three years. The Board agreed: and on that day, March 23, the prospects for an ESTC seemed brighter than ever.

The recruitment of staff commenced in the summer of 1977. R. C. Alston was designated director of the British Library operation, and since his duties would increasingly be occupied with administrative responsibilities and with developing the growth of the ESTC outside the Library, Mervyn Jannetta of the Rare Books Branch was designated deputy director. Administratively the ESTC is considered by the British Library to be an integral part of the Rare Books Branch (concerned with all books printed before 1500, English books 1501–1800, bindings, exhibitions, and the British Union Catalogue to 1800). In the context of the English printed record of the eighteenth century, whether from the resources of the Reference Division or from those of other libraries within the British Isles, the ESTC is now clearly seen by the Library as fulfilling an important function in the total concept of a National Library. A union catalogue of English printing in the eighteenth century (and of books printed in British territories) in machine-readable form would provide, for one important segment of the Library's vast historical collections, a paradigm for future projects.

The following account of the ESTC attempts to describe a project that is, fully-fledged, barely nine months old. Not to emphasise its practical achievement would do less than justice to all those who have contributed unselfishly their energies and enthusiasm, yet it is obvious that many aspects of its future development must await clarification. A first edition of a bibliographical tool of universal utility to historians of English speaking culture in the eighteenth century, though envisaged by 1984, still seems a long way off. Support for the project, now almost wholly dependent on the financial resources of the Reference Division, and those institutions which, seized by the importance of an enterprise from which manifold benefits may be expected, have offered valuable help by contributing their records, must be more broadly based if success is to be achieved.

In a project of this magnitude and complexity each specific activity or procedure must interact with every other, but it has been thought convenient to divide this account into three sections:
Scope and Content—Cataloguing Principles—Working Methods.

Scope and Content

The two existing English *Short Title Catalogues* (Pollard and Redgrave for printing up to 1640, and Wing for the period 1641–1700) attempted to record all printed material, whether letterpress or engraved, without regard for its form or content. The revised STC, with a heroic disregard for any selective principle governed by subjective notions of ephemerality, includes blank forms, printed scraps of any sort, and bookplates. The revised edition of Wing, while notionally obedient to this doctrine of inclusivity, nevertheless has settled for a somewhat more practicable definition of the material it will record.* It has always been clear that a short title catalogue for the eighteenth century, which witnessed the spread of printing to almost every locality in the kingdom and the emergence of jobbing printing on an unprecedented scale, would necessarily have to omit a wide range of materials. Arguments about what should be included or excluded have been, as we should expect, a significant feature of ESTC debate ever since the June Conference, and if the organisers have erred in their decision about what the catalogue will include they have done so in favour of those who urged comprehensive coverage.

The chronological scope of the catalogue is clear; its geographical scope includes:
1. All relevant items printed in the British Isles in any language;
2. All relevant items printed in Colonial America, the United States (1776–1800), and Canada; in any language;
3. All relevant items printed in territories governed by Britain during any period of the eighteenth century; in any language;
4. All relevant items, printed wholly or partly in English, or other British vernaculars, in any other part of the world.

It follows that, since this policy will necessitate including a Portuguese translation of

---

*As stated in Wing's original Preface, "only one kind of printed matter has been excluded—periodical literature". There are certain kinds of ephemera (e.g. blank forms), that the revision of Wing excludes.

the Book of Common Prayer printed at Calcutta, books printed in those parts of the Caribbean which came under British rule in the eighteenth century, and a host of printed ephemera connected with British trade and commerce in Europe, the burden of searching for such material is likely to be significant and will inevitably involve the project in investigating the resources of unfamiliar libraries and archives. But evidence already available indicates that such investigation will yield important discoveries. Reproduced on page 49, for example, is a previously unrecorded piece printed at Altona in 1772 recently discovered in a search being undertaken at the Royal Archives in Copenhagen. A substantial collection of letterpress music printing, pioneered by the Swedish printer Henry Fougt in London in the 1760s, has been found in the Royal Library in Stockholm. There is little doubt that if it proves possible to undertake a systematic search of important archives in Scandinavia, Holland, Germany and France, much new light will be shed on those details of commercial organisation between Britain and her trading partners which have so far eluded documentation.

Material to be Omitted

The following categories of material will not be included in the first phase of ESTC, though it should not necessarily be inferred that the eventual inclusion of some categories is thereby denied:

1. Engraved material: including maps; music; topographical views and prints; portraits, caricatures, etc. Note, however, that books wholly engraved (e.g. Pine's Horace, or engraved treatises with substantial text) and atlases will be included. Items partly engraved, but with some letterpress, will be included.
2. Printed forms intended to be completed in manuscript; indentures; warrants; passports; certificates; licences; bills of lading; and a multitude of forms associated with the administration of justice and local government.
3. Trade cards; labels; tickets; visiting cards; invitations; bookplates; currency. Note, however, that distinguishing between some of these categories and those which are included as advertisements occasionally requires the exercise of nice judgement.
4. Playbills; concert and theatre programmes. Note, however, that certain types of advertisements for entertainments (e.g. Bartholomew Fair handbills) and spectacles are included.
5. Playing cards; games; puzzles (printed "rules" are included).

Reproductions of selected examples which ESTC intends to omit will be found on pages 41–72.

Material to be Included

Though it is understandable that any omissions are likely to meet with protest from some quarter it must be emphasised that considering the vast amount of material which the printing press produced in the eighteenth century, the ESTC will record, for the first time, an impressive range of items, some of which may have escaped the attention of historians. Thus, from the uncatalogued resources of the British Library, the Bodleian, and other major research collections, a surprising number of ephemeral items have been located already. Merely to illustrate the range would require more space than can be afforded in a synoptic survey such as this, but the following categories may serve as a demonstration of the variety:

Lists of members of societies, institutions and clubs; commodities; articles for sale; elections; tariffs, etc.
Rules for societies, institutions and clubs.
Advertisements for services, products, entertainments; auction sales; meetings; lectures; demonstrations; books published, etc.
Election propaganda, including letters, handbills and circulars.
Songs and ballads, popular and political.
Catalogues of books, pictures, articles for sale or commercial products, exhibitions, curiosities.

The remarkable growth of the provincial book trade during the second half of the century—a fact well documented in the project's book trade files—brought to hundreds of townships, for the first time, the practical advantages of inexpensive printing in the service of local government, commerce, education and political awareness. The importance of much of the jobbing printing which ESTC will identify and record has yet to be assessed, since its existence has so far been inadequately documented, but it is now understood that while books, pamphlets and newspapers tell us much about the great debated issues of the day, it is to the ephemera that we must turn for a more intimate and informative picture of the everyday life of the citizen. And ephemera can, and frequently do, enlighten our understanding of the political issues. This can be clearly demonstrated in the turbulent career of a Wilkes or a Horne-Tooke, and to ignore the considerable quantity of hastily printed handbills which can be identified with the *North Briton* affair or the Jacobin movement of the 1790s is to underestimate the nationwide passions which such movements aroused.

The restrictions exercised over the printing press in the seventeenth century gradually gave way, after 1695, to a more lenient interpretation of the freedom of the press. The consequence of this change, which few perhaps could have foreseen, was the rapid spread of printing to provincial towns, encouraged by the sustained growth of literacy regarded as a prerequisite to Lockean enlightenment, and the commercial advantages waiting to be exploited. The obscurity which surrounds the early history of printing in so many localities is due, in large measure, to the ephemeral nature of the material a printer was expected to undertake. Thus, while evidence gleaned from a variety of sources discloses the existence of a printer in a particular locality, his name is unlikely to be recorded in the imprints of books and pamphlets. But occasionally a printer will bestow, on even the most trivial item, the benefit of an imprint, and we know of one printer working at Sheffield from one advertisement printed in 1799 (see the illustration on page 63). We can follow the career of a printer like J. Fowler of Salisbury who issued, over a period of years, hundreds of single-sheet songs and verses in various shapes and sizes. One of Fowler's advertisements issued about 1785 from his Salisbury shop, and again in 1789 after he had moved to London, is reproduced on page 50. A recent search of the Goodchild Collection in the Wakefield Record Office has yielded an important number of items printed in West Riding towns—none of which are in the British Library—including a number of unrecorded prospectuses for local friendly societies. The archives in the Bradford City Library have yielded some republican songs, possibly printed at Halifax, with one song represented in no fewer than twelve copies!

Whereas the spread of printing throughout North American has been well documented, there remains much to be done for areas such as the West Indies and India. A fairly typical case is that of the printer Joseph Stockdale who emigrated to Bermuda in 1784. Stockdale's newspaper, *The Bermuda Gazette* (a complete file exists in Bermuda and has been scanned), reveals over a period of sixteen years his industrious contribution to the commercial and cultural life of an island community. In addition to printing a weekly newspaper (the numerous changes in format were, confessedly, the result of difficulties experienced in securing adequate supplies of paper), supplying the local administration of government with printed forms, printing legislative documents, popular fiction, he started a subscription library. Of the fifty odd books, pamphlets and almanacs which he printed before 1800 not one has yet been located.

Printing in English in other, non-English-speaking parts of the world is a familiar phenomenon, and we know, for example, that in France, Switzerland, Germany and Holland there was a distinct, if limited, market for reprints of English "classics". Recent studies by Bernhard Fabian have shown how extensive this trade was, and the ESTC must, if it is to record such material comprehensively, establish practical arrangements with European libraries to ensure that their English holdings can be incorporated. What promises to be the first such arrangement is a project to record, under Professor Fabian's direction, the English books printed before 1800 in the University Library of Göttingen, and its importance cannot be overestimated. It may well prove the model for subsequent projects in libraries of similar size and richness.

The discovery of other varieties of English printing, more directly associated with international commerce, will depend on the extent to which ESTC can undertake, or encourage to be undertaken, searches in archival repositories. That such printing did in fact exist is proved by an intriguing collection of import and export lists in the John Carter Brown Library at Providence. An example, printed at Croisic, is reproduced on page 51.

Given the expansion of the printing press throughout the century, and given the decision to incorporate as much of the surviving output as is practicable, the ESTC will, in a way denied its precursors, be able to shed new light on a wide range of aspects of eighteenth century English civilisation, and thereby fulfil one important function of historical bibliography – the nourishment of historical disciplines.

Cataloguing Principles

For those concerned with the detailed principles which govern the cataloguing of material to be included in ESTC the revised edition of the rules, reprinted below, will suffice. What concerns us here is an attempt to express, without specific appeal to the complexities of the original material and its subordination to logical and consistent principles of cataloguing, the intellectual processes which have contributed to the evolution of these rules. There are three factors which have influenced these processes: the nature of the British Museum *General Catalogue*; the nature of previous short-title catalogues; and the novel possibilities, balanced by certain negative factors, provided for by the development of computer cataloguing.

The General Catalogue

The *General Catalogue* is, by common consent, a research tool of undisputed importance for historians of European civilisation from the invention of printing to the present day. Its utility and the universal esteem in which it is held derive from two principal factors: the richness of the collections it seeks to describe, and the principles underlying the methods of that description. Unlike most library catalogues which provide access to collections via the main entry-points of author or title, the *General Catalogue* has, from the beginning, sought rather to incorporate the best traditions of German analytic cataloguing into the general framework of an author catalogue.* The logic of its structure is derived from thesaural rather than lexical principles. Generations of scholars have testified to the benefits for research which its rich contextual organisation make possible. The juxtaposition of related materials, frequently arranged in a chronological rather than merely alphabetic sequence (in recognition of the scholar's needs), is a feature designed to encourage a systematic and exploratory response from the user. Thus, the search for a specific item (especially if that item was published anonymously) can yield a rich and perhaps unsuspected harvest of related items, and opportunities for discovery are further multiplied by the elaborate system of cross-references between authors and headings. The format of the catalogue was itself devised to encourage the user to explore sequences of entries rather than to focus upon the individual entry. It is as though Panizzi conceived of books as members of a vast related community and obligingly sought to demonstrate their relationship within the constraints of a library catalogue. For certain kinds of anonymous publication, Panizzi's rules were designed to allow a subject approach, based on the wording of the title page. But within such headings the sequences are where possible based on historical principles. Such familiar collective headings as:—ENGLAND, FRANCE, AMERICA; LONDON, ROME, PARIS; BIBLE, LITURGIES; GEORGE III, LOUIS XIV, PIUS IX; PERIODICAL PUBLICATIONS —represent the imposition of an historically understood order upon a considerable body of heterogeneous publications. For the user in search of a specific anonymous title the catalogue's disposition to arrange items in an historical context (derived from a significant element within the title) can be frustrating if only the first few words of the title are known, or if the cataloguing principles for choice of heading are imperfectly understood. But the alternative, now widely regarded as standard, procedure of entering anonymous titles under first word, while facilitating access to individual works (the title-index to ENGLAND is undoubtedly invaluable) distributes irrecoverably related items frequently crucial to the user's requirements. It is clear that for the collections of a major research library multiple access is desirable, but for a machine-readable catalogue such as ESTC the search possibilities provided by the computer fortunately make these problems less acute.

There can be little doubt that the *General Catalogue* owes its existence to a generation for which research was an intellectual occupation in which haste and urgency had no place, and which had as its objective the absorption of widely disparate intellectual components into a systematic order, and the servants of this intellectual empire (the cataloguers) required almost as much historical instinct as the users they served. It is no accident that for nearly a hundred years the cataloguing of books has nursed a continuous succession of distinguished scholars within the Department of Printed Books.

---

*The 1841 text of the 91 *Rules for the compilation of the Catalogue* is reproduced in Appendix II.

received in the light of understanding. [Being an Exposition of the Apostles Creed, with the text.] Written by A. Gil. *Anne Giffin, for J. Norton and R. Whitaker, London,* 1635. fol.
1217. k.

APPELIUS (JOANNES) A true Relation of the . . . Death of . . . Philippus Ludovicus, Earle of Hanaw . . . who . . . deceased . . . the ninth of August, 1612 . . . Translated out of the Germane by S. R. 𝕭. 𝕷. *For N. Bourne, London,* 1612. 4to. 611. e. 22. (4.)

APPIAN, *of Alexandria.* An auncient Historie and exquisite Chronicle of the Romanes warres, both Civile and Foren . . . With a continuarion [*sic*] . . . from the death of Sextus Pompeius . . . till the overthrow of Antonie and Cleopatra, etc. (The second part . . . translated . . . by W. B.) 2 pts. 𝕭. 𝕷. *R. Newbery and H. Bynniman, London,* 1578. 4to.
C. 13. a. 4.

APPIUS CLAUDIUS CRASSUS, *the Decemvir.* *See* CLAUDIUS CRASSUS (A.)

APPRENTICE. *See* P., B. The Prentises Practise in Godlinesse, etc. 1608. 8vo. 4410. aa.

AP-ROBERT (J.) The yonger Brother his Apology by it selfe. Or, a Father's free power disputed for the disposition of his lands, or other his fortunes to his Sonne, sonnes, or any one of them : as right reason, the laws of God and Nature, the Civill, Canon, and Municipall lawes of this Kingdome do command. [*London ?*] 1618. 4to. 6355. a. 1.

APULEIUS (LUCIUS) *Madaurensis.* The XI. Bookes of the Golden Asse, conteininge the Metamorphosie of L. A., enterlaced with sondrie pleasaunt and delectable Tales, with an excellent Narration of the Mariage of Cupido and Psiches . . . Translated into Englishe by W. Adlington. 𝕭. 𝕷. *Henry Wykes, London,* 1566. 4to. C. 21. b.

Interleaved.

— Another edition. 𝕭. 𝕷. *W. How, for A. Veale, London,* 1571. 4to. 244. k. 23.

— Another edition. 𝕭. 𝕷. *V. Symmes, London,* 1596. 4to.
C. 34. h. 39.

— Another edition. 𝕭. 𝕷. *T. Harper for T. Alchorn, London,* 1639. 4to. 12410. bbb.

ARAGON, *Queen of.* The Queene of Arragon. A tragicomedie [in five acts and in verse ; by W. Habington, with a prologue and epilogue by S. Butler]. *T. Cotes for W. Cooke, London,* 1640. fol. 162. m. 4.

— Another copy. 644. k. 27.
Wanting the prologue.

ARCÆUS (FRANCISCUS) A most excellent and compendious Method of curing woundes . . . Translated into English by J. Read. Whereunto is added the exact cure of the caruncle . . . With a treatise of the Fistulae . . . translated out of J. Ardern, and also the description of the Emplaister called Dia Chalciteos, etc. 𝕭. 𝕷. *T. East, for T. Cadman, London,* 1588. 4to.
549. g. 22. (5.)

ARCANDAM, *pseud.* The most excellent . . . Booke of the famous . . . Astrologian A., or Alcandrin, to finde the fatall destiny . . . of every man . . . by

Short-Title Catalogues

The rapid growth of the Department's collections in the second half of the nineteenth century, sustained by Panizzi's passionate adherence to the principle of encyclopedic acquisition, with the accompanying growth in size of the catalogue to proportions which made its comprehension by an individual virtually impossible,* determined the creation of smaller catalogues based on the limitations of geography and period. One of the earliest of these was destined to exert a powerful and still evident influence on enumerative bibliography, and has provided the model for a familiar succession of short-title catalogues. With prescience of the historical needs of a generation which, in 1880, cultivated an absorbing interest in the development of English civilisation between the waning of the Middle Ages and the Civil War, the Department of Printed Books authorised the preparation of a catalogue of books printed in the British Isles before 1640. The energy devoted to building and cataloguing, within the space of a lifetime, a library of unique richness and size was now to be concentrated in a series of catalogues which would more readily reveal that richness than the prodigal bulk of the *General Catalogue* which began to appear in printed form in the year 1881. In 1884 the Trustees published George Bullen's *Catalogue of Books in the Library of the British Museum, printed in England, Scotland and Ireland . . . to the year 1640*, thereby establishing a tradition of which ESTC is a manifest beneficiary.

Bullen's catalogue was, considering the speed with which it was prepared and printed, a remarkable achievement. Here, for the first time, was a compendious guide to the English Renaissance based on the collections of the largest library in the English-speaking world, and there is no doubt that it fulfilled the double function of providing convenient access to early English printed books and of advertising to the book trade what was lacking in the collections (see the illustration opposite). The importance of a short title catalogue as an instrument of comprehensive acquisition was not lost on A. W. Pollard, then an Assistant Keeper in the Department of Printed Books, who was later to play a significant role in the Museum's series of short-title catalogues of foreign books* in addition to his crucial part in the planning and execution of the Bibliographical Society's STC. In the note prefixed to the first of the Museum's foreign STCs for early Spanish books (1921) Pollard wrote:

> This "Short-title Catalogue of books printed in Spain . . . is intended (i) to place in the hands of students of Spanish literature a quick means of discovering what books of this period the Museum already possesses, and (ii) to facilitate further acquisitions. For both these purposes the bare fact of the presence of a book in the Museum collection is the important point, and titles have therefore been cut down to the minimum necessary for identification, leaving further information to be obtained either from the General Catalogue of the books in the Museum, or from bibliographies . . . The Spanish books which Dr. Thomas has registered probably do not amount to more than one-sixth of those still extant, but (thanks very largely to Mr. Grenville's bequest of his library) the proportion of the more important books is very much higher, and with the aid of this Catalogue it should not be difficult to make the Museum collection thoroughly representative of the period here covered.

The first attempt at an inventory of English printing up to 1640 was intended, as Pollard observed in the Preface to the Bibliographical Society's STC, as a "short-title handlist". The purpose of such a listing was clear:

---

*By 1881 when the first printed edition of the General Catalogue began to appear the Reading Room Catalogue exceeded two thousand volumes.

*The series of short-title catalogues, of which volumes for Spain and Portugal, France, Holland, Germany and Italy have been published, is still active: new catalogues for Germany (1601–1700) by David Paisey and Holland (1601–1700) by Anna Simoni are in reparation, and the volume for France is undergoing revision.

Sharpe, Leonell—*cont.*

Scotiam. *Cantabrigiæ, ex off. J. Legat,* 1603. C.

22372 — A looking-glasse for the pope. *Tr.* E. Sharpe. 4⁰. *E. Griffin,* 1616. O. BAMB.

22373 — [Anr. ed.] 4⁰. *T. Bayly,* 1623. L.

22374 — Novum fidei symbolum. 4⁰. *R. Field,* 1612. L. O. C.

22375 — Oratio funebris in honorem Henrici Walliæ principis. 4⁰. *Gull. Hall,* 1612. Ent. 17 de. L. O. C. HH. LINC.; HN.

22376 — A sermon [on 1 Kings 10. 9.]. 8⁰. *Cambridge, J. Legat, sold by S. Waterson,* 1603. L. C.

22377 **Sharpe, Lewis.** The noble stranger. 4⁰. *J. O[kes] f. James Becket,* 1640. L. O. O⁶. ETON; HN. CH. N. NY. WH.

22378 **Sharpe, Robert.** The confession and declaration of R. Sharpe, the xij of June. 1575. br. fol. *W. Seres,* [1575.] HN.

22379 **Sharpe, Roger.** More fooles yet. 4⁰. [*T. Purfoot] f. T. Castleton,* 1610. Ent. 1 jn. O.; WH.

22380 **Sharpham, Edward.** Cupids whirligig. [Init. E. S.] 4⁰. *E. Allde, solde by A. Johnson,* 1607. Ent. to J. Busby a. A. Johnson 29 jn. L. O.; HN. CL. WH.

22381 — [Anr. ed. Init. E. S.] 4⁰. *T. C[reed], sold by A. Johnson,* 1611. L.; N. WH.

22382 — [Anr. ed. Init. E. S.] 4⁰. *T. Creede a. B. Alsop, solde by A. Johnson,* 1616. L. O.

22383 — [Anr. ed. Anon.] 4⁰. *T. H[arper] f. R. Meighen,* 1630. Ent. 29 ja. L. L⁶. O.; HN.

22384 — The Fleire. 4⁰. [*E. Allde], printed and solde by F. B[urton],* 1607. Ent. to Trundle a. J. Busby 13 my. 1606; to Busby a. A. Johnson 21 no. 1606. L.; HN. CL. WH.

22385 — [Anr. ed.] 4⁰. *f. N. Butter,* 1610. L. L⁶. O.; HN.

22386 — [Anr. ed.] 4⁰. *f. N. Butter,* 1615. L. O.; HN.

22387 — [Anr. ed.] 4⁰. *B. A[lsop] a. T. F[awcet] f. N. Butter,* 1631. L. L⁶. O.; HN. CH. WH.

22388 — Entry cancelled.

22389 **Shaw, John.** Biblii summula. [Anon.] 8⁰. *R. Field f. R. Milbourne,* 1621. Ent. 28 oc. 1620. L. O. HN.

22390 — [Anr. ed. Anon.] 8⁰. *R. Field, imp. R. Mylbourne,* 1623. L. O. C.; HN.

22391 — The blessednes of Marie, the mother of Jesus. A sermon. 8⁰. *R. Field,* 1618. Ent. 25 se. L. O.

— A true christians daily delight. 1623. *See* Wastell, S.

Shawe, George. The doctrine of dying well. [By G. Shawe?] 1628. *See* Doctrine.

22392 **Sheafe, T.** Vindiciæ senectutis, or a plea for old age. 8⁰. *G. Miller, sold by J. Kirton a. T. Warren,* 1639. Ent. 24 se. 1638. L. O.; HN.

Shee-Jesuits. The suppressing of the assembly of the Shee-Jesuits. 1631. *See* Urban VIII, *Pope.*

22393 **Sheldon, Richard.** Certain general reasons proving the lawfulnesse of the oath of allegiance. By R. S[heldon], Priest. 2 pts. 4⁰. *F. Kyngston* (pt. 2: *A. Hatfield) f. W. Aspley,* 1611. Ent. 16 mr. L. O. C.

Sheldon, Richard—*cont.*

22394 — Christ, on his throne; not in popish secrets. 4⁰. *H. Lownes,* 1622. L. O. C³.

22395 — The first sermon of R. Sheldon after his conversion. 4⁰. *J. B[eale] f. N. Butter,* 1612. L. O. C. D².

22396 — Man's last end. 4⁰. *W. Jones,* 1634. Ent. 5 fb. L. O. LINC.

22397 — The motives of R. Sheldon, Pr., for his renouncing of communion with Rome. 4⁰. [*R. Braddock] f. N. Butter,* 1612. Ent. 7 ja. L. O. C. HH.; HN.

22398 — A sermon preached at Paules Crosse. 4⁰. *W. Jones,* 1625. L. O.; NY.

22399 — A survey of the miracles of the Church of Rome. 4⁰. *E. Griffin f. N. Butter,* 1616. L. O. C.

22400 **Shelford, Robert.** Five pious and learned discourses. 4⁰. *printers to the Univ. of Cambridge,* 1635. L. O. C. DUR⁴. HH. LINC.; HN.

22401 — Lectures or readings upon Proverbs xxii. 6. 8⁰. *F. Kingston f. T. Man,* 1602. Ent. 28 no. 1595. O.

22402 — [Anr. ed.] 8⁰. *F. Kyngston f. T. Man,* 1606. L³.

22403 **Shelton, Thomas.** A centurie of similies. 8⁰. *J Dawson,* 1640. Ent. 7 jy. L. O. C.; HN.

22404 — Shortwriting. Second ed. 8⁰. *J. D[awson] f. S. C[artwright],* 1630. Ent. to S. Cartwright 17 ap. 1626. O.

22405 **Shepery, John.** Hyppolitus Ouidianæ Phædræ respondens. 8⁰. *Oxoniæ, J. Barnesius,* [1586.] L². O.

— In nouum Testamentum carmen. [Pt. 2 of 'Gemma Fabri'.] 1598. *See* Smyth, W.

22406 — Summa et synopsis Noui Testamenti. 8⁰. *Oxoniæ, ex off. J. Barnesii,* 1586. L³. O. HH.

Shepherd. The affectionate Shepheard. 1594. *See* Barnfield, R.

— The passionate shepheard. 1604. *See* Breton, N.

22407 **Shepherds' Kalendar.** The kalendayr of the shyppars. [*Tr.* Alex. Barclay?] fol. *Paris,* [*A. Verard,*] 1503 (23 jn.). O. (3 ll. only), M. (imp.), Devon.

22408 — [Anr. translation.] Here begyneth the Kalender of shepherdes. fol. *R. Pynson,* 1506. L. (imp.).

22409 — [Anr. translation, by R. Copland.] The kalender of shepeherdes. fol. *W. de Worde,* 1508 (8 de.). O¹².

22410 — [Anr. ed.] Here begynneth the kalender of shepardes. fol. *Julyan Notary,* M.CCCCC [XVIII ?] L. O.; HN. (all imp.).

22411 — [Anr. ed.] The kalēder of shepeherdes. 4⁰. *W. de Worde,* 1528 (24 ja.). O. (wants title a. colophon); HN.

22412 — [Anr. ed.] Here begynneth the kalender of shepardes. Newly augmented a. corrected. fol. *W. Powell,* 1559. L³.

22413 — [Anr. ed.] fol. *W. Powell f. J. Walley,* 1559. Ent. bef. 4 my. 1560. Q.

22414 — [Anr. ed.] fol. *J. Wally,* [1560 ?] O.

22415 — [Anr. ed.] Here beginneth the kalender of

A. W. Pollard and G. R. Redgrave's Short Title Catalogue, published by the Bibliographical Society in 1926

As has already been noted, the original idea for this preliminary record of research, in preparation for a full-dress catalogue, was that of a "handlist" of books of which copies could be traced, excluding those known only from report. It was intended from the first that the list should also serve as an index to the extant books entered on the Stationers' Register, and other possibilities were kept in mind; but as long as the entry served to identify book and edition, nothing more was desired, because anything more might stand in the way of the full-dress catalogue which was the ultimate ideal. One of the discoveries, however, to which the work done for this Short-title Catalogue has led is the existence of a much larger number than had been suspected of variant editions and issues bearing the same date. The differences between these are often quite slight, and to record them demands scrupulous care. The trouble is that when scrupulous care is evident in some entries, it is expected in all, and one object of this preface is to warn all users of this book that from the mixed character of its sources it is a dangerous work for any one to handle lazily, that is, without verification. The main workers on it on the average are septuagenarians and something over, and though the task of compilation and editing has been extended from the three or four years of our anticipation to between eight and nine, it has been necessary to work with some regard to time . . . Greater completeness as well as a higher standard of uniformity and accuracy might well have been attained if the work had been conducted from the first on a more systematic plan, more especially if it had been possible to obtain at the outset the help of a larger number of American libraries and collectors. But properly to organize team-work requires more (and more evenly distributed) leisure than was available, and all that seemed practicable was to find one volunteer after another and then, as far as was possible, to fill in the gaps.

The difference between what Pollard & Redgrave sought to achieve and what Bullen regarded as the minimum detail for an entry is easily seen by a comparison of a typical page from each catalogue. In STC the transcription of titles was severely curtailed, imprints were summary, and the entries were not all based on examination of the original books (a specimen page is reproduced opposite). But Pollard always insisted that STC was only a base upon which would be built, with cooperative effort on both sides of the Atlantic, a work of unimpeachable authority. It has taken almost fifty years to complete that work, and the publication in 1977 of the second volume of the revised edition of STC* begun by F. S. Ferguson and W. A. Jackson and completed by Katharine Pantzer was, indeed, the fulfilment of the Bibliographical Society's ambitions as expressed at the historic meeting on January 21, 1918, when STC was first projected. The effort that has been necessary in order to arrive at an accurate record of English printing up to 1640 and the time it has taken to complete it was the product of that 'scrupulous care' which is evident in every entry of New STC. The lesson for ESTC is clear, and it is to be hoped that by including fairly full and detailed descriptions of every item from the start, the risk of faulty matching will be minimized and that the entries, however short of the possible total, will not require subsequent re-examination on a large scale. Some indication of the magnitude of the task may be gained by reminding ourselves, from time to time, that ESTC will attempt to describe a corpus of printing more than ten times the size of that recorded in New STC.

The dependence of STC on British Museum rules for anonymous books has advantages and disadvantages. For example, identifying a book in STC usually ensures its identification in the General Catalogue, but not necessarily in the catalogues of other libraries – hence the widespread practice in major libraries of annotating STC with shelfmarks and additions. In Wing's STC the listing of anonymous books under title is more general, but the brevity of titles recorded there frequently causes difficulties in tracing a book to its heading in the General Catalogue. The two STCs are clearly derived from two different traditions: for STC that tradition derives from British Museum cataloguing rules; for Wing it lies in the cataloguing practices evolved in America and embodied in *Anglo-American Cataloguing Rules*. Apart from these differences, which concern principally the choice of heading, the two catalogues share a number of features: entries are brief, with the maximum practicable detail afforded to the imprint; edition statements are summary; format is given, but not pagination, and copies are located in up to five libraries in Great Britain and America. New STC goes beyond

*Volume I is due to appear in 1980.

POPE, Alexander *(1688–1744)*

P8380 An essay on criticism. [Anon.] *London: printed for W. Lewis; and sold by W. Taylor, T. Osborn, and J. Graves, 1711.* 4°: [2], 43, [3], p. L (4, 3 imp.); O, C (imp.), Dt(imp.), E(imp.); NNP, CLU-C, InU, MH(imp.), TxU(imp.), CtY, NIC(imp.). Foxon P806; Griffith 2.

P8381 [—] — [Anr. ed.] *London: printed for W. Lewis, 1711.* 4°: [2], 43, [3]p. CtY; IU, TxU, CSmH(imp.), NN-B. Foxon P807, 8; Griffith 3.

P8382 [—] — [Anr. ed.] *Dublin: printed by A. Rhames, for George Grierson, [1711?].* 12°: 36p. L; MH(imp.) Foxon P809; Griffith Add. 27a.

P8383 —— The second edition. *London: printed for W. Lewis, 1713 [1712].* 8°: [4], 36p. L; Lv(2), O, C, Dk, CtY, IU MH, ICU, NJP, CaBVaU, RPB. Foxon P810; Griffith 8.

P8384 —— The third edition. *London: printed for W. Lewis, 1713.* 12°: 35, [1]p. L; Lv(2), O, MRu, ABu; CLU-C, ICU, MH, NjP, TxU, DFo, Foxon P811; Griffith 26.

P8385 —— The fourth edition. *London: printed for W. Lewis, 1713.* 12°: 35, [1]p. L; O, Ot; ICN, ICU, MH, NjP, TxU, CoU, Pv, CtY, NN, NcD, NcD-MC. Foxon P812; Griffith 27. A re-issue.

P8386 —— The fifth edition. *London: printed for Bernard Lintot, 1716.* 12°: 35, [1]p. L; O; CtY, MH, TxU, NIC(imp.), DLC, CLSU. Foxon P813; Griffith 71.

P8387 —— [Anr. ed.] *London [The Hague]: printed for T. Johnson, 1716.* 8°: 51, MH. Foxon P814.

P8388 [—] — [Anr. ed.] *Dublin: re-printed for George Grierson, 1717.* 8°: 34p. L; NIC. Foxon P815; Griffith 102. Re-issued in *Works*, no. P8310 above.

P8389 —— The sixth edition. *London: printed for Bernard Lintot, 1719.* 8°: 48p. L; Lv, O, Ct; CtY, ICU, IU, MH(2), ICN, NjP, NIC. Foxon P816; Griffith 107.

P8390 —— The seventh edition. *London: printed for Bernard Lintot, 1722 [1721].* 8°: 48p. L; O, LEu; CtY(2), ICU(2), ICN, PU, NIC, NjP, NcD, IU, MH, TxU. Foxon P817; Griffith 129.

P8391 —— The seventh edition. *London: printed for Bernard Lintot, 1728.* 12°: 36p. ICU. Foxon P818.

P8392 —— [Anr. ed.] *[London: printed for M. Cooper, 1744].* 4°: [4], 60p. L(4); O, C, E, Gu; IU, MH(2), NjP CtY, NIC, NSchU, NN, TxU, MdBJ, CLU-C, CSmH, CSt. Foxon P819, 20; Griffith 590.

P8393 —— [Anr. ed.] *London: printed for Henry Lintot, 1749.* 8°: [2], 89, [1]p. O; Lv; CtY, MH(2), MB, InU, FU, NN. Foxon P821; Griffith 635.

P8394 —— [Anr. ed.] *London: printed for William Owen, 1751.* 8°: [2], 89, [1]p. L; DFo(imp.). Griffith 654.

P8395 —— [Anr. ed.] *Glasgow: printed by R. Urie, 1754.* 8°: 60, [25]p. L; MH.

P8396 —— [Anr. ed.] *Halle: J. J. Gebauer, 1758.* 8°: 28p. MH.

P8397 —— [Anr. ed.] *London: 1765.* 16°: 28p. MH.

P8398 Essai sur la critique. *Londres: par J. Delage, et se vend par P. Dunoier, 1717.* 4°: 19, [1]p. E; IU. Foxon R228. Tr. by J. Robethon.

P8399 —— Nouvelle édition. *Londres: (Imprimé chez G. Smith), 1737.* 4°: 193, [7]p. NIC; IU, NNC, CSmH, MiU; P.

P8400 Essais sur la critique et sur l'homme. Nouvelle édition. *Londres: chez Guillayme Darres, et Claude Du Bosc [imprimé chez G. Smith], 1741.* 4°: 193, [7]p. L; IU, ICU, FU. Griffith 539. Tr. by E. de Silhouette.

P8401 Versuch über die Critik. *Dressden: bey George Conrad Walther, 1745.* 8°: [12], 164p. L; GOT. Tr. by M. G. E. Mueller.

P8402 Tentamen de modis criticis. *Londini: typss Joh. Purser; prostant apud R. Dodsley & Jac. Robinson, [1745]* 8°: [2], x, [2], 31, [1]p. L; C, Ct, E; CLU-C, IU, TxU. Foxon K88. Tr. by James Kirkpatrick.

P8403 Tentamen de re critica. *Londini: prostant ap d M. Cooper; apud J. Hinton, 1747.* 8°: [4], xv, [1], 88p. L; O, ABu; IU, TxU, NIC NjP. Foxon G6. Tr. by U. Gahagan.

POPE, Alexander *(1688–1744)*

P8380 An essay on criticism. [Anon.] *London: printed for W. Lewis; and sold by W. Taylor, T. Osborn, and J. Graves, 1711.* 4°: [2], 43, [3], p. L (4, 3 imp.); O, C (imp.), Dt(imp.), E(imp.); NNP, CLU-C, InU, MH(imp.), TxU(imp.), CtY, NIC(imp.). Foxon P806; Griffith 2.

P8381 [—] — [Anr. ed.] *London: printed for W. Lewis, 1711.* 4°: [2], 43, [3]p. CtY; IU, TxU, CSmH(imp.), NN-B. Foxon P807, 8; Griffith 3.

P8382 [—] — [Anr. ed.] *Dublin: printed by A. Rhames, for George Grierson, [1711?].* 12°: 36p. L; MH(imp.) Foxon P809; Griffith Add. 27a.

P8383 —— The second edition. *London: printed for W. Lewis, 1713 [1712].* 8°: [4], 36p. L; Lv(2), O, C, Dk, CtY, IU MH, ICU, NJP, CaBVaU, RPB. Foxon P810; Griffith 8.

P8384 —— The third edition. *London: printed for W. Lewis, 1713.* 12°: 35, [1]p. L; Lv(2), O, MRu, ABu; CLU-C, ICU, MH, NjP, TxU, DFo, Foxon P811; Griffith 26.

P8385 —— The fourth edition. *London: printed for W. Lewis, 1713.* 12°: 35, [1]p. L; O, Ot; ICN, ICU, MH, NjP, TxU, CoU, Pv, CtY, NN, NcD, NcD-MC. Foxon P812; Griffith 27. A re-issue.

P8386 —— The fifth edition. *London: printed for Bernard Lintot, 1716.* 12°: 35, [1]p. L; O; CtY, MH, TxU, NIC(imp.), DLC, CLSU. Foxon P813; Griffith 71.

P8387 —— [Anr. ed.] *London [The Hague]: printed for T. Johnson, 1716.* 8°: 51, MH. Foxon P814.

P8388 [—] — [Anr. ed.] *Dublin: re-printed for George Grierson, 1717.* 8°: 34p. L; NIC. Foxon P815; Griffith 102. Re-issued in *Works*, no. P8310 above.

P8389 —— The sixth edition. *London: printed for Bernard Lintot, 1719.* 8°: 48p. L; Lv, O, Ct; CtY, ICU, IU, MH(?), ICN, NjP, NIC. Foxon P816; Griffith 107.

P8390 —— The seventh edition. *London: printed for Bernard Lintot, 1722 [1721].* 8°: 48p. L; O, LEu; CtY(2), ICU(2), ICN, PU, NIC, NjP, NcD, IU, MH, TxU. Foxon P817; Griffith 129.

P8391 —— The seventh edition. *London: printed for Bernard Lintot, 1728.* 12°: 36p. ICU. Foxon P818.

P8392 —— [Anr. ed.] *[London: printed for M. Cooper, 1744].* 4°: [4], 60p. L(4); O, C, E, Gu; IU, MH(2), NjP CtY, NIC, NSchU, NN, TxU, MdBJ, CLU-C, CSmH, CSt. Foxon P819, 20; Griffith 590.

P8393 —— [Anr. ed.] *London: printed for Henry Lintot, 1749.* 8°: [2], 89, [1]p. O; Lv; CtY, MH(2), MB, InU, FU, NN. Foxon P821; Griffith 635.

P8394 —— [Anr. ed.] *London: printed for William Owen, 1751.* 8°: [2], 89, [1]p. L; DFo(imp.). Griffith 654.

P8395 —— [Anr. ed.] *Glasgow: printed by R. Urie, 1754.* 8°: 60, [25]p. L; MH.

P8396 —— [Anr. ed.] *Halle: J. J. Gebauer, 1758.* 8°: 28p. MH.

P8397 —— [Anr. ed.] *London: 1765.* 16°: 28p. MH.

P8398 Essai sur la critique. *Londres: par J. Delage, et se vend par P. Dunoier, 1717.* 4°: 19, [1]p. E; IU. Foxon R228. Tr. by J. Robethon.

P8399 —— Nouvelle édition. *Londres: (Imprimé chez G. Smith), 1737.* 4°: 193, [7]p. NIC; IU, NNC, CSmH, MiU; P.

P8400 Essais sur la critique et sur l'homme. Nouvelle édition. *Londres: chez Guillayme Darres, et Claude Du Bosc [imprimé chez G. Smith], 1741.* 4°: 193, [7]p. L; IU, ICU, FU. Griffith 539. Tr. by E. de Silhouette.

P8401 Versuch über die Critik. *Dressden: bey George Conrad Walther, 1745.* 8°: [12], 164p. L; GOT. Tr. by M. G. E. Mueller.

P8402 Tentamen de modis criticis. *Londini: typss Joh. Purser; prostant apud R. Dodsley & Jac. Robinson, [1745]* 8°: [2], x, [2], 31, [1]p. L; C, Ct, E; CLU-C, IU, TxU. Foxon K88. Tr. by James Kirkpatrick.

P8403 Tentamen de re critica. *Londini: prostant ap d M. Cooper; apud J. Hinton, 1747.* 8°: [4], xv, [1], 88p. L; O, ABu; IU, TxU, NIC NjP. Foxon G6. Tr. by U. Gahagan.

A sample page of ESTC in short-title format

these bare essentials and incorporates detailed information on printing history, date, imperfections of copies, and distinctions relating to variants and issues, and has set a standard for short-title catalogues difficult to follow. It is not surprising, therefore, that throughout the June Conference, and in much of the debate about bibliographical standards which has occupied the various meetings held since, the expectations for ESTC were expressed as attempting no more than a "Pollard & Redgrave". That the project has chosen to identify its objectives more closely with those of New STC, as far as practicably possible, is due to the irresistible appeal of machine-readable cataloguing (MARC) to which research libraries are increasingly committed. Those who attended the June Conference were in no doubt that a wholly manual ESTC was an impossibility and, if the computer was to be used at all, there were persuasive arguments in favour of enhancing the records for ESTC up to a standard which was at least compatible with the requirements of the revision of *Anglo-American Cataloguing Rules* (AACR2) and MARC. As an example of what a page of ESTC, produced according to the traditions of STC might have looked like, a sample page enumerating the editions of Pope's *Essay on Criticism* is reproduced opposite. Such a catalogue would, no doubt, be less expensive to compile, less bulky, and easier to use. But by the time the British Library had completed the second pilot project it had become clear that, if ESTC was to win the support of major libraries, the records would have to conform to the broad principles of MARC cataloguing.

Machine-Readable Cataloguing

The practical application of the computer to bibliographic cataloguing has been necessitated by the realisation that the traditional role of the cataloguing department of a large library was becoming increasingly difficult to sustain in the face of ever-increasing demands to acquire ever-increasing numbers of books published throughout the world in a multitude of languages. The sheer bulk of acquisitions flowing into research libraries in the post-war publishing expansion, stimulated in part by the correlative expansion in higher education, threatened to overwhelm the resources of even the largest institutions. Some way had to be found to obviate the need for every library acquiring a "standard" book to catalogue its copy. The principle of one definitive bibliographic record for a book was not itself new: the Library of Congress card distribution service had been performing this important function for subscribing libraries since 1901. What was new was the principle that a catalogue record, stored in a machine-readable file and capable of virtually instantaneous indexing, could be consulted via electronic means, amended, enhanced, and copied at will by any user connected to the file. Furthermore, in constructing a dictionary catalogue requiring several copies of a record the ability of the computer to generate printed copies of a record is a clear advantage.

The development of MARC cataloguing in the United States and Britain has proceeded during recent years in parallel with the revision of AACR, for it was clear that as increasing numbers of libraries subscribed to on-line computer cataloguing systems (OCLC, BALLOTS, BLAISE) and shared cataloguing became the rule rather than the exception, there was an urgent requirement to develop a cataloguing code for modern books which would ensure uniformity in practice. Since the individual library is no longer necessarily responsible for the creation of a bibliographic record of a book it acquires, it follows that universal acceptance of a cataloguing code becomes a matter of crucial importance. One principle embodied in the operation of a shared-cataloguing system – that redundant intellectual effort devoted to the near-simultaneous cataloguing of the same book in several libraries represents a prodigal waste of resources – clearly requires a collective trust in the construction of a record according to a code (to which the cooperating libraries collectively subscribe) by any member of the co-operative. The importance of this principle is underlined by the intricate difficulties experienced by the Library of Congress in compiling, maintaining, editing and finally publishing a vast National Union Catalogue based on cards submitted from a wide variety of libraries. The problems encountered in matching records compiled according to different cataloguing rules are nowhere more evident than in the duplicate records for the same book which are a conspicuous feature of NUC. More disturbing perhaps is the fact, to which any bibliographer who has used NUC as a primary source will testify, that a single record with multiple locations frequently disguises the existence of different bibliographical entities. Since ESTC has, in its day-to-day operation, continuous recourse to NUC as a reference work, ESTC is well aware of the problems created in a union catalogue by the absence of uniform conventions.

It was inevitable that the principle of shared cataloguing for modern books would, in time, be extended to include books of all periods, and it is significant that the revision of AACR, together with its international offspring ISBD (International Standard Book Description) has gone some way to incorporate early printed books within its prescriptions. It is regrettable that the architects of AACR2 and international standards for the description of all printed books were unable to accommodate within their proposals one self-evident fact that books printed by hand, before the widespread use of mechanical printing in the middle of the nineteenth century, belong to a different species, and cannot adequately be described according to the rules devised for modern books. Furthermore, there is the equally self-evident fact that those who need access to older material have expectations of a bibliographic record different from those who use a record for a modern book. To these simple propositions may be added the recognition that copies of early printed books are rare. The economic argument for shared cataloguing cannot be said to apply when there is abundant evidence that a very high proportion of the items which ESTC will record will be represented by fewer than five copies. In the case of ephemera it seems quite possible that the majority will prove to be unique. The development of an international standard for the description of older books (ISBD-A), while in principle a commendable aim, has, it appears, required some rejection of the tradition accumulated in over a century of bibliographical endeavour. ESTC has resisted the tendency to dismiss the "tradition" as obsolete and incapable of adaptation to the seemingly inflexible requirements of the computer.

Conceived as a tool for historical research ESTC owes its existence to the imagination and determination of individuals for whom an accurate and intellectually revealing record of the printed word is a necessity. The *General Catalogue*, whatever its shortcomings, has always, in spite of numerous changes since 1841, sought to provide such a record, and the evolution of Panizzi's rules (see Appendix II) has consistently tended in the direction of providing readers with an accurate description of the individual item and suggesting, by virtue of its sequential position, the historical context of that item. The capability of the *General Catalogue* to reveal by its ordering of entries is a feature which ESTC is unwilling to abandon in favour of a mere alphabetic or indeed random arrangement. It is a matter of concern to those who are responsible for the execution of ESTC that it should strive to fulfil the expectations of its users whether they are students of literature seeking a copy of a book, the history of a text, a conspectus of an author's work, or historians whose needs are often less defined and specific requiring access to a wide variety of bibliographically unrelated items.

The failure of AACR2 and ISBD-A wholly to satisfy the needs of ESTC is due, in large measure, to the absence of experience in accommodating within a large retrospective file complex sequences of editions and issues, a problem which seldom occurs in a file comprehending modern printed books. No substantial retrospective file currently exists and, in the absence of any contradictory experience available to the architects of AACR2 and ISBD-A, it was assumed that principles found adequate for modern books would suffice for their elder brethren. It is the experience of ESTC that this assumption is false. The catalogue of the British Library's holdings of the works of Alexander Pope printed before 1800 provided in this book – submitted as a model of the project's bibliographical ambitions – could not have been produced in that form without certain modifications to both AACR2 and MARC. Its evolution was accompanied by a succession of refinements to the cataloguing rules over a period of months. The problems daily encountered by cataloguers required to accommodate the book in hand, with all its idiosyncrasies, within the textual tradition of which it is merely an evidential unit, and to do so in a manner which permits subsequent additions from the resources of other libraries possessing other units as yet undisclosed, require a continuous re-appraisal of the limitations, as well as the opportunities, provided by the computer. The responsibility to contribute solutions to the problems created in automatic filing is a challenge to which ESTC has responded with enthusiasm and has added a dimension of some significance to the project unforeseen by many at the June Conference.

The principles governing the creation of a valid isolative record, i.e. one which, like a LC card, contains, and if necessary repeats, all the relevant details concerning an individual publication – are relatively simple to formulate once agreement has been reached as to the essential data such a record should contain. These data will include, as a matter of course, the choice of heading, the ordering of the information on the titlepage, the collation (not necessarily the register), and the physical characteristics of the copy. While in the majority of records for straightforward books ESTC rules involve no conflict with AACR2, there are cases where modifications have been necessary. It should be stressed that the differences between ESTC methods and AACR/MARC have been kept to a minimum; none have been shown to result in records which are unacceptable to the British national data base. In the purely descriptive part of the record these differences are confined to small, but for scholarly purposes, important details. On the record card the title and edition statement are transcribed *literatim*, including the original punctuation, in accordance with the standards of title page transcription traditionally associated with scholarly catalogues. Thus, all subfield delimiters and the associated prescribed punctuation marks are omitted; all omissions, including preceding epithets are indicated by ellipses; no author statements are transposed; and edition statements are not standardised.

It has been found through experience that the grouping and filing facilities provided by AACR/MARC are inadequate for complicated headings and sequences of editions. This inadequacy has been supplied by the introduction of three additional fields, which are not prescribed in standard MARC. They are used in ESTC cataloguing, either singly or in combinations, to provide the computer with the instructions necessary to ensure a correct filing sequence. In order to appreciate the reasons for these precise instructions it must be remembered that in computer filing the slightest deviation from the alphabetic progression at any point in the individual title may disrupt the sequence. It is also evident that in a sequence of editions all having the same title and imprint date but belonging to different impressions the computer will, unless otherwise instructed, file them randomly. In a manual file the ordering of editions can be simply effected, but the computer scrupulously obeys an alphabetical logic. Thus, in a sequence of titles for an identical work established as follows:

Reasons presented to the House of Commons . . . 1711
Reasons humbly presented to the House of Commons . . . 1711
Reasons humbly offered to the House of Commons . . . 1711
Reasons humbly offered to the Honourable House of Commons . . . 1711

the computer will file them in reverse order unless the title field (245) is overridden in some way.

Normal application of a uniform title will still not achieve a correct sequence, unless some *additional* filing element is included. The field in which this filing information is inserted has been designated 249, subfield $a. The filing data may be in simple numerical form: 010,020,030, subfield $a; or, to allow a greater degree of hospitality for future insertions, in alphabetical form D,E,F, etc.

The exercise of vigilance which is required when cataloguing and filing different editions of the same work places a considerable burden on those editing the file before it is keyboarded, especially since the method of working does not normally permit one cataloguer to be responsible for all the records of an individual author or title. Anonymous works present particular difficulties since they never get collected under a heading other than the first word of title, and titles such as *Poems on several occasions* require an intricate uniform title description to ensure correct filing.

This device will allow the imposition of a sequence on editions of one *work* with a complicated publishing history. For large complicated *headings*, of which that for Alexander Pope is a representative example, it has been necessary to construct a special filing field (not prescribed in MARC) designated 239, and the catalogue of Pope's work provided below was mechanically sorted in strict accordance with the instructions implicit in the use of 239. But the use of this field is necessarily dependent upon the completion of a heading, and is therefore not used by cataloguers unless or until an entire heading has been catalogued. The application of this filing field will, therefore, have to be the concern of the editors when the manual file at the British Library is completed.

The third additional field is designated 259, subfield $a, and is used to ensure correct chronological filing when the form entered at 260 $c has been subject to modification (e.g. it was misprinted in the original imprint, or is known to be incorrect). Thus, in three consecutive editions dated 1726 [1725 in fact], 1726, and 1726 [1727 in fact] the correct date is given in 259, thereby ensuring the sequence [1725]–1726–[1727].

In certain cases it may be necessary to use these additional fields in conjunction with each other, i.e. they are not mutually exclusive, as different filing data may be required for the main and added entry sequences.

It can be asserted with some confidence that while much attention has been devoted to the creation of an international standard for the description of a book in its isolative context, very little has been devoted to the problem of how such records can be accommodated in a substantial file so that sequences of an author's works and sequences of editions are preserved in a historically meaningful order. The problems which will inevitably arise from negligence in this crucial area are likely to be serious and, if unforeseen, render inoperable one of the distinctive features of a machine-readable file: the capability to produce, on demand, printed lists of retrospectively converted records from a wide variety of collections which have the authority and integrity of a conventionally produced bibliography or catalogue. Identification of an isolative record has a defined if limited purpose: the larger purpose, in which that record can reveal contextually its ancestry and its offspring, is for most students of cultural history of far greater significance. This, it is assumed, is what Richard Christophers implied when he asserted (page 3 above) the British Library's interest is in "a catalogue of the highest possible bibliographical standard is an objective of prime importance".

Working Methods

It has already been noted that many of the routines adopted in the execution of the first stage of ESTC were established during the second pilot project. They fall into four principal stages: (1) the description of the book based on simultaneous examination of "duplicates"; (2) verification of transcription by another cataloguer; (3) addition of bibliographical data assembled from reference works; (4) filing. All four stages are, inevitably, interactive, as illustrated in the following example. Cataloguer A describes the book in hand (which may contain numerous individual items) and checks the record against the project's set of the *General Catalogue*. It is there discovered that of the ten items in the volume the Library possesses other copies of five. These are fetched, and it is determined whether or not they are genuine duplicates. The General Catalogue is then marked with an "E" to indicate that these items have been described and verified. The records, and the books, are then passed to cataloguer B who checks transcription, and may make suggestions about details included or excluded, form of heading, etc. A then consults the authority file in order to verify the author's established form of name, epithet, and any other data which the authority cards might contain, and if no title by that author has yet been catalogued establishes an authority card, based on information culled from various biographical (e.g. *DNB*) or bibliographical (e.g. *NUC*) sources. If the item(s) in question appear(s) to present complications the cataloguer will, as a matter of course, consult other bibliographies and catalogues. With all this preliminary checking completed the record(s) can be xeroxed for insertion in the various files maintained by the project. The filing of the main card, the final step in the process before keyboarding, frequently requires alterations to be made if other editions of the title are already on file: the length of title may have to be adjusted, the uniform title may have to be changed, and where the records for different editions of a title appear to be identical they will all be withdrawn for closer inspection. Only thus can a re-issue, perhaps calling itself the "fifth" edition, be accurately identified. As the enlargement of the file from the resources of other libraries progresses, there is some likelihood that a record may be filed immediately adjacent to a record submitted by another library whose copy may contain information missing from the Library's copy. Such information may take the form of ascriptions of authorship (sometimes derived from contemporary annotations) or date. If the source appears to be reliable, then this information will be taken over, and any emendation of the *General Catalogue* necessary will be incorporated in the project's set. The verification of ESTC's cataloguing by comparison with records compiled in other libraries is an important way of ensuring accuracy and consistency.

The project maintains a number of manual files which are indispensable for the systematic creation of a large retrospective data base according to the principles described in the section on cataloguing above. The most important of these is undoubtedly the book trade index, started during the second pilot project, which now extends to several thousand cards. Data are culled from a wide variety of sources: directories, poll-books, imprints, studies of printing and bookselling in journals, the scanning of provincial newspapers, information voluntarily supplied by a large number of provincial public and university libraries, and records for provincial imprints contributed by a growing number of libraries throughout Britain. Thus, the nearly complete file of records for Aberdeen printing in the library of Aberdeen University has enabled the index for that town to be more or less comprehensive. As the project's links with other regional studies of the book trade are increasingly close, the amount of accurate and bibliographically revealing data available to cataloguers similarly increases, thereby contributing significantly to the quality of the records being compiled. Much guesswork in dating is obviated, and in many cases it is becoming possible to ascribe, with some degree of confidence, the printing of a work to a particular printer.

A companion to the book trade index, recently begun, is a file of printers' ornaments based on photographs taken by a Polaroid camera. The extension of this file to include ornaments found in the collections of other libraries has already begun, and much useful raw material is being abstracted from the photocopies which the project has acquired of ephemera in the Bodleian Library and Cambridge University Library, as well as in several smaller provincial libraries.

Information derived from the systematic scanning of learned journals for information about any aspect of eighteenth century printing and publishing is noted in the project's set of the *General Catalogue*. In this way a study of a particular author can be drawn to the attention of cataloguers. Attributions of authorship for anonymous works discovered in articles, books or bibliographies are similarly noted. The project is fortunate in receiving from scholars throughout the world information about the progress of their work which sometimes takes the form of a donated typescript prior to publication. Much of this invaluable cooperative help derives from the project's newsletter – *Factotum* – which is distributed gratis to a wide variety of institutions and individuals.

There are five main files which are based on the master record: an authority file; an imprint file; a genre file; a chronological file; and a file devoted to items not hitherto separately catalogued in the *General Catalogue*. The maintenance of these files is the responsibility of a clerical officer, who xeroxes the master record as many times as necessary. Thus, an almanac with an author statement, printed at Nottingham, and not separately catalogued, will be xeroxed five times; an anonymous pamphlet printed in London will be xeroxed once only for the chronological file.

The authority file is constructed from information about an author drawn from a variety of sources: an authority card will provide an established form of the name, alternative forms or spellings, an established epithet, and dates of birth and death if ascertainable. A separate authority file is kept for corporate authorship and provides details of established headings and subheadings. On the completion of the British Library project it is proposed that these two files be made available in machine-readable form in order to facilitate enrichment of ESTC records in America and elsewhere.

The imprint file, arranged (chronologically) by place (other than London) has proved of great value: for new facts about a particular printer can be used to revise earlier less well-informed cataloguing. In the absence of any contradictory information, cataloguers will normally rely on the *General Catalogue* to date undated publications. The book trade and imprint files have, however, shown that these dates should not be accepted uncritically. For example, a recently discovered collection of single sheet poems printed by J. Fowler of Salisbury (dated in the General Catalogue as *ca.* 1841) can be confidently dated as *ca.* 1785 from evidence available in both the imprint and book trade files. And the discovery that S. Harward of Tewkesbury was printing in the 1760s has led to the redating of a whole series of garlands and chapbooks previously catalogued as *ca.* 1785. The book trade index is particularly valuable for books and pamphlets printed between *ca.* 1690 and *ca.* 1710, and many items recorded in Wing have been brought forward to a date in the eighteenth century.

The genre file is restricted to certain categories of material which it was felt required to be brought together in order to make a huge quantity of mostly ephemeral items accessible. These categories are: almanacs, advertisements, directories, prospectuses, and songs (including ballads). A substantial number of these have "authors" and will be entered in ESTC under the appropriate heading, but, in view of their evidential value for historians, it was thought useful to provide an additional point of access. In the case of advertisements, for instance, the required AACR2 heading is likely to be some such word as *In, To, At*, making such items difficult to locate unless the precise wording is already known. A researcher seeking evidence likely to be provided by an advertisement will, by consulting that genre heading, have his search reduced to manageable proportions.

The chronological file, which duplicates the main file, is arranged so that each year of the century has three divisions: works stated to be printed in a year; works reliably attributed to a year; and works for which the year is an intelligent guess. Thus, for the year 1714, records are arranged as follows: 1714 (given in the imprint and no modification suggested)—[1714] (attributed on reliable internal or external evidence; the imprint may well have 1713)—[1714?] (an unverified date from a secondary source, including the General Catalogue). With nearly 100,000 records already incorporated, the chronological file is becoming a tool of considerable value for historians.

The file devoted to items not separately catalogued in the General Catalogue already includes over 10,000 records and is frequently used by visiting scholars. When completed this file will constitute an important supplement to the General Catalogue.

Although samples of records compiled during the first and second pilot projects were keyboarded and processed in the British Library's central computer, keyboarding on any scale did not begin until November 1977. Since then some 9,000 records have been converted into machine-readable form and are held on a BLAISE file in the British Library computer at Harlow. The diagnostic (or edit-list) for these records (see opposite) has been corrected and the records will, in due course, be amended. There is, however, uncertainty about the extent to which ESTC can continue to have its records converted, since it is clear that the first responsibility of the project's staff must be to complete the cataloguing of the British Library's holdings by the end of 1980. Keyboarding on a large scale will inevitably require the deployment of additional resources. The correction or amendment of records no longer, mercifully, requires the marking of diagnostic and the completion of record-amendment forms: the project now has an ICL 1501 terminal (and line-printer) which can, with software specially designed for the British Library, retrieve BLAISE records in batches. The 1501 mini-tapes are capable of holding over three hundred MARC records which can be amended at will and then despatched to the central computer. On-line charges are thus reduced to the absolute minimum. A sample of line-printer output from the 1501 is reproduced on page 33.

Enlargement of The British Library File

At an early stage in the second pilot project it was realised that the success of ESTC would depend upon the extent to which adequate procedures could be devised for incorporating into the file the records of other libraries. As already indicated above, the matching of bibliographical records and the management of a union catalogue present numerous problems. There are five basic kinds of evidence which can be employed in

t005529

          +RI+   PRCVENANCE=dp   TYPE=a   CLASS=m

                             *ben *c *d   *e *f *g *h *i *j *k *leng *m *n *o   *p

008 0 00 / 0   013 780412 *as1726+

049 0 00 / 0   *aL+

090 0 00 / 0   *a643.l.24(49)+

090 0 00 / 1   *a163.n.13+

100 0 10 / 0   *aPope*hAlexander*fthe Poet+

239 0 00 / 0   *a70090+

245 0 14 / 0   *aThe discovery: or, the squire turn d ferret. An excellent new ballad. To the tune of High boys! up go we;

               Chevy Chase; or what you please.+

260 0 00 / 0   *aWestminster*bprinted by A. Campbell, for T. Warner, and sold by the booksellers*cl727 1726 +
                                                                                                (　)

300 0 00 / 0   *a8p.*c2 +
               H

500 0 00 / 0   *aAscribed to Alexander Pope, in collaboration with William Pulteney, by Spence on Pope s authority.

               Publication date from Twickenham edition.   On the imposture of Mary Toft+

503 0 00 / 0   *aFoxon D328+

700 0 10 / 0   *aPulteney*hWilliam*fEarl of Bath+

956 0 00 / 0   *bwith a folding engraved plate by William Hogarth inserted+

A proof-list as produced on the British Library's central computer

33

```
#RI#T005570#
008 $as1711$ben$1en9#
049 L#
090 Cup.402.f.4#
090/1 161.m.24#
090/2 Ashley 3765#
090/3 C.57.i.49#
245.13 An essay on criticism.#
239 70500#
260 London$bPrinted for W. Lewis; and sold by W. Taylor, T. Osborn, an
d J. Graves$c1711#
300 [2], 43, [3]p.$c4°#
500 Anonymous.  By Alexander Pope. - With a half-title and a final lea
f of advertisements#
100.1 Pope$hAlexander$fthe Poet#
956/0 Uncut; half-title mutilated#
956/1 $bImperfect; wanting the advertisement leaf.  Luttrell's MS. dat
e on titlepage:  17 May#
956/2 $bImperfect; wanting the half-title and advertisement leaf#
956/3 $bImperfect; wanting the half-title and advertisement leaf#
089 $aO(made-up);$aC(imp.); $aE(imp.); $aOt(imp.); $aCLU-C; $aInU; $aM
H(imp.); $aNNP; $aTxU(imp.); $aCtY; $aNIC(imp.)#
503 Foxon P806; Griffith 2#

#RI#T999917#
008 $as1711$ben$1en9#
049 CtY#
090 xxxxx#
245.13 An essay on criticism.#
239 70505#
260 London$bPrinted for W. Lewis$c1711#
300 [2], 43, [3]p.$c4°#
500 Anonymous.  By Alexander Pope. - A variant; the change in imprint
was apparently made at press#
100.1 Pope$hAlexander$fthe Poet#
089 IU(made-up); $aTxU; $aCSmH(imp.); $aNN-B(fine paper)#
503 Foxon P807,8; Griffith 3#

#RI#T005571#
008 $as1711$bie$1en9#
049 L#
090 1488.de.46(5)#
245.13 An essay on criticism.#
239 70510#
260 Dublin$bPrinted by A. Rhames, for George Grierson$c[1711?]#
300 36p.$c12°#
500 Anonymous.  By Alexander Pope. - Includes John Philips's 'The sple
ndid shilling', pp. 33-36#
100.1 Pope$hAlexander$fthe Poet#
956 $bImperfect; wanting pp. 29-32#
089 MH(imp.)#
503 Foxon P809; Griffith Add. 27a#

#RI#T005572#
008 $as1712$ben$1en9#
049 L#
090 11631.bbb.45#
245.03 An essay on criticism.  Written by Mr. Pope.#
250 The second edition#
239 70520#
260 London$bPrinted for W. Lewis$c1713[1712]#
300 [4], 36p.$c8°#
500 With a half-title. - Publication date from Foxon#
100.1 Pope$hAlexander$fthe Poet#
089 $aLv(2); $aO; $aC; $aOk; $aCtY; $aICU; $aIU; $aMH; $aTxU(Griffith
1); $aNIC#
089.1 NJP; $aCaBVaU; $aRPB#
503 Foxon P810; Griffith 8#
```

A specimen of a machine-readable proof-list as produced on the ICL computer system in use in the British Library Project the construction of a union catalogue: (1) a reproduction of the titlepage marked for format and pagination; (2) a record card containing a transcription of most of the essential elements of the title page with format and pagination added; (3) a very brief record accompanied by a fingerprint; (4) a library catalogue card; and (5) an entry in a printed catalogue or bibliography. After a considerable amount of testing of all five methods ESTC has decided to accept as evidence of a verified location (1) and (2); evidence from (4) and (5) is used for unverified locations; and method (3) is not used.

During the second pilot project all five methods were tested: for (1) a sample of 200 items was selected by staff in the Cambridge University Library; for (2) a sample of 300 items was selected from the British Library*; method (3) was, for obvious reasons, under continuous assessment; for (4) a sample of 500 items from the chronological files at Yale University and Trinity College, Dublin; for (5) a sample of 200 items in the catalogue of the Goldsmiths' Library at London University.

The items selected from Cambridge University Library covered various types of publication, printed at London and in the provinces, represented a variety of formats, and spanned the century. The xeroxes were marked for pagination, format, and shelf-mark, and sent to the project. They were distributed among the staff and the books were identified (where possible) in the General Catalogue. The British Library copies were then catalogued in the normal way, and the staff were asked to attempt a match where the evidence of the xerox and the record card seemed identical. The Cambridge xeroxes were then compared with the actual copies. In two cases changes in title page setting were undisclosed in the record, and could have been detected by no other means. One disadvantage of the titlepage method is the fact that it does not necessarily provide the author's name, and some items from Cambridge were not identified in the General Catalogue because the author-statements occurred at the end of a preface or dedication (all apparently anonymous books were referred back to Cambridge for checking). This disadvantage becomes less significant as the file grows, since a title is always matched against the main title file. The main advantage of the title page evidence in xerox form is that where any discrepancy is found between the pagination statement and the pagination given in the ESTC record a comparison between the two title pages is possible, and it is the experience of ESTC that whereas identical impressions of a text are commonly preceded by slightly different titlepages, it is extremely rare to find identical titlepages concealing different impressions. The one exception to this rule is the work consisting of several parts, each of which could have an independent existence, where the collective titlepage can conceal a variety of issues and states. Matching copies of works in parts requires a considerable body of detailed evidence.

The opportunity to provide ESTC with xerox titlepages does not always occur: an increasing number of libraries prohibit absolutely the xeroxing of early printed books. And many of the smaller libraries, with special collections of great interest to ESTC, simply have no facilities for providing photcopies on any scale. As an alternative, a modified record card, with a brief set of rules to ensure that essential data is recorded, was designed. After much experiment it was decided to adhere strictly to the format of the British Library card, but with those areas which contributing libraries had no responsibility to complete shaded in blue. In this way the task of completing a record is reduced to a minimum, and subsequent up-grading of the record to include all the data and tagging can be simply effected if no copy exists in the British Library. If more primary information about the book is required to construct a MARC record, at least there will be no need for re-transcription of the titlepage information. The volunteer record card, together with the rules governing its completion is reproduced on pages 37–39. Volunteer contributions to ESTC derive not only from library staff: a growing

---

*In a recent test carried out with the cooperation of London University Library (Porteous Collection), 118 abridged record cards were matched against the British Library file: when all the Porteous copies were checked against those in the British Library the match proved correct in 109 cases.

number of university staff, in departments of history and English studies, are undertaking to compile records for books in their libraries, and every such contribution brings a little nearer the completion of this massive cooperative enterprise.

It is a well known fact that library catalogues are compiled according to a disconcerting variety of rules, and though it would be foolish to disregard the evidence of a catalogue compiled according to the most scrupulous principles of historical bibliography (such as that for the Rothschild Collection at Trinity College, Cambridge), great care has to be taken in using library catalogues, and it is essential to establish beforehand the principles adopted in each. It must also be remembered that few library catalogues possess homogeneity- they reflect changes in cataloguing methods over a number of years. Few catalogues rigidly adhere to the details of the original titlepage, and detailed pagination is rarely given. The same observations apply to bibliographies and catalogues of authors, subjects, localities or individual presses. ESTC willingly accepts the evidence of a Foxon, a Todd, a Gaskell, but where books are described according to principles which fail to reflect the integrity of the titlepage or the precise details of its pagination, such evidence is treated with caution, and a location will be provided in the unverified field.

The value of the "fingerprint", devised as a technique for matching records in Project LOC (see further J. W. Jolliffe, *Computers and Early Books*, 1974), has been much debated. After much deliberation it was decided not to employ the fingerprint in the British Library on a comprehensive scale for the following reasons: recording, checking, keyboarding, and proofreading them would have added an unacceptable burden to the staff of ESTC and the financial resources available; to be effective they must be recorded with great precision according to a complex set of rules; they are not widely used as a bibliographical device; no international standard has yet been agreed; and, in cases where a text has been reset *literatim*, the fingerprint is unable to discriminate. Although the standard being used in France and Scotland derives from the formula described in the report on Project LOC, there is still much doubt about the standard which should be applied to single sheet material. A report on the fingerprint undertaken by John Feather at the request of the Research and Development Department of the British Library in 1977 is currently undergoing statistical analysis with a view to establishing whether the standard sixteen character fingerprint is capable of reduction to four. The outcome of this analysis is awaited with considerable interest. In the meantime, for purposes of further analysis, the fingerprint is being used in certain cases.

The enrichment of the ESTC at the British Library is currently based on records being submitted from over forty libraries. The largest contribution is being made by Manchester University where a team of twenty-five graduates is currently recording every eighteenth century English book in the University's Collections. The cataloguing team is using ESTC rules, the volunteer record card, and is directed by senior staff at the John Rylands University Library. The richness of Manchester's holdings in eighteenth century books and pamphlets has never been fully appreciated, and there is no doubt that their records will prove a most valuable addition to ESTC. The importance ESTC attaches to the contributions made by other libraries cannot be overstressed for, since the records submitted are based on a physical examination of the original books, a considerable amount of otherwise unavailable information is yielded. Thus, contemporary annotations frequently reveal authorship and date; the existence of half-titles, often suspected, is confirmed; a diligent cataloguer at another library may have discovered facts about a book not available to the cataloguer who compiled the entry in the General Catalogue. Two records recently submitted by Liverpool University Library illustrate the evidential significance of other copies: *The bride-woman's counsellor*, by John Sprint, and *Concerning holy resolution*, by Thomas Tenison, both printed by Henry Hills, are found in a chronological sequence of pamphlets collected by Lancelyn

Title	Author	Place	Heading
			967 $a a d p s v

* RI * 008 $a s $b en $1 eng 049 $a $c 1 2 3 $d 1

090 $a

245 [ ][ ] $a

240 [ ][ ] $a

250 $a

260 $a $b

$c

300 $a $b $c

500 $a

100 [ ] $a $h
110 $f

GK 3 519 $a

---

600 [ ] $a $h
6I0 [ ] $u

645

700 [ ][ ] $a $h
710

956 $b

Ver. locs. 089 0 $a $b $a $b $a $b
$a $b $a $b $a $b
$a $b $a $b $a $b

Unver. locs. 089 1 $a

Bibl. refs. 503 $a

Conservation

Provenance

Notes

The record card used by contributing libraries

37

RULES TO BE OBSERVED IN COMPLETING ESTC RECORD CARDS

The ESTC record card has been designed to accomodate the information necessary for compiling a machine-readable catalogue according to the standards embodied in AACR2 and MARC (UK version). The card has been pre-printed with a number of field and subfield tags, together with boxes for indicators. In completing your record cards these may be ignored, and you are required to complete only the unshaded areas:

    049 $a........the symbol for your library......090 $a........shelfmark(s)
    245 $a........transcription of the title.......250 $a........edition
    260 $a/$b/$c..imprint (place/printer(s)/date)..300 $a/$b/$c..pag./ill./format.

Providing that all the required details are provided in these fields it will be possible to match the record against the British Library file, and if the item is not there then a MARC record can be constructed. The following rules have been kept as simple and unambiguous as possible, and presuppose very little knowledge of either bibliographical principles or library cataloguing, and it is understood that certain books and pamphlets will inevitably present difficulties. In such cases do not hesitate to explain what you have before you in an extended note in the area marked *NOTES* on the back of the record card. Remember that difficult cases are always better described in detail rather than attempting to reduce information to a structured formula.

049 $a   Write here the symbol which has been allocated to your library.

090 $a   Write here the shelf-mark of the copy you are describing. If your library has more than one copy list them as follows:

          090 $a Ho.45.63 090/1 $a Ho.45.63/2 090/2 $a ... 090/3 $a ...

245 $a   Transcribe the title-page as fully as you judge necessary in order to convey the contents of the work, including sub-title, and details of authorship. Always include the names of editors, revisers, translators. Always include the opening words of the title-page unless they fall into the following categories:
          An author statement not grammatically linked to the title:
          THOMAS SMITH. / An appeal to Christians...
          An edition statement:
          Bell's edition. / The injured lady...
          An imprint statement:
          Printed at Paris, now reprinted at London. / The voice of the people...
          A date:
          London, 13 March, 1792. / At a meeting...
Adhere as closely as possible to the punctuation of the title-page, but only capitalise proper names, honorific titles (*Sir, Right Honourable, His Majesty, Lord, etc.*) Any omissions should be indicated by the use of ... preserving any mark of punctuation preceding. Transcribe as found all author statements:
...By James Harrison, M.A....   ...By a Lover of Truth.   ...By N.N., M.A.
Note: author statements found elsewhere than the title-page (dedication, preface, end) should be mentioned in the *NOTES* area.

250 $a   Transcribe here the edition statement (if any):
          The fifth edition, corrected...
          A new improved edition (No punctuation - see below)
          The fifteenth edition, revised by Thomas Martin, F.R.S.
Indicate if the edition statement is taken from elsewhere than the title-page (e.g. the half-title). Note: the computer generates a full point automatically at the end of this field.

260 $a   Give here the place of publication or printing. In complex imprints such as: *London printed: Dublin reprinted...* record *Dublin* in $a and repeat the whole statement in $b. If no place of publication is given (and you feel unsure about suggesting one) write *[No place]* in $a. If the imprint occurs elsewhere than the title-page (verso of title-page, end) note this fact. Note: the computer generates a comma automatically at the end of $a.

The rules used in the compilation of record cards for ESTC by contributing libraries

260 $b   Give here the names (but not the addresses) of up to seven persons named in the imprint, retaining the wording and punctuation of the original so as to indicate their responsibility for the book:

> *printed by John Hargreaves for Thomas Bell, and sold by J. Pardoe, T. Waller, and F. Lye*
>
> *sold by G.G.& J. Robinson, B. Collins, Salisbury, and F. Angus, Newcastle*

In the first example it is understood that all the persons named carried out their business in the place given at $a. In long imprints where more than seven names are given, indicate those after the fifth as follows:

> *...[+ 4 in London, 2 in Oxford, 1 in Cambridge]*

Note: the computer automatically generates a comma at the end of this field. If the imprint contains no names transcribe as found:

> *[London?] Printed in this present year [1750?]*
>
> *[London?] Printed for the booksellers of London [1780?]*

260 $c   Write here the date (if any) in arabic numbers. If the date is, or appears to be, erroneous then give the form as you find it, with the real (or probable) date in square brackets after. If the book has no date, and you feel unsure about ascribing one, write *[No date]* in $c. In such cases it will be helpful to acquire a photocopy.

300 $a   Record here the pagination exactly as it is given in the book, indicating the total of all unnumbered pages in square brackets. Do not record pagination for works in more than one volume where each volume has a separate sequence. If the work is unpaginated, count the pages giving the total within square brackets. The following examples illustrate the principles to be adopted:

> 2v.   6v.   2v. (690p.) *i.e. pagination continuous.*
>
> *[6], 140 p.*   *[8], viii, 112 p.*
>
> *164, [4] p.*   *xii, [4], 36, 124 p. i.e. two arabic sequences.*

Note: a book paginated *viii 9-60* would be described as *60p.* If the page numeration begins after i or 1, count back to the page which would have been so numbered. If this page constitutes what could be considered a reasonable place to start (i.e. not half-way through the Preface), record the sequence as though it had been so numbered. If this procedure produced ambiguity then record the pagination as accurately as possible:

> *[i-vi], 5-80 p. 6 preliminary pages, text begins on p. 5.*

Although blank pages should be included and indicated, do not count blank leaves. Engraved matter (unless printed on leaves forming part of the signatures) is not included in $a. The only exception to this rule is for an engraved title-page unaccompanied by a letterpress title-page. The presence of an engraved title-page, whether used as the basis for the description or not, should always be indicated.

300 $b   Give here details of any illustrations, plates, maps, music, folding tables, etc. Indicate folding tables whether or not they constitute part of the pagination sequence.

300 $c   Give here the format, according to the principles adopted in most manuals of bibliographical description. For single sheet items write *1 sheet* in $a, and give the proportion (as nearly as you can) of the item in question to a whole sheet of the period, expressed as a fraction: 1/2o, 1/4o, 1/8o. For example, a 1/2o will be approximately the size of a sheet from a folio with vertical chain-lines. Where no attempt to determine the fraction of a whole sheet can be made give the measurements in mm., height before width. Note: single sheet items usually present great difficulties in description, and where possible a photocopy of the whole item is preferred.

Any details regarding the book in hand which you feel should form part of the description (imperfections, provenance, presence of MS. notes, ascriptions of authorship, etc.) should be given in the *NOTES* area on the back of the card. References to standard bibliographies are desirable where possible.

The rules used in the compilation of record cards for ESTC by contributing libraries

Green. Their position in the collection suggests that they appeared in 1708. They are dated in the General Catalogue [1699?] and [1695?] on the evidence of the dates on which the sermons were preached, and are accordingly entered in Wing at S5084 and T689. Hills is well known as a reprinter and it seems likely that Wing S5084 (printed by W. Bowyer and sold by A. Baldwin) is the first edition of Sprint's sermon, and that a first edition of Tenison's has yet to be found. ESTC, on the Liverpool evidence, has dated both items as [1708?], especially since Hills's piratical activities seem to have begun in that year.

The problems presented by ephemera are such that it has been decided to incorporate locations only on the evidence of a photocopy. And, since a photocopy of a single sheet item provides the complete text, the British Library collections are significantly enriched if the item happens—often the case—to be a different setting or unrecorded. The project has now acquired a complete photographic file of the songs and ballads in the Madden Collection at Cambridge University Library, and photocopies of the eighteenth century ephemera in the John Johnson and Harding Collections at the Bodleian. The Bodleian survey of ephemera, based on various stack collections in addition to Johnson and Harding (e.g. Gough adds., Douce adds., Douce Prints, etc.) has yielded a harvest of over 16,000 items, of which it is estimated that the British Library possesses no more than twenty percent. Since ephemera tend to be found in archives, plans are being prepared for searching a number of county archives, and a massive operation at the Public Record Office is under consideration. The association of printed material with contemporary manuscripts is often a circumstance which contributes to the dating of these problematical pieces.

In the *Feasibility Study*, which brought about the June Conference, Paul Korshin wrote:

> In any scholarly project of the size of the Eighteenth-Century STC, it is inevitable that a feasibility study must face, and prepare solutions to, a number of critical questions concerning geographical and chronological scope, methodology, the use of computers, personnel, libraries, and funding.

It is our belief that, given the support of the British Library, evident at every stage in the project's development as outlined above, much has been accomplished, and that the expectations of those who were present at the Conference in June 1976 have been, in some measure, fulfilled. The willingness to contribute to ESTC manifested by a growing number of institutions and individuals is reassuring to all those who have contributed their energies and skills to the establishment of ESTC as a practical project, and testifies to the importance which so many attach to it. As a cooperative venture in historical bibliography ESTC has no precedent, and has had to learn all its lessons the hard way, but there is now sufficient evidence to suggest that the project so tentatively conceived at the June Conference in 1976 is established, and that success is within its grasp.

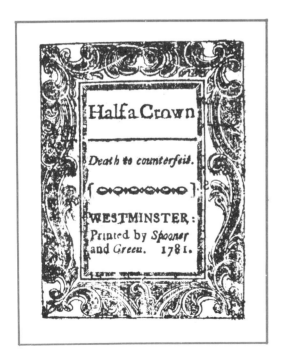

An engraved trade card, currency, and a theatre ticket (not included in ESTC)

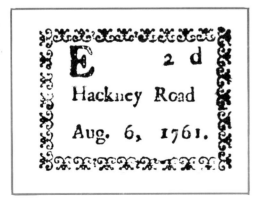

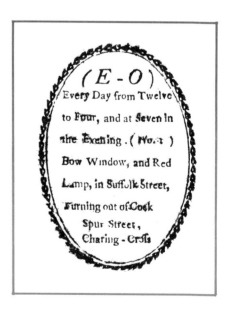

A funeral ticket, a turnpike ticket, and a brothel ticket (not included in ESTC)

THEATRE,

STRAWBERRY-HILL,

NOVEMBER, 1800,

Will be prefented a COMEDY in Two Acts called

The Old Maid.

Mr. Harlow, Mr. B U R N,
Clerimont, EARL of MOUNT EDGCUMBE,
Captain Cape, Mr. B E R R Y.

Mrs. Harlow, Mifs B E R R Y,
Mifs Harlow, Mrs. B U R N,
Trifle, Mifs A. B E R R Y.

TO WHICH WILL BE ADDED, THE

Intriguing Chambermaid.

Goodall, Mr. B U R N,
Valentine, EARL of MOUNT EDGCUMBE,
Oldcaftle, Mr. B E R R Y,
Trufty and Col. Bluff, Mr. H E R V E Y,
Slap and Security, Mr. C A M P B E L L.

Mrs. Highman, Mrs. B U R N,
Charlotte, Mifs. A. B E R R Y,
Lettice, Hon. Mrs. D A M E R.

The PROLOGUE to the Performance to be fpoken by the
EARL of MOUNT EDGCUMBE.

The EPILOGUE by the Hon. Mrs. DAMER.

Richmond : Printed for G. WALL, at his Circulating Library, Hill-ftreet.

A playbill (not included in ESTC)

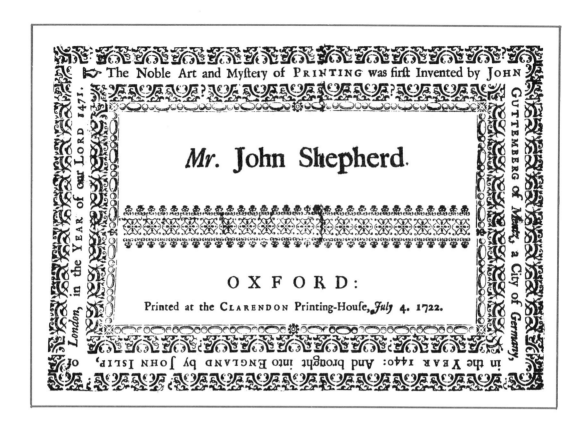

Mr. John Shepherd.

OXFORD:

Printed at the CLARENDON Printing-House, *July* 4. 1722.

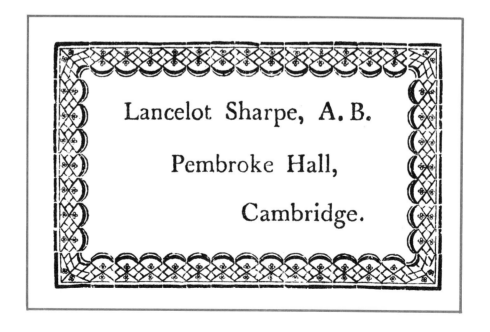

Lancelot Sharpe, A. B.

Pembroke Hall,

Cambridge.

A printer's keepsake and a bookplate (not included in ESTC)

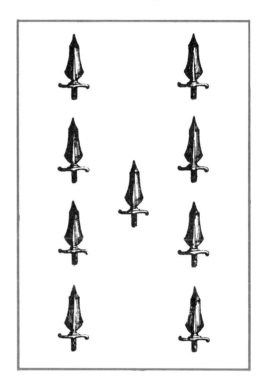

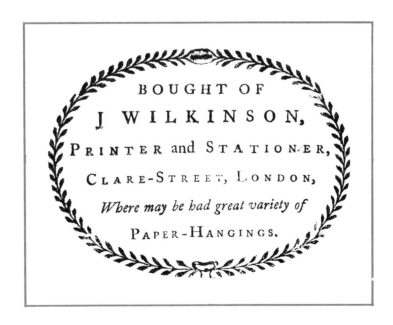

An engraved card, a playing card (woodcut), and a bookseller's label (not included in ESTC)

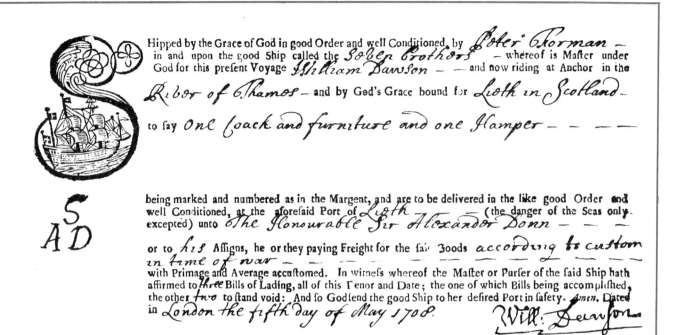

Shipped by the Grace of God in good Order and well Conditioned, by *Peter Forman* — in and upon the good Ship called the *Sober Brothers* — whereof is Master under God for this present Voyage *William Dawson* — — and now riding at Anchor in the *River of Thames* — and by God's Grace bound for *Leoth in Scotland* — to say *One Coack and furniture and one Hamper* — — — —

5
AD

being marked and numbered as in the Margent, and are to be delivered in the like good Order and well Conditioned, at the aforesaid Port of *Leoth* — — (the danger of the Seas only excepted) unto *The Honourable Sir Alexander Donn* — — — or to *his* Assigns, he or they paying Freight for the said Goods *according to custom in time of war* — — — — — with Primage and Average accustomed. In witness whereof the Master or Purser of the said Ship hath affirmed to *three* Bills of Lading, all of this Tenor and Date; the one of which Bills being accomplished, the other *two* to stand void: And so God send the good Ship to her desired Port in safety. *Amen.* Dated in *London the fifth day of May 1708.* *Will: Dawson*

John Granger Esqr.

Bought of T. PALMER,
Printer, Bookseller and Stationer,
At his China, Glass & Earthenware *Warehouse,* E. GRINSTEAD.
☞ Licenced to deal in Medicines, Perfumery and HATS.

1794	The London Chronicle March 5. 1793 to March 2 1794 inclusive 156 Papers —	£		
		3	5	—

A bill of lading and a tradesman's receipt (reduced: not included in ESTC)

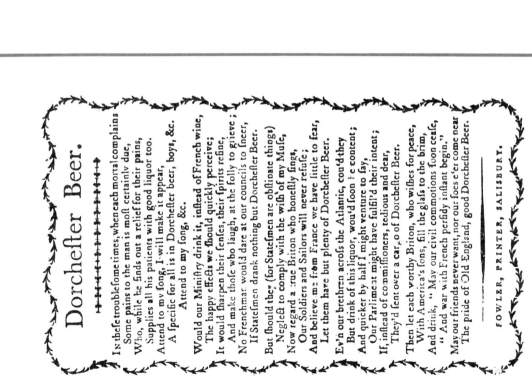

Joseph Braffet, Bookseller in Poole,

Sells the following Articles as cheap as in London, viz.

ALL Sorts of Books and Stationary-Wares, Magazines, Weekly Numbers, Prints, &c. Mariners and Pilots Charts and Maps.

Hadley's and Davies's Quadrants.

Scales and Compasses.

Journals and Pocket-Books.

Letter-Cases, Bills of Lading and Shipping Paper.

Best gilt, black-edg'd, post and plain Writing Paper.

Ink and Ink Powder, Sealing-wax, Wafers, and Office Quills and Pens.

Black and Red Lead Pencils.

Accompt Books ruled and plain.

Ivory Folding Sticks.

Violins, Flutes, Hautboys, Fiddle Strings, Music Books and Paper.

Instruments for drawing; Drawing Paper and Indian Ink.

Box and Ivory Rules.

Cephalic Snuff, Mustard and best Roll Pomatum.

Money Scales and Weights

Best Blacking Balls for Shoes and Ivory Black.

Temple and common Spectacles.

Best and common Spy-Glasses

Best Salisbury Razors, Scizzars and Penknives.

Birmingham and Sheffield Cutlery and Ironmongers Wares.

Shaving Powder, Boxes, Hones, and Razor-Straps

Ivory and Horn Combs

Sailors Buckles.

Greenough's Tincture and Ward's Powder for the Teeth.

Turlington's Balsam of Life, and all Dr. Ward's Medicines.

Daffey's Elixir.

Bateman's Drops.

British Oil.

Godfrey's Cordial.

Hooper's and Scots Pills.

Dr. James's Powders, &c.

N.B. BOOKS let out to read at 3d. a Volume per WEEK, and if kept longer, to pay in Proportion.

Any one that borrows a Book is not to lend it to any Person out of his House, and if the Book is damag'd to pay for it. Money for old Books.

Dorchester Beer.

In these troublesome times, when each mortal complains
Some pains to the man is most certainly due,
Who, while he finds out a relief for their pains,
Supplies all his patients with good liquor too.
Attend to my song, I will make it appear,
A specific for all is in Dorchester beer, boys, &c.
Attend to my song, &c.

Would our Ministry drink it, instead of French wine,
The happy effects we should quickly perceive;
It would sharpen their senses, their spirits refine,
And make those who laugh, at the folly to grieve;
No Frenchman would dare at our councils to sneer,
If Statesmen drank nothing but Dorchester Beer.

But should they (for Statesmen are obstinate things)
Neglect to comply with the wish of my Muse,
Now regard a true Briton who honestly sings,
Our Soldiers and Sailors will never refuse;
And believe me from France we have little to fear,
Let them have but plenty of Dorchester Beer.

Ev'n our brethren across the Atlantic, cou'd they
But drink of this liquor, wou'd soon be content;
And quicker by half I might venture to say,
Our Parliament might have fulfil'd their intent;
If, instead of commissioners, tedious and dear,
They'd sent over a car_ of Dorchester Beer.

Then let each worthy Briton, who wishes for peace,
With America's sons, fill the glass to the brim,
And drink, "May our civil commotions soon cease,
"And war with French perfidy instant begin."
May our friends never want, nor our foes e'er come near
The pride of Old England, good Dorchester Beer.

FOWLER, PRINTER, SALISBURY.

A popular song printed at Salisbury ca. 1785 and a provincial bookseller's advertisement (included in ESTC)

A PROCLAMATION.

WHEREAS it is in the Power of His Majesty's Generals, and of the Forces under their Command, entirely to destroy all those who have risen in Rebellion against their Sovereign and his Laws; yet it is nevertheless the Wish of Government, that those Persons who, by traitorous Machinations, have been seduced, or by Acts of Intimidation have been forced from their Allegiance, should be received into His Majesty's Peace and Pardon:

commanding in the County of   specially authorized thereto, does hereby invite all Persons who may be now assembled in any Part of the said County against His Majesty's Peace, to surrender themselves and their Arms, and to desert the Leaders who have seduced them; and for the Acceptance of such Surrender and Submission, the Space of fourteen Days, from the Date hereof, is allowed, and the Towns of

are hereby specified, at each of which Places one of His Majesty's Officers, and a Justice of the Peace, will attend; and upon their entering their Names, acknowledging their Guilt, and promising good Behaviour for the future, and taking the Oath of Allegiance, and at the same Time abjuring all other Engagements contrary thereto, they will receive Certificates which will entitle them to Protection so long as they demean themselves as becomes good Subjects.

And in order to render such Acts of Submission easy and secure, it is the General's Pleasure, that Persons who are now with any Portion of Rebels in Arms, and willing to surrender themselves, do send to him or to   any Number from each Body of Rebels not exceeding ten, with whom the General or   will settle the Manner in which they may repair to the above Towns, so that no Alarm may be excited, and no Injury to their Persons be offered.

29th June, 1798.

DUBLIN: Printed by GEORGE GRIERSON, Printer to the KING's Most Excellent Majesty.

A genuine hybrid (both a text and a blank form), a public notice posted at Dublin Castle (included in ESTC)

From the LONDON CHRONICLE, *for* February 4, 1772, No. 2363.

To the PRINTER.

SIR,

THE concern and vexation, which appeared in every countenance at the report which seems to have gained full credit respecting the Consort of a Northern Potentate, are very great; but as there is reason to believe the said report is a wicked and gross falshood and imposition on the English nation, should we not suspend our judgment? We seem to have judged *ex parte;* and have, in this case, gone even beyond credulity, let us have a little patience. Recollect the manner in which that Lady was educated, and that, when delivered into the hands of her husband, she was in full possession of every virtue. All the graces were in her; she nothing knew but what was good. Can it then, with any degree of reason, be concluded, that in so short a time the Lady can forget every virtuous precept, and abandon herself to infamy? My dear Countrymen, it cannot be; and until we have a certainty of guilt, believe it not, though an angel from Copenhagen should affirm it. It was but the other day we were made happy in being told of certain regulations which had taken place, and are for the advantage of the people of that kingdom, and which were wholly attributed to the counsel of that Lady. Alas! there is too much reason to fear the exalted character, justly acquired with the populace, hath produced in those of rank, envy, hatred, confusion, and ruin.

The intrigues and disputes in that Court have long existed, and the exceeding wickedness of it is universally known. The Minister who has the greatest sway there, is well known in Germany to be a bad man; confusion is his forte; and I make no doubt it well at length appear, that the young and amiable pair owe their present misery to the diabolical intrigues of him and his associates. Peace and quietness would have ruined him long ago.

Hence the source of all their troubles; and the cause of this Minister's intrigues is, that, in the midst of confusion, he may revel in security on the spoils of others. Accept from me then, by way of voucher, the outlines of the life of this man, and amongst an hundred actions, each of which deserved a halter, but which I have forgot, permit me to present you with a few of equal merit which I do remember. This extraordinary person is now a Baron, and was Treasurer to that amiable Monarch on his tour. A few years before the invasion of Saxony by the King of Prussia, this man was a Merchant's Clerk in Hamburgh, and being discharged for some offence, became very poor; but gaining the assistance of a person on whom he waited as — and whom he sufficiently duped for his kindness, he became a petty Merchant in Hamburgh, but shortly decamped *a la sourdine.* After some time, he appeared as an inferior Clerk either in the Court of the late Elector of Saxony, or in one of the Offices belonging to the China Manufactory, and was in a place that gave him the knowledge of the most secret repository of the most valuable effects belonging to the Court; but no sooner was Dres-

den, &c. in possession of the King of Prussia's troops, but away flies this faithful servant, and, for a reward of promise and favour, makes a full discovery of the said repositories, to the extreme vexation of his royal and unhappy Master.

The invaluable sets of china found therein, the King of Prussia ordered to be sold; but this artful genius privately conveyed out of every set one piece, so that the Merchants finding them incomplete, and thinking on that account to have them very low, refused at that time to purchase, being privately advised by him so to do. He immediately informs the King that the Merchants would not buy, but said he would undertake to sell them: having by his address gained the King, he was permitted, and caused many waggons to be loaded and sent away to Hamburgh, &c. at the expence of the King and the poor country people. The Nobility, Gentry, and connoisseurs, all flocked to the sales; and the stolen pieces being restored to the respective sets, an immense sum was raised. However, it afterwards appeared, that the allowance he thought proper to make to his Royal Employer was at the rate of 1 s. 9 d. per pound sterling; nor had the King, being duped by his address and seeming sincerity, the least suspicion of being cheated, until our hero's next exploit, respecting the contract for coining of a large quantity of silver, fully opened the King's eyes: but it was then too late: he had decamped, and flown to the court of Denmark; where, taking the advantage of the then King's want of money, he advanced it, and got himself appointed Danish Resident at Hamburgh, with the title of Baron; consequently he became protected by the Senate of Hamburgh as well as by the King of Denmark. His hatred to the English is rooted, and publickly spoken of, and the disgrace lately suffered by a young and noble Count is attributed to the advice of our Baron, as the Count loved the English, and his King and Queen. Thus, my countrymen, I have endeavoured to shew, that it is more than probable that our amiable and Royal country woman, as well as the King her husband, have fallen by the wicked art and cunning of this monster. I should also have observed, that he is most assiduous in his court to one of the Dowager Queens, whose hatred to the reigning Queen is enormous.

It is wickedly asserted, that the Monarch's illness is attributed to some medicine given him by his Physician, &c. " Hear this, O Heaven, and be astonished, O Earth!" The truth is, that you ought rather to wonder that his Majesty is now alive, than that he is afflicted with nervous or paralytic disorders. My eyes were witness to the manner and excess of his living when he was at Altena. I could say a great deal, but it does not become me. I shall only say this one thing, which is an indisputable truth: That many who then saw his Majesty concluded, from his delicate constitution, it could not hold long, and execrated our Baron for his introducing him to, and encouraging him in, the most destructive vices. Therefore, if any disorder affects the head of his Majesty, may it not be more justly attributed, either to such excess, or to the diabolical act of the Baron, than to the Queen, who was educated in the fear of God?

C. P.

A single sheet printed by Haberkorn at Altona in 1772 in the Royal Archives at Copenhagen: the recto bears the German text

49

FOWLER's ADDRESS,

TO

LADIES AND GENTLEMEN.

SHOP BILLS in profe are now fo trite,
So eafy, too, for folks to write;
So dull the catalogue appears,
So grating to a poet's ears,
That I'm determin'd now to crofs
My little fav'rite Hobby Horfe,
Juft take a fip at *Helicon*.
Recount my wares, and thus jog on :

First, then, at *Fowler's* fhop are fold
Sermons for both young and old;
Rules for drawing, painting, gilding,
Farming, gardening, and building;
Hiftories of ancient days,
Poems, magazines, and plays;
Books of roads, and books of fairs,
Bibles, teftaments, and prayers;
Fenning, Dyche, & Dilworth's fpelling,
Such as children may read well in;
Primers, horn books, books of pictures,
Pleafing toys for infant lectures.

Books whole bound, or only half,
In morocco, fheep, or calf;
Marble-paper'd, green or blue,
Neatly gilt, and letter'd too.

Paper, ev'ry kind you'll mention,
Ev'ry country's beft invention;
Marble, from the *French* and *Dutch*,
Englifh worth but half as much;
Brown for packing, purple, green,
Mufic, lawn, and mazarine;
Royal medium, quite inviting,
Pot and foolfcap cut, for writing;
Elephant, and cartridge too,
Whited brown, and common blue;

Blotting, black, and gold embofs'd,
Plain, or gilt, and mourning poft;
Glaz'd, or having lines upon it,
Colour'd pafteboard for a bonnet.
Quills and pens, a beauteous fhew,
From the turkey, goofe, and crow,
Suited to the different hands
Us'd in this, and other lands;
Thofe which are efteem'd the beft,
(Being harder than the reft)
Late from *Hamburgh* wing'd their way
Or the fhores of *Hudfon's Bay*;
Ink as black as darkeft night,
Truly flowing as you write;
Ink from wood of *Brazil* made,
Growing bright with ruby red;
Ink of genuine *Indian* make,
Ink in powder, or in cake;
Ink-ftands, elegant and neat,
Furnifh'd for the defk compleat,
There attract the Hiftic's eye,
Tempting many a one to buy;
Side by fide, in order, ftand
Ebon, glafs, and book japann'd;
Lead, and pewter ones, with fockets,
Mix'd with others for the pockets.

Wafers ftain'd with motley hue,
Yellow, black, white, red, and blue;
Wax that holds the ftrongeft paper,
Wax to burn in rolls or taper;
Folding knives to fit your hand,
Rulers, pounce, and fhining fand;
Drawing pencils, white and red,
Reed and cedar, fill'd with lead;
Slates and pencils, fmooth and clear,
Brufhes made with camel's hair;

Bailey's cakes for liquid blacking,
Balls to keep your fhoes from cracking
Handy books that have within
Ivory leaves, or affes fkin;
Cards for meffages, or play,
Or that inftruction do convey.

Mufic next my verfe invites—
Mufic! fource of foft delights;
There, collected, you may fee
Songs in great variety;
Solos, overtures, duettos,
Trios, fymphonies, quartettos;
New concertos that would charm ye,
Fav'rite marches for the army;
Country dances, and cotillons,
Jigs and minuets by millions;
Catches, glees, and pleafant airs,
Books to guide unpractis'd play'rs;
Strings of catgut, or of wire,
And what elfe you may require,
When with mild and fweet controul
Mufic reigns within the foul!

Next his *Printing Room* we view,
Rolling-prefs, and letter new,
Here he works his copper-plates,
Here he prints the moiften'd fheets;
There difpos'd, in order, lie,
Types, beautiful, by *Edmund Fry*:
Round the room, behold, are hung,
Songs which fav'rite bards have fung;
Party fquibs, and birth-day odes,
Epigrams, and Epifodes.

The favors which his friends have fhewn
His heart with gratitude will own;
And in all inftances expedient,
He'll gladly be their moft obedient.

FOWLER, PRINTER, NO. 21, NEWCASTLE-STREET, STRAND. *1789*

A bookseller's advertisement (included in ESTC)

Croisic PRICE CURRENT.

Calculated in french livres one of which are equal to about 9 ⅜ British Sterling. Croisic may 2d. 1789.

EXPORTS.

SALT. *Per* Moy of 21 Meaſures, and from 550 to 6000 Ct. Wt. free on board.

Beſt. { £30 in Croiſic Harbour, good Anchorage for Ships under 14 Feet Draft of Water,
{ £29 in Pouliguen ——————————— 10 ditto
Inferior. £27½ in Meſquer. — — — — — — — — — 10 Do.

For Ships of any ſize to load always a-float.

Beſt { £34 —— in Croiſic Road }
{ 40 —— in Nantz River } On Account of the Additional Freight and Charges from
{ 34 —— in Vilaine ditto } hence thither.
inferior 54 —— in Vannes River } Per Moy of 32 Meaſures, and from 7000 to 7400 Ct.
good 50 —— in Penerf ditto } Weight.

As all Ships on their Way to either of theſe various Places moſt Times come in the Sight of this Harbour, which lies in the midſt of them and foremoſt to Sea, the Maſters ſhould come off the Croiſic Point, and then hoiſt a Signal of a Jack at the Fore-Top-Gallant Maſt-Head, or bring up in the Road which is ſafe, and write a Line when inſtant Advice will be ſent them with Directions, and a Pilot to the Place, beſt calculated to load them in the eaſieſt, cheapeſt, quickeſt, and moſt convenient Manner.

	or 54 gall		
Brandy - - - £ 135 to 140: per 29 Vts	Wheat - £ 345 : 360 per Ton of 2250 to 2400 Wt.
Vinegar - - - 16. 13: — — Bar.	Rye - - - 230 : 240	
White Country Wines 40 . 500 — Hhd.	Barley - - 150 : 176	
Ditto Bordeaux - 50. 70: — — ditto	Oats - - - 130 : 133	Weight in
Red ditto - - - 75 .150: — — ditto	Peaſe - - - 345 : 355	Proportion.
Coffee - - - 1 : 2 d. : to 3 :/d.per lb	French Beans - 360 : 400	
Tea, Bohea - - - 1 :3/4 2 — — ditto	Small ditto - 170 : 140	
Green - - 0 : 8 — — ditto	Honey - - - 26: 25 } per Ct. Wt.
Flour - - - - 24 - 26 — per Ct. Wt.	Butter - - - 44: 50 }

IMPORTS. or 60 gall		COURSE OF EXCHANGE.	
Cod Oil - - £ 60 : 70 per 30 Vts.	London - - - - 29 3/4 }
Coals - - - - 300 : 440 Qr.	Amſterdam - - - 55 }
Beef - - - - 60 : 65 Bar.	Hamburgh - - - 189 } ⅟Uſ.
Pork - - - - 65 : 66 }	Paris - - - 1 : 6 4 }
Butter - - - - 50 : } per Cwt.	Ditto Sight Par.
Rice - - - - 23 : 24 }	

maſters of Ships alſo coming for a cargo, had better follow the above Directions

Maſts, Planks, Deals, Staves, Spars, Tin, Lead, Iron, Copper, Steel, Buttons, Stuff, Sail Cloth, Earthenware, and any ſort of Goods, the Produce of Foreign Countries and Manufactories, as are admitted to an Entry by the Treaties, and fit for France, will anſwer here BETTER THAN any where elſe in this Province; as this Port, from its being ſituated between and near the Mouths of three Rivers, has the beſt Opportunity of ſelling here and ſending far up into the Country Places, and with very little Expence, whatever Goods are wanted for Home Conſumption, and likewiſe ſuch Goods as are only fit or admitted for Exportation to Foreign Countries or French Iſlands.—This Place is allowed the Privilege of receiving and ſhipping, with an *Acquit a Caution,* and by that means FREE OF DUTIES, all Foreign and Inland Goods; as alſo all Eaſt and Weſt India produce, in the ſame Manner as the MOST FAVOURED PLACES of France.

It is Optional either to PAY THE DUTIES of Goods on Importation, or if Warehouſed under the King's Locks, then to be paid ONLY for what is taken out for HOME CONSUMPTION; but NO DUTIES for what is exported Abroad or to French Plantations.

Pleaſe to direct to DE LA MARQUE, SENIOR, at CROISIC, in *France.*

An export list printed at Croisic in 1789 (included in ESTC)

HENRY BRADFORD,

Draper, Salesman and Upholder,

NEAR THE CHURCH,

In the Market-Place, Wallingford,

HAVING just laid in a fresh and compleat Assortment of the under-mentioned Articles, hopes to merit the Favour of his Friends and the Public in general, by selling them on the most reasonable Terms, viz.

Superfine and other Broad Cloths, Forest ditto, Beavers, &c. of the most fashionable Colours; Clouded, Embossed, and Plain Velverets; Corderoys, Thicksets, Fustians, Dimities, &c.; Printed Linens and Cottons, Irish Cloth of the various Widths and Prices; Lancashire, Scotch, and Irish Sheeting; Dowlas, Blues, and Checks; Silk, Cotton, and Linen Handkerchiefs; Stuffs, Shaloons, and Camblets; Bays, Flannels, and Linsey; Mens and Boys ready made Cloaths; Mens, Women, and Childrens Worstead, Thread, and Cotton Hose; Mens and Boys Hats; Womens and Childrens Stays; fine Down, Goose and other Feather Beds, Flock ditto, Mattresses, Cotton Counterpanes, Quilts, Blankets, Coverlids, Bed Ticks of sundry Widths and Prices, Hara-teen, Moreen, and Check Furniture for Hangings, Furniture Papers, with the various other Articles in the above Branches.

Rooms neatly and expeditiously Papered.

Those who please to favour him with their Commands may depend on their being executed with the utmost Care and Dispatch.

₊ Estates, Houshold Furniture, &c. Bought, Sold, or Appraised by Commission, by W. BRADFORD and SON, Wallingford.

A tradesman's advertisement printed at Wallingford in 1786—the verso bears a dated receipt—(included in ESTC)

At the Theatre in GUILDFORD,

On Monday FEBRUARY 4th, 1782,

WILL BE PERFORMED

By a Party of GENTLEMEN,

The TRAGEDY of

TANCRED and SIGISMUNDA,

Tancred,	Mr. DAYSH,
Matteo Siffredi,	Mr. WILLIAMSON,
Earl Ofmond,	Mr. DUNCUMB,
Rodolpho,	Mr. RICKMAN,
Sigifmunda,	Mr. HOWELL,
Laura,	Mr. S. COLE.

With an occafional PROLOGUE and EPILOGUE.

The Doors will be opened at FIVE, and the Play begin exactly at SIX.

Againft the Royal Exchange, Cornhill.

London, 26 Day of April 1748

Bank Stock - - - - -	121
India - - - - - - - -	175
South Sea - - - - -	104
Ditto Old Annuity - -	
Ditto New - - - - -	56
3 per Cents. - - - -	94
4 per Cent. Bank Ann. 1746	
Ditto 1747 - - - - -	94 3/4
Ditto 1748 - - - - -	93
India Bonds - - - - -	11s
Tickets - - - - - - -	10.10
Lottery 1767 —	93 3/4

SIR,
Your humble Servants,
Cotton and Lambert.

A stockbroker's quotation slip and an advertisement for a play (not included in ESTC)

AT a meeting of the inhabitants of the parish of St. Andrew, held in the town of Grenville the 20th day of February 1793: Capt. John Mann being called to the Chair as President, and Mr. Gordon Turnbull appointed Secretary of the said meeting, the following resolutions were separately proposed, and passed *unanimously*.

Resolved 1. That every subject in every part of the British dominions, is bound to pay due allegiance to his Majesty Geo. III. King of Great Britain, the father of all his people.

2d, That the Constitution of *King, Lords, and Commons* as by law established, is the best and wisest form of Government for a free people.

3d, That the Constitution of Great Britain is, and of right ought to be, the Constitution of her Colonies.

4th, That we will defend and support the said Constitution with our lives and properties; and that we will endeavour, to the utmost of our power, to bring to justice all those evil-minded persons, who shall attempt to disturb the peace and good order of the Community, by disseminating doctrines incompatible with the principles of the established Government, and tending to create dissension, anarchy, and ruin.

5th That such of us as are electors will give our suffrages only to those Candidates, who are firm and approved friends to the Constitution, to be our representatives in the General Assembly of these islands.

6th, That an Address be presented to the Hon. Ninian Home, Esq; Commander in Chief of these islands, expressive of the sentiments contained in the above resolutions, and congratulating him on his safe arrival in his Government.

7th, That an address be likewise presented to the Hon. Samuel Williams, Esq; thanking him for his upright and impartial conduct, during the time he was Commander in Chief of these islands.

Both addresses were then read, and signed by upwards of sixty Gentlemen present. The following resolutions were then moved, and agreed to unanimously.

Resolved, That the Gentlemen present at this meeting, do attend the burning *the Effigy of Thomas Paine* this evening; as well to preserve order and decorum, as to shew our detestation of all such traitors.

Resolved, That the above Resolutions, signed by the Secretary of the meeting, be published in the *St. George's Chronicle*.

C. TURNBULL.

III.

With grief sincere I pity those
Who've drawn themselves this scrape in;
Since from this dreadful gripe, Heaven knows,
Alas! there's no escaping!

R. DEATH,
AT THE
FALCON,
BATTERSEA RISE,
ON THE
WANDSWORTH ROAD.
DEALER IN FOREIGN SPIRITUOUS LIQUORS,
WHOLESALE AND RETAIL.

I.

O! stop not here, ye forlorn wights,
For purl, nor ale, nor gin;
For if you stop, whoe'er alights
By DEATH is taken in.

II.

Where having eat and drank your fill,
Should ye (O hapless case!)
Neglect to pay your landlord's bill,
DEATH stares you in the face!

IV.

This one advice, my friends, pursue,
Whilst yet ye've life and breath;
Ne'er PLEDGE your Host; for if you do,
You'll surely—drink to DEATH!

The VERSES by E. T. PILGRIM.

From the EUROPEAN MAGAZINE for NOVEMBER, 1785.

A tradesman's advertisement with added text, and a handbill printed in Grenada in 1793 (included in ESTC)

THE YOUNG ENGLISHMAN

O r

A Collection of Moral and Entertaining pieces, taken out of the best English writers, wherein are marked both the pronunciation, accents of every word, and all the expressions peculiar, to the language; to which is, likewise added a little dictionary containing the words of the book, for the use of the beginners at the University of Mosco.

МОЛОДЫИ АГЛИЧАНИНЪ,

И Л И

Собранїе Нравоучительныхъ пїэсъ, взятыхъ изъ лучшихъ Аглинскихъ писателей, въ которомъ показаны правила о выговорѣ и ударенїе словъ, съ прїобщенїемъ Словаря на всѣ слова въ книгѣ находящїяся, и показанїемъ выраженїй свойственныхъ Аглинскому языку.

И З Д А Н Н О Е

Для начинающихъ учиться сему языку въ Гимназїяхъ при ИМПЕРАТОРСКОМЪ Московскомъ Университетѣ.

M O S C O .

A book in English and Russian printed at Moscow, ca. 1790

THE curious SMELLING-BOTTLE, called LE SEL POIGNANT d' ANGLETERRE, held in the higheſt Eſteem by all the Quality and Gentry throughout Europe, who conſtantly carry it in their Pocket; and is infinitely ſuperiour to every other Kind of Salts hitherto invented, and far more fragrant and refreſhing than either Lavender, Hungary, or any Kind of Eſſence, or odoriferous Water.

By ſmelling to it, it gives inſtantaneous Relief in all Sorts of Head-Aches, Sickneſs, Faintings, ſudden Frights, Hyſterick and Hypochondriacal Diſorders, Lowneſs of Spirits, Convulſive and Epileptick Fits, Apoplexies, Vertigoes, and all the whole Train of nervous Diſorders. Add to theſe moſt excellent Qualities, only by opening the Stopper now and then, it gives a moſt agreeable Flavour to a Room, or any publick Place; and by its penetrating and diſcutient Effluvia, is a certain Preventive from the Small-Pox, Meaſles, and every Kind of infectious Diſorder. In ſhort, conſidering the many ſudden Diſorders we are liable to, no one is really ſafe without it.

This celebrated Smelling-Bottle is prepared only by DAL-MAHOY, Chemiſt to her Majeſty, on Ludgate-Hill, London; and ſold at 1s. 2s. 6d. 5s. and 10s. 6d. each; alſo at Mr. Hendrie's, Perfumer, Shug-Lane.

Artful and deſigning Perſons are offering for Sale Bottles of an inferior Quality, who, in Order to colour over the Deception, have meanly made an Alteration in a Letter of Dalmahoy's Name, to the great Diſcredit of the genuine Bottles, as well as Impoſition upon the Publick. The Publick are intreated to obſerve, that the Name engraved upon each Bottle as well as in the Label and Bill of Directions, which conſtantly accompany the genuine Sort, is ſpelt exactly agreeably to this Advertiſement; by which Caution the Fraud will be diſcovered, and the Impoſition expoſed.

N. B. All Sorts of Drugs, Medicines and chemical Preparations, prepared and ſold, Wholeſale and Retail, in their utmoſt Perfection.

WANTED to PURCHASE, The PERPETUAL ADVOWSON of a RECTORY, or PERPETUAL or DONATIVE CURACY, of about the Value of TWO HUNDRED POUNDS per Annum, with immediate or moſt probable Proſpect of a very ſpeedy Avoidance. As the Advertiſer is a Gentleman and profeſſional Man, no Broker or Attorney need apply. The greateſt Secreſy and Honour may be depended upon; and all Letters (Poſt-paid) addreſſed to L. M. at No. 75, Borough High-Street, will command the moſt immediate Attention.

For the EUROPEAN EVENING POST.

TOO TRUE A PROPHESY,

Written ſome time ago,

TO breechleſs blockheads round his board
   Gulping down wine, yet never merry,
Nods ARCHY, proud ſententious lord,
   " I mean to taſte a *Kentiſh cherry.*"

The ſycophantick chorus cries,
   Your Lordſhip's right, you ne'er can rue it.
I ſhall ſay nothing, he replies;
   But damme Gentlemen I'll do it.

Give me a hawk of a good neſt;
   My FANNY comes from ancient Roydon;
And though in Chriſtendom the beſt,
   She's quite a ſimple pretty Hoyden.

O *Archy*, *Archy*, doating fool,
   To think an artful ſleek deceiver,
Bred in the wanton JERSEY's ſchool,
   Timid and ſcrupulous could leave her.

Truſt me, old cully, whilſt ſhe's kind,
   (So let not pregnancy ſurprize you)
Aſſiſtant vigour ſhe ſhall find
   To do what *John Adair* denies you.

Keith Stewart firſt ſhall feel the ſhock,
   For all his cunning, all his flummery,
And ſoon a ſecond harder knock
   Shall blaſt the hopes of *Hugh Montgomery.*

THROUGH.

A small single sheet, perfected in such a way that if cut in half, two copies of the piece would result. Presumably intended to simulate a newspaper cutting or off-print. James Boswell has been credited with its composition (included in ESTC)

Advertisement.

JUST printed in 8vo. at the Theatre in Oxford, and ready to be delivered to Subscribers, *Joannis Rossi, Antiquarii Warwicensis, Historia Regum Angliæ. E Codice MS. in Bibliotheca Bodlejana descripsit, notisque & indice adornavit* Tho. Hearne, *A. M. Oxoniensis. Accedit Joannis Lelandi Antiquarii Nenia in mortem Henrici Duddeleji Equitis; Cui præfigitur Testimonium de Lelando amplum & præclarum, hactenus ineditum.*

The Publisher is now printing, *Titi Livii Foro-Juliensis Vita Henrici V^{ti} regis Angliæ. Accedit, Sylloge Epistolarum ab Henrico VIII^{vo}. Edvardo VI^{to}. aliisque quibusdam Angliæ Principibus scriptarum,* 8vo. The Price of this Work will be twelve shillings the large, and eight shillings the small Paper; whereof half is to be paid at the time of Subscribing, and the Remainder when the Copies are delivered. Those that do not Subscribe are to pay twenty shillings for the large, and twelve shillings for the small Paper. Subscriptions are taken in either by the Publisher at Edmund-Hall, or by John Rance at the Theatre Printing House in Oxford.

Febr. 10. 1715:

A voting list for Directors of the Court of the East India Company and an advertisement for one of Thomas Hearne's books (included in ESTC)

The House List amended.

Anno 1773.

1 H Enry Crabb Boulton, *Esq*;
2 Charles Boddam, *Esq*;
3 Benjamin Booth, *Esq*;
4 * Charles Chambers, *Esq*;
5 Sir James Cockburn, *Bart.*
6 William Devaynes, *Esq*;
7 Peter Du Cane, *Esq*;
8 Henry Fletcher, *Esq*;
9 * Richard Hall, *Esq*;
10 * John Harrison, *Esq*;
11 * John Hawkesworth, *Esq*;
12 Joseph Hurlock, *Esq*;
13 * William James, *Esq*;
14 Peter Lascelles, *Esq*;
15 John Michie, *Esq*;
16 * Frederick Pigou, *Esq*;
17 * Samuel Peach, *Esq*;
18 * Thomas Bates Rous, *Esq*;
19 * Joseph Sparks, *Esq*;
20 Henry Savage, *Esq*;
21 * John Smith Jun. *Esq*;
22 George Tatem, *Esq*;
23 Edward Wheler, *Esq*;
24 * John Woodhouse, *Esq*;

N. B. *These mark'd with* *, *are new Ones.*

☞ *If any List shall contain more than 24, or less than 22 Persons Qualified for Directors, then such List, and all the Names therein, will be totally rejected.*

REIGATE - TURNPIKE,

25th *September*, 1786.

THE GENERAL MEETING of the *TRUSTEES* will be held at the *Swan Inn*, in *Reigate*, on *Monday*, the thirtieth Day of *October* next, at 10 o'Clock in the *Forenoon*, for letting by Auction, for two Years and three Quarters from *Chriſtmas* next, the Tolls of the Gates called *Sutton* Gates, *Tadworth* Gate, The *Ruffett* Gate and *London-Lane* Gate, which produced, the laſt Year, the Sum of *Three Hundred* and *Fifty-three* Pounds *Four Shillings* and *Six-pence*, above the Expences of collecting them : And for electing a Treaſurer and Clerk, on the Reſignation of *Richard Ladbroke* Eſquire, the preſent Treaſurer, and Mr. *Barnes* the preſent Clerk ; and to conſider the State of the *Roads*, and other Affairs relating to the Truſt.

RICHARD BARNES, Clerk.

A turnpike auction notice (included in ESTC)

April 13, 1763.

HE North Briton makes his appeal to the good fenfe, and to the candour of the English nation. In the prefent unfettled and fluctuating ftate of the *adminiftration*, he is really fearful of falling into involuntary errors, and he does not wifh to miflead. All his reafonings have been built on the ftrong foundation of *facts*; and he is not yet informed of the whole interiour ftate of government with fuch *minute precifion*, as now to venture the fubmitting his crude ideas of the prefent political crifis to the difcerning and impartial public. The Scottish minifter has indeed *retired*. Is his influence at an end? or does he ftill govern by the *three* wretched tools of his power, who, to their indelible infamy, have fupported the moft odious of his meafures, the late ignominious *Peace*, and the wicked extenfion of the arbitrary mode of *Excife?* The North Briton has been fteady in his oppofition to a *fingle*, infolent, incapable, defpotic minifter; and is equally ready, in the fervice of his country, to combat the *triple-headed, Cerberean* adminiftration, if the Scot is to affume that motley form. By him every arrangement *to this hour* has been made, and the notification has been as regularly fent by letter under his Hand. *It therefore* feems clear to a demonftration, that he intends only to retire into that fituation, which he held before he firft took the feals; I mean the dictating to every part of the king's adminiftration. The North Briton defires to be underftood, as having pledged himfelf a firm and intrepid affertor of the rights of his fellow-fubjects, and of the liberties of Whigs and Englishmen.

Printed for G. Kearsly, in *Ludgate-Street.*

Wilkes' handbill issued the week before the appearance of No. XLV (included in ESTC)

A CARD.

A FONT of Types in the Banian or Guzerat Character, having been invented and Caſt by Behramjee Jeejeebhoy and Nurſunjee Cowaſjee, and added to the Printing Stock of the Bombay Courier Office; the Public are hereby informed, that buſineſs will hereafter be executed in this Type, with the exception for the preſent of Advertiſements in the News Paper, upon the ſame terms as in the Engliſh Character.

Bombay Courier Office, Novr. 9th, 1796

An early Indian type specimen (included in ESTC)

60

JAMES  MILES,

From *Sadler's* Wells, at *Iflington*;

NOW keeps the GUN-MUSICK-BOOTH, in *Bartholomew*-Fair. Whereas Mr. *Miles*, by his Care and Diligence to oblige the Gentry, and all Others that are Lovers and Judges of good Mufick, has put himfelf to an extraordinary Charge, in getting fuch Performers, as, no doubt, will give a general Satisfaction to all. This is alfo to give Notice to all Gentlemen, Ladies, and Others, That they may be accommodated with all Sorts of Wine, and other Liquors; with feveral extraordinary Entertainments of Singing and Dancing, which was never perform'd in the Fair, *viz*. (1.) A New Dance between Three Bullies and Three Quakers. (2.) A New Dance between Two Spirits and Two Scaramouches. (3.) A New Dance between Four Swans and Four *Indians*, riding in on their Backs. (4.) A Wreftlers Dance, performed by Two Youths. (5.) Likewife Dancing on the Tight Rope, and a Young Man that Vaults the Slack Rope, with Variety of Tumbling. (6.) A New Dance of Eight Granadiers, who perform the whole Exercife of War, in their proper Accoutrements, to the juft Time of Mufick. (7.) A New *Scotch* Dance, with their Habits and Bonnets, perform'd by Two Boys, to Admiration. (8.) A New Entertainment between a Scaramouch, a Harliquin, and a Punchanello, in Imitation of Bilking a Reckoning. (9.) A New Cane-Chair Dance by Eight Perfons. (10.) A New Dance by Four Scaramouches, after the *Italian* Manner. (11) A New Dance by a Scaramouch and a Country Farmer. (12.) A New Swans Dance, perform'd by Four young Lads, to the Amazement of all Spectators. (13.) We fhall alfo prefent you with the Wonder of her Sex, a young Woman, who dances with the Swords, and upon the Ladder with that Variety, that fhe challenges all her Sex to do the like. (14.) A Cripples Dance by Six Perfons with Wooden Legs and Crutches, in Imitation of a Jovial Crew. (15.) A Pofture Dance, perform'd by Eight Perfons. (16) A Dance by Six Men, wherein Two Coopers, Two Grinders, and Two Butchers perform every thing natural to their Trades. (17.) The *Vigo* Dance, perform'd by an *Englifh* Man, a *Dutch* Man, a *French* Man, and a *Spaniard*. (18.) A Black-Smiths Dance. (19.) A Tinkers Dance; together with other extraordinary Entertainments too long to be inferted.

VIVAT REGINA.

An advertisement for a Bartholomew Fair entertainment, ca. 1708 (included in ESTC)

61

A

Descriptive Plan

of the

NEW OPERA HOUSE,

with the NAMES *of the*

Subscribers to each Box

taken from the Theatre itself

by

A LADY of FASHION.

Published by T. Becket, *Pall Mall,*

Bookseller to His Royal Highness, the Prince of Wales.

PRICE 5 SHILLINGS.

A wholly engraved book (included in ESTC)

Whereas,

MANY of the principal Inhabitants of *Sheffield* have expreſſed great unwillingneſs to part with the BELLS lately taken down from the Pariſh Church; and are alſo deſirous to have them placed in the Steeple of St. Paul's; ~~and~~ as they muſt be ſent to London immediately, if not purchaſed, the Churchwardens of Saint Paul's think it their Duty, to give the People an opportunity of declaring their Sentiments:

THEREFORE

They hereby give Notice,

That a Meeting will be held at the TOWN-HALL, on MONDAY next, at eleven o'Clock in the Forenoon, for taking the Senſe of the Town on the ſame; and if approved of, to open a Subſcription for the Purchaſe of the ſaid Bells, or any Part thereof.

April 3, 1799.

PIERSON, PRINTER:

A handbill printed at Sheffield in 1799

Appendix I

The ESTC in America

The Washington Meeting (November 1976—described briefly above, page 11) confirmed two developments of crucial importance for the development of ESTC: the commitment of the British Library to the Second Pilot Project, and the nomination of a Drafting Committee to prepare a series of proposals which could be submitted to foundations for securing the funds necessary to ensure a positive strategy for ESTC in the United States. The Drafting Committee (T. R. Adams, P. J. Korshin, R. C. Alston and R. J. Roberts) has met on several occasions (in Oxford, London and New York) and was responsible for a successful application to the National Endowment for the Humanities (NEH) for funds to establish a pilot project at the New York Public Library. This project commenced in March 1978 and is scheduled to last six months. Its objectives as expressed in the proposal submitted to NEH, were clearly derived from the experience gained in the British Library. The New York Public Library was chosen as an ideal institution in which to test the relevance of the Second Pilot Project in the British Library to the ESTC in America for numerous reasons:

It is a very large, comprehensive library, covering in its various departments most areas of human knowledge; it is a complicated amalgamation of several collections, physically dispersed throughout several buildings; it has substantial collections of uncatalogued material (particularly in the general stacks); it is rich in all varieties of printed materials (including ephemera); and its various catalogues represent different degrees of bibliographical control (from the typed cards for the broadside collections through the miscellaneous nature of the imprint catalogue, to the sophisticated catalogues of the Berg and Arents Collections) . . . Although it is clear that no library in the world exactly duplicates the problems which have had to be solved in the British Library, it is nevertheless important that the nucleus of an American editorial team be developed in a library which presents similar sorts of problems. If the strategy we envisage for the whole of Phase I (1977–84) is to succeed, it must be predicated on the development of an American editorial team capable of responding to the challenges which will have to be faced in the early years of the project.

The purposeful ambitions envisaged for the New York Public Library Operational Test (NYPLOT) were:

(1) to create a team in the United States similar to the one already working in the United Kingdom; (2) to give this team an understanding of the problems that the full Project will inevitably face in the United States as it deals with difficult libraries and their local problems; (3) to encode a certain number of records (several thousand) for entering into the full Project's data base later, and to convert a portion of these records into machine-readable form; and (4) to give the ESTC project and its aims further publicity in the United States library and academic communities.

The second stage in the development of ESTC in America was determined as a two year project to convert into machine-readable form the total output of the printing press in North America during the eighteenth century. A proposal for this stage, entitled the American Imprints Publications Project (AIPP), has been submitted to the National Endowment for the Humanities and, if successful, will be followed by applications to other foundations for matching funds. The objective of this second stage in American ESTC activity is, in essence, to produce a machine-readable file of approximately 45,000 items printed in America and Canada between 1701 and 1800, based on the existing bibliographical guides.

The second stage of the ESTC in America will, it is planned, be based at Brown University. The project will be directed by T. Belanger, and it is expected that a machine-readable file of North American imprints, the ultimate administration and enlargement of which will be the responsibility of the American Antiquarian Society at Worcester, will be available by the end of 1980 when the British Library holdings have been encoded.

The ESTC in America will be governed by a National Committee consisting of the following:

Carl Bridenbaugh *(Chairman)*, Emeritus Professor, Brown University.
T. B. Belanger, *(Editor)*, School of Library Service, Columbia University.
T. R. Adams, Librarian, John Carter Brown Library.
J. M. Beattie, Professor of History, Toronto University.
F. T. Bowers, Emeritus Professor of English, University of Virginia.
D. W. Bryant, Director of Harvard University Library.
A. H. Epstein, Former Director of BALLOTS.
A. M. Fern, Director, Research Department, Library of Congress.
J. D. Hart, Director, Bancroft Library, Berkeley.
B. Hindle, Director, Smithsonian Institution.
Mary M. C. Hyde, Princeton, New Jersey.
G. J. Kolb, Professor of English, University of Chicago.
P. J. Korshin, Professor of English, University of Pennsylvania.
W. J. Matheson, Chief, Rare Books Division, Library of Congress.
M. A. McCorison, Director, American Antiquarian Society.
E. S. Morgan, Stirling Professor of History, Yale University.
G. N. Ray, President, John Simon Guggenheim Memorial Foundation.
H. L. Snyder, Professor of History, University of Kansas.
G. T. Tanselle, Associate Professor of English, University of Wisconsin.
W. B. Todd, Professor of English, University of Texas.
E. Wolff, 2nd, Librarian, Library Company of Philadelphia.

The first meeting of the American National Committee is scheduled to take place late in 1978.

If the experience of the revision of Pollard & Redgrave and Wing is of any importance for ESTC it surely lies in the fact that no historical bibliography of English printed materials can be comprehensive without the active support and cooperation of libraries in North America. The outcome of those steps which have been taken to ensure that support and cooperation is awaited with optimism.

RULES

FOR THE COMPILATION OF THE CATALOGUE.

I. TITLES to be written on slips, uniform in size.

The entries of works in the collection of George the Third presented by George the Fourth to the Nation to be distinguished by a crown.

II. Titles to be arranged alphabetically, according to the English alphabet only (whatever be the order of the alphabet in which a foreign name might have to be entered in its original language) under the surname of the author, whenever it appears printed in the title, or in any other part of the book. If the name be supplied in MS. the work must nevertheless be considered anonymous or pseudonymous, as the case may be, and the MS. addition deemed merely a suggestion to which the librarian will attach such importance as he may think proper, on his own responsibility, in supplying the author's name between brackets, as hereafter directed.

In the alphabetical arrangement, initial prepositions, letters or articles to be taken in connection with the rest of the name.

III. If more than one name occur in the title, by which it may appear that the work is the production of more than one person, the first to be taken as the leading name.

IV. The works of sovereigns, or of princes of sovereign houses, to be entered under their Christian or first name, *in their English form.*

V. Works of Jewish Rabbis, as well as works of Oriental writers in general, to be entered under their first name.

VI. Works of friars, who, by the constitution of their order, drop their surname, to be entered under the Christian name ; the name of the family, if ascertained, to be added in brackets. The same to be done for persons canonized as well as for those known under their first name only, to which, for the sake of distinction, they add that of their native place, or profession, or rank. Patronymics, or denominations, derived from the ancestors or names of other persons, to be used as surnames.

VII. The respondent or defender in a thesis to be considered its author, except when it unequivocally appears to be the work of the Præses.

VIII. When an author uses a Christian or first name only (either real or assumed), such name to be taken as a heading ; and if more than one be used, the first to be preferred for the principal entry. The surname or family name, when known, to be added in brackets after the first name.

IX. Any act, resolution, or other document purporting to be agreed upon, authorized, or issued by assemblies, boards, or corporate bodies, (with the exception of academies, universities, learned societies, and religious orders, respecting which special rules are to be followed,) to be entered in distinct alphabetical series, under the name of the country or place from which they derive their denomination, or, for want of such denomination, under the name of the place whence their acts are issued.

X. Names of persons that may have been altered by being used in various languages, to be entered under their vernacular form, if any instance occur of such persons having used it in any of their printed publications. With respect to places, the English form to be preferred.

XI. Works of authors who change their name or add to it a second, after having begun to publish under the first, to be entered under the first name, noticing any alteration which may have subsequently taken place.

XII. Foreign names, excepting French, preceded by a preposition, an article, or by both, to be entered under the letter immediately following. French names preceded by a preposition only, to follow the same rule ; those preceded by an article, or by a preposition and an article, to be entered under the initial letter of the article. English surnames, of foreign origin, to be entered under their initial, even if originally belonging to a preposition. Foreign compound surnames to be entered under the initial of the first of them. In compound Dutch and English surnames the last name to be preferred, if no entry of a work by the same person occur in the catalogue under the first name only.

XIII. German names, in which the letters *ä, ö* or *ü* occur, to be spelt with the diphthong *ae, oe* and *ue* respectively.

XIV. Surnames of noblemen, though not expressed in the book, to be ascertained and written out as the heading of the entry. A person who has assumed titles not generally acknowledged, to have the words "calling himself," between brackets, to precede the assumed title.

XV. The same rule to be followed with respect to archbishops and bishops.

XVI. Christian names, included in parentheses, to follow the surname, and all to be written out in full, as far as they are known. In case of doubt on this or any other point, when the librarian is directed to supply any information in cataloguing, a note of interrogation to follow in such a position as to indicate clearly the point on which any doubt is entertained.

XVII. An author's rank in society, in cases in which he enjoyed any eminent honorary distinction, or office for life, not lower than that of knight, admiral, or general, to be stated in italics. Younger sons of dukes and marquesses, and all daughters of dukes, marquesses and earls, when not enjoying a distinct title, to have the designation *Lord* or *Lady* prefixed to the Christian name. All other younger branches of the nobility to have the word *Hon.* prefixed. The words *Right Hon.,* in the same situation, to distinguish privy councillors. Knights to be indicated merely by the appellation *Sir* prefixed to their first name. Titles of inferior rank, whether ecclesiastical, military, or civil, to be given only when necessary to make a distinction between authors having the same surname and Christian name.

Proper names commencing with Mc. or M' to be entered under Mac, with cross-references from the other forms.

Where a person is referred to in a title-page by a description sufficiently clear to render his or her iden-

a

tity obvious, the proper name of such person to be adopted as a heading, whether the work be historical or otherwise.

XVIII. The title of the book next to be written, and that expressed in as few words, and those only of the author, as may be necessary to exhibit to the reader all that the author meant to convey in the titular description of his work; the original orthography to be preserved. The number of the edition to be stated when appearing in the title.

In cataloguing sermons, the text always to be specified. The date at which preached to be inserted when it differs from that of publication.

XIX. Any striking imperfection in a book to be carefully noted; and any remarkable peculiarity, such as that of containing cancelled or duplicate leaves, &c. to be stated.

XX. When the book is without a title-page, its contents to be concisely, but sufficiently, stated in the words of the head-title, preceded by the word *begin. (beginning)* in italics; if there be no head-title, in those of the colophon, preceded by the word *end. (ending)*; and when the want of title is owing to an imperfection, the words taken from either head-title or colophon to be included between parentheses. If both head-title and colophon be wanting or insufficient, then some idea of the work to be briefly given in English, between brackets, and the edition so accurately described as to be easily identified without fear of mistake.

XXI. Whenever one or more separate works are mentioned in the title of any publication, as forming part of it, the same to be particularly noticed in cataloguing the principal publication; and, if not mentioned in the title-page, this information to be added to the title between brackets or parentheses, as the case may be.

XXII. All works in Oriental characters or languages, except Hebrew, to be separately catalogued in a supplementary volume, according to special rules to be framed. The Bible and its parts, however, in whatever language or characters, to be entered in the general catalogue as hereafter directed.

XXIII. Works in more languages than one, accompanied by the original, to be entered in the original only, unless the title be accompanied by a translation or translations, in which case such translation also to be given. If no original text occur, the first language used in the title to be preferred. In all cases the several languages used in the book to be indicated at the end of the title, in italics.

XXIV. Works with a title in a language different from that used in the body of the book to be entered according to the above rule, merely stating at the end of the title in italics in what language the work is written.

XXV. The number of parts, volumes, fasciculi, or whatever may be the peculiar divisions of each author's work, to be next specified, in the words of the title.

XXVI. When nothing is said in the title respecting this point, if a work be divided into several portions, but the same pagination continue, or, when the pages are not numbered, if the same register continue, the work to be considered as divided into parts; if the progressive number of the pages or the register be interrupted, then each series of pages or letters of the register to be designated as a volume.

XXVII. Then the place where the book was printed; and in particular cases, as in the instance of early or very eminent typographers, the printer's name to be

specified. Next the date: when no date or place is specified, then either or both to be given, if known to, or conjectured by, the librarian; but in these instances to be included in brackets. The form to follow, whether fol., 4to, 8vo, &c.

XXVIII. If an early printed book, and in Gothic or black letter, the circumstance to be mentioned at the end of the title, thus :—G. L. or B. L.

XXIX. If printed on vellum, satin, on large or fine paper, or if an editio princeps of a classical or very distinguished writer, who flourished before 1700, or if privately printed, or a fac-simile or reprint of an early edition; if only a small number of copies were struck off, or if there be any manuscript notes, these peculiarities to be stated.

XXX. If the author of the manuscript notes be known, this information to be added between brackets. If the volume belonged to some very distinguished personage, the fact to be recorded in few words at the end of the entry, also between brackets.

XXXI. An editio princeps to be designed by the words *ED. PR.*, in italic capitals, at the end of the title. Manuscript notes to be indicated in italics at the end of the title, previous to the size of the volume, as follows :—*MS. NOTES.* If the notes be remarkably few, or the reverse, the circumstance to be noticed by prefixing to the above the word *FEW* or *COPIOUS.* Works printed *ON VELLUM* to be distinguished by these words, in small italic capitals, at the end of the title. The letters *L.P.* or *F.P.* in the same situation, to indicate copies on large or fine paper.

XXXII. Works published under initials, to be entered under the last of them; and should the librarian be able to fill up the blanks left, or complete the words which such initials are intended to represent, this to be done in the body of the title, and all the supplied parts to be included between brackets.

The rules applicable to proper names to be extended to initials.

XXXIII. When the author's name does not appear on the title or any other part of the work, the following rules to be observed. Anonymous publications relating to any act, or to the life of a person whose name occurs on the title of a work, to be catalogued under the name of such person. The same rule to be followed with respect to anonymous publications addressed (not merely dedicated) to any individual whose name occurs on the title.

XXXIV. When no such name of a person appears, then that of any assembly, corporate body, society, board, party, sect, or denomination appearing on the title to be preferred, subject to the arrangement of Rule IX.; and if no such name appear, then that of any country, province, city, town or place so appearing, to be adopted as the heading.

Articles to be inquired of within an ecclesiastical district to be entered under the name of such district.

XXXV. If no name of any assembly or country, to be preferred as above, appear on the title, the name of the editor, (if there be any,) to be used as a heading; or, if no editor's name appear, that of the translator, if there be one. Reporters to be considered as editors.

XXXVI. Adjectives formed from the name of a person, party, place or denomination, to be treated as the names from which they are formed.

XXXVII. If two names occur seeming to have an equal claim, the first to be chosen.

Reports of civil actions to be catalogued under the

name of that party to the suit which stands first upon the title-page.

In criminal proceedings the name of the defendant to be adopted as a heading.

Trials relating to any vessel to be entered under the name of such vessel.

XXXVIII. In the case of anonymous works, to which none of the foregoing rules can be applied, the first substantive in the title (or if there be no substantive, the first word) to be selected as the heading. A substantive, adjectively used, to be taken in conjunction with its following substantive as forming one word; and the same to be done with respect to adjectives incorporated with their following substantive. The entries which may occur under the same heading to succeed each other in strict alphabetical order.

XXXIX. Whenever the name of the author of an anonymous publication is known to, or conjectured by, the librarian, the same to be inserted at the end of the title, between brackets.

XL. Works without the author's name, and purporting to comment or remark on a work of which the title is set forth in that of such publication, to be catalogued under the same heading as the work remarked or commented upon.

XLI. In the case of pseudonymous publications, the book to be catalogued under the author's feigned name; and his real name, if discovered, to be inserted in brackets, immediately after the feigned name, preceded by the letters *i. e.*

XLII. Assumed names, or names used to designate an office, profession, party, or qualification of the writer, to be treated as real names. Academical names to follow the same rule. The works of an author not assuming any name but describing himself by a circumlocution, to be considered anonymous.

XLIII. Works falsely attributed in their title to a particular person, to be treated as pseudonymous.

XLIV. Works of several writers, collectively published, to be entered according to the following rules, [and the separate pieces of the various authors included in the collection to be separately entered in the order in which they occur; excepting merely collections of letters, charters, short extracts from larger works, and similar compilations.]

That part of the foregoing rule which is inserted between brackets has not been acted upon, in order to accelerate the printing of the catalogue.

XLV. In any series of printed works, which embraces the collected productions of various writers upon particular subjects, such as Ugolini Thesaurus Antiq. Sacrarum, Gronovii Thesaurus Antiq. Græcarum, the work to be entered under the name of the editor.

Works of several authors published together, but not under a collective title, to be catalogued under the name of the first author, notwithstanding an editor's name may appear on the work.

XLVI. If the editor's name do not appear, the whole collection to be entered under the collective title, in the same manner as anonymous works.

In cataloguing collections without an editor's name, and having a collective title, the heading to be taken from such collective title without reference to that portion of the title which may follow.

XLVII. General collections of laws, edicts, ordinances, or other public acts of a similar description, to be entered under the name of the state or nation in which or by whom they were sanctioned, signed, or promulgated. Collections extending only to one reign or period of supreme government by one person, as well as detached laws and documents separately enacted and issued, to be catalogued under the name of the person in whose name and by whose authority they are enacted or sanctioned; such names to be entered alphabetically under the principal entry of the state or nation, after the general collections. When more than one name occurs, the first to be preferred.

XLVIII. Collections of laws, edicts, &c., of several countries or nations to be catalogued according to rules XLV. and XLVI.

XLIX. The same to be done with respect to laws on one or more particular subjects, either merely collected or digested in some particular order, or used as text to some particular comment or treatise.

L. The names of translators or commentators to be stated in cataloguing and entering a work, if they occur in the title page; and when they do not occur, but are known to or conjectured by the librarian, to be supplied between brackets.

LI. The works of translators to be entered under the name of the original author. The same rule to be observed with respect to the works of commentators, if the same be accompanied with the text complete.

LII. Translations to be entered immediately after the original, generally with only the indication of the language into which the version has been made, in italics; but if any material alteration in the title have been introduced, so much of the title of the translation to be given as may be deemed requisite, or a short explanation in English added, between brackets.

LIII. Commentaries unaccompanied by the text, to be entered under the commentator's name; if without a name, or with an assumed name, then according to the rules laid down for anonymous or pseudonymous works.

LIV. No work ever to be entered twice at full length. Whenever requisite, cross-references to be introduced.

LV. Cross-references to be divided into three classes, from name to name, from name to work, and from work to work. Those of the first class to contain merely the name, title, or office of the person referred to as entered; those of the second, so much of the title referred to besides, as, together with the size and date, may give the means of at once identifying, under its heading, the book referred to; those of the third class to contain moreover so much of the title referred from, as may be necessary to ascertain the object of the reference.

LVI. Cross-references of the first class to be made in the following instances:

From the titles of noblemen, and from the sees of archbishops or bishops, to the family name, or the first name under which the works of such personages are to be entered according to the foregoing rules.

LVII. From the family name of persons whose works are to be entered under the Christian or first name, to such Christian or first name; excepting in the case of sovereigns, or princes belonging to sovereign houses.

LVIII. From any surnames either spelt, or in any way used, in a manner differing from the form adopted in the principal entry, to such entry.

LIX. From any of the names or surnames used by an author besides that under which the principal entry is made, to the one so preferred.

a 2

LX. From the real to the assumed name of authors; adding *pseud.* to the entry referred to in the cross-reference.

LXI. Cross-references of the second or third class, according to circumstances, to be made in the following instances:

From the names of editors, or of biographers who have prefixed an author's life to his works, (provided such names appear in the book,) to the principal entry.

LXII. From the names of authors of anonymous or pseudonymous works supplied in the title, as well as from the names of authors who have shared with another in writing a work, or have continued it, and also from the names of translators, commentators, or annotators, either appearing on the title, or supplied as above directed, to the main entry.

LXIII. From the name of any person the subject of any biography or narrative, to its author; stating briefly, in italics, after the name referred from, the peculiar designation of the biography in the work referred to; or, if this cannot be done, using the nearest English word, in brackets and italics, that may give an idea of the object of the cross reference.

In this description of cross-reference the first words of the title of the work referred to to be given, but not its date or size, so that the cross-reference may serve equally for all editions.

LXIV. From any name which may be reasonably conceived to have an equal claim to that selected for the principal entry, to such entry.

LXV. From any author, any whole work of whom or any considerable part of it may be the subject of a commentary, or notes, to the name of the commentator or annotator. No notice to be taken of the name of authors, fragments or inconsiderable parts of whose works are observed upon by the commentator or annotator.

LXVI. From any author whose works, or considerable part of them contained in a collection, are considered so important as to be distinctly specified in the entry of the collection itself, to the principal entry; the volume, or part of the collection in which the article so referred to is found, to be specified.

LXVII. From the names of authors whose entire works or any considerable part of them are included among the collected works of a polygraphic writer, or translator, to the principal entry.

LXVIII. From the name of a state or nation to which a collection of laws, entered under any other heading, belongs, to the main entry.

From the name of the superior of any ecclesiastical district who promulgates articles for inquiry to the name of such district.

From the name of any party to a civil action to the principal entry.

LXIX. Entries to be made in the following order:

Cross-references to be placed at the beginning of the entry, from which they are made, in the alphabetical order of the entries referred to.

LXX. Collections of all the works of an author in their original language only, to be entered immediately after the cross-references; the editions without date, and those of which the date cannot be ascertained even by approximation, to precede all those bearing date, or of which the date can be supplied either positively or by approximation. The latter to follow according to their date, whether apparent in any part of the book, or supplied. Editions by the same editor, or such as are expressly stated to follow a specific text or edition, and

editions with the same notes or commentary, to succeed each other immediately in their chronological order after the entry of that which is, or is considered to be, the earliest.

LXXI. The text of the collected works, accompanied by a translation, to follow those having the text only, and in the same order.

LXXII. The translations of such collected works into the Latin language only to precede those in any other language in the above order; the Latin translations to be followed by those in English. Translations in any other language to follow according to the alphabetical order of the name of the language in English. If the volume contain two or more translations, without the text, the entry to be made according to the alphabetical order of the first of the languages employed. Translations into the same language, and their several editions, to be entered in conformity with the rules laid down for the entries of the originals.

LXXIII. Collections of two or more works of an author to be entered in the order and according to the rules laid down for the collections of all the works of a writer, after the translations of the whole works; such partial collections to precede, as are known or are supposed to contain the largest number of an author's works.

LXXIV. Selections, or collected fragments, from the works of an author, to follow the partial collections of his works, and to be entered according to the above rules.

LXXV. Separate works of an author to succeed each other alphabetically; the several editions and translations of each of them to be entered in the same manner as directed for the collected works of a writer.

LXXVI. Entire portions of a separate work to succeed the work from which they are taken, in the order above directed. If the whole work to which they belong do not occur, such portions to be entered after all the separate works, but according to the principles laid down for the latter.

LXXVII. Works not written by the person under whose name they are to be catalogued according to the foregoing rules, to be entered alphabetically as an appendix, and in chronological succession, when more than one article occurs in the same alphabetical series, after all the works of the person whose name is selected, if any occur in the catalogue. Volumes without date, or the date of which cannot be supplied, to be entered first.

LXXVIII. The same rule as to the alphabetical and chronological arrangement to apply to works entered under any other heading than the name of a person.

LXXIX. The Old and New Testament and their parts, to be catalogued under the general head "Bible," and arranged in the following order:—

1st. The Old and New Testaments in the original Hebrew and Greek only, chronologically arranged.

2d. The same, in polyglot editions, which include the original texts; beginning with those editions which contain most translations.

3d. The same, translated into other languages, but without the original; those editions to precede which contain most languages; then translations into one language only, arranged as directed in rule LXXII.

4th. Editions, with comments, to follow those having the text only, in the same order and according to the same principles. Bibles accompanied by the same comment to follow each other immediately in chronological succession.

5th. The Old Testament only to be next entered, according to the same principles and rules.

6th. Detached parts of the Old Testament then to follow, in the same order in which they are arranged in the English authorised version of the Scriptures, and to be entered as directed for the whole Bible.

7th. The Apocrypha, as declared by the Church of England, to be next catalogued and entered according to the same rules.

8th. The New Testament to be next catalogued, and then its parts, according to the foregoing rules.

9th. General cross-references to be made from the several names of the inspired writers, as well as from the names of the several parts of Scripture, to the general head " Bible." Particular cross-references to be made from the names of editors, commentators, translators, &c., to the precise entry under which the part of Holy writ referred from in the cross-reference occurs.

10th. The names of parts of the Bible, as well as of inspired writers, to be expressed in the form adopted in the authorised English version of the Scriptures.

LXXX. All acts, memoirs, transactions, journals, minutes, &c., of academies, institutes, associations, universities, or societies learned, scientific, or literary, by whatever name known or designated, as well as works by various hands, forming part of a series of volumes edited by any such society, to be catalogued under the general name " Academies" and alphabetically entered, according to the English name of the country and town at which the sittings of the society are held, in the following order. The primary division to be of the four parts of the world in alphabetical succession, Australia and Polynesia being considered as appendixes to Asia ; the first subdivision to be of the various empires, kingdoms, or other independent governments into which any part of the world is divided, in alphabetical order ; and a second subdivision of each state to follow, according to the various cities or towns, alphabetically disposed, belonging to each state, in which any society of this description meets. The acts, &c., of each society, when more than one meet at the same place, to be entered according to the name under which the society published its first work, in alphabetical series ; and the acts, memoirs, &c. of each society to be entered chronologically. Continuations to follow the original entry.

LXXXI. The same rule and arrangement to be followed for " Periodical Publications," which are to be catalogued under this general head, embracing reviews, magazines, newspapers, journals, gazettes, annuals, and all works of a similar nature, in whatever language and under whatever denomination they may be published. The several entries under the last subdivision to be made in alphabetical order according to the first substantive occurring in the title.

LXXXII. All almanacs, calendars, ephemerides of whatever description they be, as well as their companions, appendixes, &c., to be entered under the general head " Ephemerides." The several works under this head to be entered alphabetically according to the first substantive occurring in the title.

LXXXIII. There shall be cross-references from the name of any author, editor, or contributor to any of the above works, appearing in any of the title-pages of any of the volumes, as well as from the peculiar name or designation of any of the societies, from the place at which they hold their meetings, from any place forming part of the peculiar name of a journal, almanac, calendar, &c., from the name under which such publications are generally known, to the main entries of such works.

LXXXIV. Religious and military orders to be designated by the English name under which they are generally known, and entries to be made accordingly.

LXXXV. Anonymous catalogues, whether bearing the title catalogue or any other intended to convey the same meaning, to be entered under the head " Catalogues," subdivided as follows :—1st. Catalogues of public establishments (including those of societies, although not strictly speaking *public*). 2d. Catalogues of private collections, drawn up either for sale or otherwise. 3d. Catalogues of collections not for sale, the possessors of which are not known. 4th. General as well as special catalogues of objects, without any reference to their possessor. 5th. Dealers' catalogues. 6th. Sale catalogues not included in any of the preceding sections.

LXXXVI. Catalogues of the first subdivision to be entered under the name of the place at which the collection exists, as directed for Academies : those of the second, under the name of the collector or possessor : those of the third, in strict alphabetical order, according to the first substantive of the title : those of the fourth, to follow the same rule : those of the fifth, under the dealer's name : those of the sixth, strictly chronologically, supplying the year in brackets whenever omitted, but known to, or conjectured by, the librarian ; and when it is impossible to ascertain the precise day and month, for catalogues coming under the same year, in strict alphabetical order before those having a precise date. Catalogues without any date, and the date of which cannot be supplied, to be entered at the beginning of this subdivision in strict alphabetical order, as just directed. With respect to mere dealers' and sale catalogues compiled since the beginning of the present century, such only to be catalogued and entered as may be considered of peculiar interest.

LXXXVII. Cross-references of the second class to be made from the name of the compiler of a catalogue (when supplied by the librarian, and other than the collector or possessor of a collection, a dealer or an auctioneer) to the principal entry.

LXXXVIII. Anonymous Dictionaries of any description, including Lexicons and Vocabularies, to be catalogued under the general head " Dictionaries," and entered in strict alphabetical order according to the first substantive in the title, with cross-references from the author's name, when supplied.

LXXXIX. The same rule to be applied to Encyclopædias, the name of the editor of which does not appear on the title, and which shall be catalogued under the general head " Encyclopædias," with a cross-reference from the editor's name, when supplied in the principal entry, to such entry.

XC. Missals, Breviaries, Offices, Horæ, Prayer Books, Liturgies, and works of the same description (not compiled by private individuals and in their individual capacity, in which case they are to be catalogued and entered according to the general rules laid down for other works,) to be entered under the general head " Liturgies," in one strict alphabetical series, according to the English denomination of the communion, sect, or religious order for whom they are specially intended ; if drawn up for any particular church, congregation, or place of worship, then according to the English name peculiar to such church, congregation, or place of worship ; if any work of this description occur not coming under either of these two classes, then the first substantive in the title to be preferred as a heading. Entries under the same heading to be made in strict alphabetical order.

XCI. Cross-references of the second class to be made from the peculiar name or designation of any of the churches, communions, sects, religious orders, or places of worship, as well as from the name under which any of the works mentioned in the preceding article is generally known, to the main entry.

Appendix III

Libraries contributing records to ESTC

Aberdeen University Library
Barbados Museum
Barbados Archives
Bedford County Library
Bermuda Library, Hamilton
Bexley Public Library
Birmingham Public Library
Bodleian Library, Oxford
Bradford Public Library
Brent Central Library
Brighton Public Library
British School at Athens
Cambridge University Library
Canterbury Cathedral Library
Colchester Public Library
Croydon Central Library
Derby Central Library
Durham Cathedral Library
Glasgow University Library
Hackney Central Library
Hammersmith Central Library
Haringey Borough Library
Hereford Cathedral Library
Heythrop College, London
Huddersfield Public Library
John Rylands University Library,
    Manchester

Kent County Library
Kingston upon Thames Central Library
Lambeth Borough Library
Lincoln Cathedral Library
London School of Hygiene and
Tropical Medicine
Merton Borough Library
Newham Borough Library
Nottingham County Library
Richmond upon Thames Public Library
Royal Archives, Copenhagen
Royal College of Surgeons
Royal Library, Stockholm
Saffron Walden Library
St. Pancras Library
Stoke Newington Public Library
Trinity College, Dublin
University College of Swansea
University College of Wales, Aberystwyth
University of Essex Library
University of Lancaster Library
University of Liverpool Library
University of Southampton Library
Wakefield City Record Office
Wandsworth Public Library
Wolverhampton Public Library
York Minster Library

CATALOGUING RULES

FOR

THE EIGHTEENTH-CENTURY
SHORT-TITLE CATALOGUE

IN

THE BRITISH LIBRARY

Revised Edition

Preface

In an earlier edition of the *Rules* used in cataloguing material for the Eighteenth-Century Short-Title Catalogue* it was remarked that the principles governing the compilation of ESTC records had evolved over a period of several months. Methods and principles have remained relatively stable, but the process of evolution continues, and the consequences are incorporated in this revised edition. Most of the changes concern minor points of detail—changes made, for the most part, in the interests of clarity and consistency.

However, it must be admitted that some changes have been made necessary as a result of the experience gained in the production of a logical, bibliographically ordered sequence of records, automatically generated, for the works of Alexander Pope printed before 1801, reproduced in the final section of this book. In the section above dealing with machine-readable cataloguing and the working methods used in the British Library much attention has been devoted to the problems which have had to be solved in reconciling isolative demands made of a machine-readable file with the more intricate demands implicit in sequences of entries such as are expected by students of literature and history. Accordingly, the section dealing with uniform and collective titles has been subject to most revision. Largely rewritten, it now incorporates the fruit of greater experience in imposing order and intellectual structure upon heterogeneous material, and demonstrates the necessity of superimposing filing-fields (additional to standard US and UK MARC) if the computer is to have any chance of producing, if required, a listing of an author's work in a sequence other than merely alphabetical. Three new fields are introduced: one, which will normally only be used in cases of extreme complexity (major, and frequently printed authors, such as Pope), can only expediently be employed once the bibliographical profile of an author has been established—field 239; one which has relevance solely to the correct chronological filing of an individual entry—field 259; and one which is used for complex texts within an otherwise straightforward bibliographical sequence—field 249. Of the three fields only 259 can be constructed at the time of cataloguing without reference to the existing or anticipated file: both 239 (applying to a complete heading) and 249 (to selected parts of a heading) must be used with editorial discretion since they predetermine, to a large extent, interrelations which may be made at a later date. It is important to observe here that the use of both 239 and 249 cannot be anticipated by a cataloguer contributing records to the base file, since the bibliographical complexities of a particular author or text may be unknown, or at best unexpected. Ensuring an accurate and, from the point of view of agreed international standards, an acceptable bibliographical description of an individual book is the object of the following rules: a more interesting, and in the context of mechanical handling a more challenging objective is ensuring that every individual record occupies its proper place in the bibliographical sequence.

In framing the rules governing ESTC cataloguing no claim is made that every peculiarity or idiosyncrasy of eighteenth-century printing has been catered for, but it is our hope that some advance has been made towards resolving the problems created by the conflicting principles of mechanical and intellectual logic, thereby bringing a little closer the day when the capabilities of the computer can be fully exploited in the service of scholarship.

R. C. Alston
M. J. Jannetta
R. A. Christophers

*This provisional edition was not intended for general circulation but was produced for those libraries contributing to ESTC.

Title HOMERIDES	Author [BURNET T.]	Place [EDINBURGH]	Heading 967 $a a d p s v
* RI * T 600327 008 $a s 1714 $b ~~en~~ st $1 eng 049 $a L			$c ① 2 3 $d 1

090 $a C. 316. b. 1 (3)   090|1 $a T. 1087. q. 25 (2)

245 | 1 | 0 | $a Homerides : or, a letter to Mr. Pope, occasion'd by his intended translation of Homer. By Sir Iliad Doggrel.

240 | 1 | 0 | $a Letter to Mr. Pope

250 $a The second edition, amended and enlarged   259 $a 1714

260 $a London [i.e. Edinburgh] $b printed [by Thomas Ruddiman], and sold by J. Roberts

     $c 1715 [1714]

300 $a [4], iv, 23, [3] p. $b ill. $c 8ᵛ

500 $a Sir Iliad Doggrel = Thomas Burnet and George Duckett. – With a half-title and a final leaf of errata. – A reissue, with a cancel titlepage and additional material, of 'A letter to Mr. Pope,' 1714. – Advertised in 'The Grumbler,' November 3, 1714. – The imprint is false; printed by Ruddiman on the evidence of the ornaments

100 | 1 | $a Burnet $e Sir $h Thomas
~~110~~ $f One of the Justices of the Court of Common Pleas

GK3   DOGGREL   519 $a

---

600 | | $a $h
610 | | $u

645

700 | 1 | 0 | $a Duckett $h George
~~710~~

956 /1 $b Imperfect ; wanting the half-title

Ver. locs. 089 0	$a O	$b Douce 38	$a	$b	$a	$b
	$a C	$b Don 3.4	$a	$b	$a	$b
	$a	$b	$a	$b	$a	$b

Unver. locs. 089 1 $a Ct Y

Bibl. refs. 503 $a Guerinot, p. 361

Conservation

Provenance   Pope's copy (C. 316. b. 1 (3))

Notes   A specimen entry, founded on fact

THE RECORD CARD

Uncoded Areas

Areas contained within double rules on the recto, and below the double rule on the verso of the record card have no field tags. Information inserted in these areas will *not* be keyboarded.

Top line

Title   Write here in capitals the first word of the title other than an article, as given in field 245.

Author   Write here in capitals the surname and initials of a personal author in field 100.
If the work is anonymous enclose it all in square brackets.
Write here in capitals the name of a government or body and in lower case any addition to this as given in field 110.

Place   Write here in capitals the place(s) in 260 $a with the exception of LONDON.
Use the accepted modern form of the name in English, e.g.: Shrewsbury, not Mwythig or Salop; Glasgow, not Glasguæ.
N.B. If the place in 260 $a is Londres, Londra, or other forms which appear to be false, enter the form as it stands in the place box.

Heading Write here in capitals the following form-headings as coded in 967:
        ADVERTS (see below page 32)
        DIRECTORIES (see below page 29)
        PROSPECTUSES (see below page 32)
        SONGS (see below page 31)
        ALMANACS (see below page 29)

Bottom Line

The box marked GK3 facilitates record of the heading in the General Catalogue under which an item is to be found. This may be abridged, but should be full enough to make subsequent reference to the item easy; in this respect volume and column number from GK3 may help.

Note—On the verso of the record card are three uncoded areas for including notes on the physical condition of the book, its provenance, and other information relevant to it, but which need not or will not become part of the keyboarded record.

Local coded information

Indicate here any of the following characteristics of the work:
967   $a   a   for advertisements
           d   for directories
           p   for prospectuses
           s   for songs
           v   for almanacs
     $c   1   for pseudonymous works entered under author's real name
           2   for pseudonymous works entered under pseudonym
           3   for works entered under initials
     $d   1   a reserve subfield

INFORMATION FIELD

Information codes

RI : Leave this blank. This is reserved for use at the keyboarding stage.

008 : $a   Date of publication.
Give the date(s) of the imprint, *without* brackets or question marks or circa, preceded by s (preprinted) if there is only one date, by *m* for multi-volume works covering more than one date e.g.:
s1797
m17621765 (no space between years)

$b   Country of publication.
Give the two letter code in the MARC manual pp. 69–71. The most common are:
- *en* England (preprinted)
- *ie* Ireland
- *st* Scotland
- *wl* Wales
- *us* America
- *gw* Germany (all parts)

Note: Boundaries at time of publication apply.

$1   Language of publication.
Give the three letter code for the predominant language as in the MARC manual pp. 73–75.
The most common are:
- *eng* English (preprinted)
- *fre* French
- *ita* Italian
- *wel* Welsh
- *lat* Latin
- *ger* German

If the work is in more than one language use the code for the language of the translation, of the prefatory material, or the first in alphabetical order in that order of preference.
If the work is in three or more language with no one language predominating use *mul*.

049 : Location field for the master record. British Library cards have *L* preprinted. For use in other libraries, write here the approved library symbol (in the U.S. and Canada the Library of Congress approved list).

090 : Shelf-mark(s) for copy/copies in the holding library entered at 049. Where multiple copies exist, indicate them as follows:
090 $a 090/1 $a 090/2 $a, etc.
Shelf-marks should be written in accordance with the prevailing practices of the holding library entered at 049.
For notes relating to specific copies (field 956) see below, page 27.

Punctuation generated by subfields.
Note that certain subfield marks are converted automatically into punctuation marks at the print-out stage. In some cases this may result in unavoidable double punctuation; in others it may be possible to avoid double punctuation by suppressing the marks a cataloguer would normally expect to provide (e.g. in the imprint field). Where necessary an explanatory note will be found in the relevant sections below.

4

TITLE

245 Title and statement(s) of authorship

General rules for transcription

The first word of the title, proper nouns and proper adjectives *only* should begin with capitals. Proper nouns and adjectives not capitalized in the original are transcribed as found. (See further AACR Appendix II, pp. 270–84 and below.)

Follow the punctuation of the titlepage. If some or all punctuation is omitted from the titlepage, the omission should be mentioned in a note. Guided at all times by the letter forms on the titlepage in question, initial capitals should be retained for those words which would clearly in conventional terms mark the beginning of a new sentence.

Where punctuation is generated by the computer retain the original punctuation even if this results in double punctuation.

Indicate all omissions in transcription (other than quotations and texts) by three dots. Preserve original punctuation before ellipses, e.g.: . . .
In general, transcribe the title as fully as necessary to ensure a correct filing sequence, to avoid confusion with other similar titles, and to indicate the content of the work.

Author statements, of whatever kind, must be transcribed. This includes pseudonyms, phrases, and initials. Supplementary wording describing the author may be omitted (e.g. "Rector of Little Gidding") and such omissions indicated by three dots.

Misprints are indicated [sic] after the affected word. If the misprint and inclusion of the word [sic] would affect the filing sequence, construct a uniform title in field 240 with the correct spelling. See further notes on uniform titles below.

Unusual spellings, punctuation or other conventions which are not in fact incorrect in the context are indicated by a pencilled tick in a circle above the appropriate character(s). This is intended to assist keyboarders and proofreaders.

Characters in non-roman alphabets are transliterated according to the standards laid down by the Library of Congress (see appendix) and a note is given in the 500 field indicating the language and extent of the transliterated matter. e.g.:

> *The first three words are transliterated from the Greek.*

Rules for transcription within subfields.

In the initial stage only subfield $a (preprinted) is to be used.

Write down the title proper*, including alternative titles and parallel titles, as found on the titlepage. Start with the opening words of the titlepage (unless these constitute the imprint, edition statement, a dedication or motto, the date or price). These should be omitted from the 245 field, but noted in 500, and transcribed in 250 or 260 if appropriate.

Retain the spelling and punctuation of the titlepage.

---

* Defined as that part of the title necessary for the identification and distinguishing of the work or edition in hand.

If there is no titlepage, use the following sources in this order of preference:
    Half-title
    Docket title*
    Caption/Drop-head title
    Colophon
    Running title
    Cover title
    Incipit or *Explicit*

Give the source of the title in a note if it is not taken from the titlepage, or from the caption of a single sheet (see 500).

If there is no title proper in any of the above sources, record the opening words of the text as far as is required to make sense, and indicate that you have done this in a note.

Precede a parallel title with an equals sign.

Where two letterpress titlepages occur, generally transcribe the first recto. Mention the other titlepage in a note, and make out a yellow cross-reference card for it.

For collections of works known to have been (or likely to have been) issued separately, make out a separate record card for each title not found in the library as a genuine separate item, in addition to a main entry card taken from the collective titlepage. Linking footnotes should then be added to each card. On the card for the collection it is preferable to give a list of contents, but where there are too many items to list separately, a note in the following form will suffice:

   Consisting of 38 pt., each with separate titlepage, pagination and register

On the cards for each individual part the footnote should refer to the whole collection as follows:

   In: 'A collection of modern poems', London, 1716

If examples of the separate parts are to be found in the library, the footnote on the record for the part should be in the following form:

   Also issued as part of: 'A collection of modern poems', London, 1716

Use of indicators

First indicator
This indicates whether an entry under the title is required. Write 1 if the work has no heading in the 100/110 field, or if the author statement has been supplied from elsewhere than the titlepage, or if the heading in 100 is a pseudonym or initialism. Write 1 if there is a 110 heading, unless a uniform title has been provided in the 240 field.
0 in all other cases.

Second indicator
This indicates how many characters must be ignored to enable the title to be filed. Write 0–9 according to the number of characters, including spaces and punctuation marks (except initial single inverted comma), to be ignored, e.g.:

* Docket titles are used in preference to captions only if the caption is not a title. If a docket title varies from a chosen caption title, mention it in a note, and complete a yellow cross-reference card leading from the variant to the chosen form. If the docket title is taken as the title proper, complete a yellow cross-reference card for the first words of the caption, or text.

0   Sermon . . . .
0   'Taxation no tyranny'
1   "Britannia triumphant"
1   Laigle de France
2   A sermon on ingratitude
2   'L'esprit des lois'
3   Le bourgeois gentilhomme
4   The Craftsman vindicated
6   [The] 'Craftsman' vindicated

Rules for Uniform and Collective Titles

Uniform Title: Field 240. The uniform title is designed to bring together all editions, translations, etc. of a particular work, whatever form of title appears on the titlepage. It may also be used to keep together, and file such genres as treaties, laws, proclamations. It is to this extent a filing device, but the use of 240 $a does not of itself guarantee that a number of items so described will, at print-out stage, file in a desired sequence. This may be achieved by the inclusion of further subfields (see below); but for some complex sequences an additional filing element may have to be inserted, as an added qualification.

An entry in field 240 will be needed where the title of the work on the titlepage:
(i) is not one by which it is generally known, e.g.:
   The tragical history of Hamlet.
   Uniform title—*Hamlet.*
(ii) is that of a translation. *A treatise on the social compact.*
   Uniform title—*Du contrat social. English.*
(iii) begins with words not required for filing, e.g. *Dean Swift's Gulliver's Travels.*
   Uniform title—*Gulliver's Travels.*
(iv) differs from that used for earlier editions as a title proper.
(v) is that of an act, treaty or proclamation or collection of such items, or other special category, e.g. prize court proceedings.

Note that in general, once a uniform title has proved necessary, as in examples (i), (iii), (iv) and (v) above, it will have to be included in all entries for editions of the same work.

Rules for transcription within subfields

Subfield mark	Definition	Punctuation generated
240 $a	uniform title	[ ]
$o	year of imprint	.
$p	qualifications added	.
$q	version	.
$r	language/version	.
$s	part of work	.

Give $a in modern spelling and capitalization of the language concerned and in as short a form as possible. Give other subfield information in English in the *reverse* order of the alphabet. If data which is not listed in the table above is required give it in the appropriate subfield, usually $a, with the elements of the data separated by a full stop. (See the fourth example below):

7

Examples: 240 $a *Gulliver's Travels* $s *Selections* $o *1732*
240 $a *Iliad* $s *Books 1–5* $r *English and Greek* $o *1770*
240 $a *Bible* $s *New Testament* $s *Luke* $r *English* $q *Coverdale* $o *1751*
240 $a *Proclamation. 1707. May 2* (Where 1707 is the year of the proclamation and not necessarily the year of imprint.)
240 $a *Essay on criticism* $r *Latin* $p *Prospectus*

Note the form in $r for bilingual texts, with the language of the translation coming first.

Rules for use of indicators. Within field 240 the first indicator is used to call for an entry under the uniform title, and to suppress or include the uniform title at the print-out stage, as circumstances require.

First indicator 0   The uniform title will be suppressed; no added entry will be generated. Its purpose is solely to give filing instructions to the computer.

Its particular uses are:
(a)   to file in a required order different editions of the same work which have the same title and the same date, or have different dates but the wording of the whole title area as transcribed in 245 $a changes in such a way that strict alphabetical filing will produce an incorrect sequence unless structured information to cover all variable elements is incorporated at 240 (see also below);
(b)   to allow misprinted titles to be filed under their correct spelling when there is no doubt as to the correct title;
(c)   to eliminate as filing elements genitive forms of an author's name preceding a title which is acceptable in itself as an access point.

First indicator 0 does not call for an entry under the uniform title; it is therefore appropriate in the instances given above only when the author's name appears on the titlepage.

First indicator 2   The uniform title will be suppressed, but entries will be generated both under the uniform title and under the title as given in 245.

Its purpose is again to give filing instructions to the computer, in circumstances similar to those in (a) and (b) above for which first indicator 0 is used. The difference here is that two entries will be generated, one under the uniform title, and another under the title of the edition or version in hand. First indicator 2 is therefore used in such instances, when no author's name appears on the titlepage.

First indicator 1   The uniform title will be printed as part of the main entry, enclosed within square brackets before the title proper; no added entry will be generated.

Its particular uses are:
(a)   to bring together works published under significantly different titles, including translations;
(b)   to make obvious the filing arrangement when the genres mentioned above are used to structure official headings;
(c)   to clarify the correct form of a misprinted title, where the correct reading is not obvious.

Since first indicator 1 does not call for an entry under the uniform title it is appropriate in the instances given above only when the author's name appears on the titlepage, and for works of special genres entered under official headings.

First indicator 3   The uniform title will be printed as part of the main entry, within square brackets before the title proper. Entries will be generated both under the uniform title and under the title as given in 245.

Its particular uses are:

(a) to bring together under at least one heading *all* editions and versions of an anonymous work, including translations and all editions of the Bible;

(b) to provide a useful additional access point for all editions and versions of a work published anonymously with different titles, but of which the authorship is known;

(c) to clarify the correct form of a misprinted title, where the correct reading is not obvious, and where no author's name appears on the titlepage.

Second indicator. As in 245 this indicates the number of characters to be ignored in filing. Articles should normally be omitted from uniform titles; the indicator will therefore most often be 0. In inflected languages, quotations, etc., however, an indicator of a different value may be required.

Collective Title: Field 243. The collective title is designed to bring together all publications consisting of three or more whole or partial works by the same author. There are three basic sub-divisions within the collections, as designated by the indicators in the table below. The precise denomination for these sub-divisions will, apart from 'Works', vary according to the requirements of the individual author concerned.

In most cases the choice of the collective title will be left to the editorial stage. Where such a title will be required change 240 on the bibslip to 243 in ink and where possible supply a suggested collective title in pencil; see examples below.

Rules for transcription within subfields.

Subfield mark	Definition	Punctuation generated
243 $a	collective title	[ ]
$o	year of imprint	.
$q	qualifications added to the collective title	.
$r	language of translation	.
$s	collective subtitles	.

Examples: 243 $a *Works*
        $a *Works* $r *French*
        $a *Selections* $r *English*
        $a *Poems* $s *Selected poems* $r *French*
        $a *Plays* $r *German*
        $a *Letters* $o *1735*

Give $a in English, in modern spelling and capitalisation. Give other subfield information in English in the *reverse* order of the alphabet.

Rules for use of indicators.

First indicator 0: use for Works—i.e. editions of complete or allegedly complete works at time of publication. Includes works in one genre if the author wrote only in one genre.

First indicator 2: use for Selections—i.e. three or more whole or partial single works.

First indicator 3: use for works in single genres as specified.

First indicator 1 is not used.

Second indicator: In 243 second indicator is always 0.

SPECIAL PROVISIONS FOR FILING

Field 249. On occasion the normal provisions in 240 and its subfields will be found inadequate for ensuring an established sequence. Thus successive editions of the same work with exactly the same title and with the same imprint date will file randomly, even if the edition statement, place of publication, pagination, and/or format is/are different. On the other hand, the smallest variation in wording on the titlepage may, through alphabetical filing, result in one (incorrect) sequence, even though the dates in the imprint call for another. If there is a requirement for a particular order, filing data should be included in 249, subfield $a in simple numerical form, allowing for possible later interpolations (e.g. 010,020,030, etc.) or in alphabetical form, which allows greater freedom in the interpolation of additional records (e.g. DDC,DDD,DDE, etc.). The numerical device as exemplified above will accommodate a maximum of nine insertions without further alteration to numbers already allocated; the alphabetical system however permits change or addition to the letter code in such a way that hospitality to new insertions is greatly increased.

Where normal cataloguing calls in any case for a 240 uniform title this should be provided in the standard form.

Field 239. The above method should serve to sort complicated sequences of an individual title, whether anonymous or of known authorship. Where it is possible to foresee the requirements of whole headings, in particular the major authors of the period, a further device may be necessary. This technique involves the addition of an extra field, *purely as a filing device*. The field number is 239: it thus overrides *all* other fields for filing purposes. The subfield code is $a. The device itself may be numerical, or preferably, for the reasons outlined above with reference to 249, alphabetical.

Generally speaking it will only be possible to implement this technique at the editorial stage, when the contents of a single heading are substantially complete. The inclusion of a 239 will be mandatory *wherever* it is desirable to bring editions of an author's complete works to the beginning of the heading, and to arrange other collections, etc., in a sequence which is *not* alphabetical. Once the decision to use field 239 as a filing device has been taken, it must, however, be added to *every* entry under the particular heading.

Within a complex heading up to five basic divisions may be used. They are designated and ordered by the choice of first digit or letter, as follows:

First character 1 or A designates   Works.

First character 2 or B designates   Selections, including Selected Works, in more than one genre.

First character 3 or C designates   Collections of single works in single literary forms, arranged alphabetically by genre, e.g. Plays, Poems. No single works are subsumed.

First character 4 or D designates   Other works, of which it is desirable to keep together both collections and single manifestations, arranged alphabetically by genre, e.g. Letters.

First character 5 or E designates   Single works.

The first character is followed by others which determine the sequence of records to hand, whilst allowing for possible later interpolations. In the case of the numerical device this will probably be a four figure number, e.g. 10010, 10020, etc. The alphabetical device may be a straightforward single-character progression, or more elaborate, as necessary, e.g. AL, ALL, AM, AN, ANO, etc.

Field 259.

In all cases where the date in the imprint has had to be modified after transcription in 260 $c, the modified form should again be given in 259 $a. This will be in the simple 4- or 6- arabic figure form, without brackets, and is designed to ensure a correct chronological sequence for editions of the same work. Thus, in the case of a misprinted date, 260 $c might read MDCXLVI [1746]; 259 $a will record, simply, 1746. Similarly, in cases where the imprint date is known to be wrong, the amended date will be added within square brackets in 260 $c, e.g. 1734 [1733]; 259 $a will record 1733. The same principles apply to multivolume works. E.g. 260 $c 1724 [1725]–26 becomes 259 $a 1725–26.

NOTE (1)   Modification here means any change made to the form of date as given in the imprint of the work in question. Supplying a date, for an undated publication, within square brackets, with or without a query mark, does not of itself mean that the date should be repeated in 259 $a.

NOTE (2)   Once this field has had to be used for one edition of a work it will have to be added to records for *all* editions of the same work, even though the dates in 260 $c have no need of modification.

11

EDITION STATEMENT

250 Edition Statement

General rules for transcription

'Edition' refers only to numbered or revised editions or printings, not to the editing of a received text.

If the edition information is an integral part of the title or statement of authorship area, give it as such in 245 only. However, if the titlepage is headed with the edition statement, give it in 250 and record its position in a note in 500.

If an edition statement such as 'newly reprinted' appears in the imprint, give it in the imprint field only.

For capitalization, punctuation, and omissions, employ the general principles laid down at 245, reading 'edition' for 'title' as appropriate.

Rules for transcription within subfields.

In the initial stage only subfield $a (preprinted) is to be used.

Subfield mark	*Definition*	*Punctuation generated by computer*
$a	edition statement, author statement, and other information relating to the edition.	[Null]

Transcribe all information relating to the number or state of the edition and any editorial author statements at $a. If this information is taken from the same source as the title proper, the preliminaries or colophon, it is recorded as found, otherwise it is recorded in a note. If it is not taken from the titlepage give the source of the statement in a note.

IMPRINT

260 Imprint

General rules for transcription

The imprint is taken wherever possible from the titlepage.

If there is no titlepage the imprint may be found in the colophon, or (in the case of single-sheet material) at the end of the text, or elsewhere. Give the source of the imprint in a note if it is not the titlepage or the final words of a single sheet (see 500).

If there is no imprint on the titlepage, it is taken from the preliminaries or the colophon in that order of preference.

If information on any *element* of the imprint appears in two or more places give only that appearing in the preferred source in the imprint area without square brackets.

If supplementary or contradictory information covering any element, already supplied from the preferred source is found elsewhere in the book or outside the book, give it in square brackets. e.g.:

> *London: printed [by J. Wright] for Lawton Gilliver, 1730*
> *London [i.e. Edinburgh]: printed for L. G. [or rather, by Thomas Ruddiman], 1735*

The source and nature of this additional information should be explained in a note. E.g.:

> *Printer's name from colophon*
> *Printed by Wright on the evidence of the ornaments*
> *The imprint is false; "Printed by Ruddiman on the evidence of the ornaments" (Foxon)*

For capitalization and punctuation employ the general principles laid down at 245, reading 'imprint' for 'title' as appropriate.

Indication of omissions is not required in the 260 field.

Rules for transcription within subfields

Subfield mark	Definition	Punctuation generated by computer
$a	place of publication	[Null]
$b	rest of imprint	:
$c	date	,

Give the chief place(s) of publication or printing in $a in the form in which it occurs/they occur in the book. E.g.:

> *Exon, Oxonii, Glocester, Leipzig & Züllichau.*

Note the form: Dublin printed, and London reprinted for T. Warner, 1728—which requires the transcription of *London* in $a, and the repetition of the *whole* imprint in $b. More than one place of publication should be included in $a only in those cases where the form of the imprint is such that no one place can be said to predominate.

If no place of publication or printing is given in the book supply one within square brackets, if necessary followed by a query, in $a. Use an English form of the contemporary name of the place, e.g.:

> [*St. Petersburg*] not [*Leningrad*]

260 $a should not be left blank.

Boroughs, villages, or localities within the London area specified in the imprint should be entered as given in $a, e.g.:

> *Southwark, Spitalfields, Westminster, Hammersmith, etc.*

Give all the rest of the imprint with the exception of addresses of publishers/ booksellers/ printers (unless grammatically linked to the name or town of the publisher or if the address only, with or without the town, appears in the imprint) in $b. Where the imprint gives simply a phrase such as "printed in the Savoy", "printed in the year", this should be transcribed. E.g.:

> $a [*London*] $b *printed for E. & S. Harding, no. 98 Pall-Mall, and sold by R. Cruttwell, Bath* $c *1798*
> $a *London* $b *sold at the sign of the Black Boy in Paternoster Row* $c *1729*

If the place of publication and the rest of the imprint are inseparably linked give it all in $b and repeat the place of publication in $a. If the place cannot be grammatically isolated in $a in the form in which it occurs in the imprint, give it in English, using square brackets.

If up to six publishers, etc. are given in this element, record them all. If seven or more are given, record the first five as they appear and add in square brackets a summary of the rest, e.g. [*and 6 others in London, 1 in Bath*]. If, however, this statement would be as complex and lengthy as full transcription, record the full statement.

Give the date of the publication in arabic figures in $c, whether or not it is linked to the rest of the imprint. If the date is not expressed in years of the Christian era, or the figures (arabic or roman) make no sense, transcribe it as found and add the true date in square brackets.* If the date is not in the book, give it in square brackets, with a question mark if the assigned date is in doubt, supplemented in cases of possible ambiguity with a 500 note. Where a date cannot be ascertained with any degree of accuracy, you may indicate in a 500 note a period within which the work probably appeared: e.g.:

> *Ca. 1750–1760   Not before 1730   Not after 1776   Printed between 1731 and 1737*

On the use of field 259 see above, *Special Provisions for Filing.*
Multivolume works. In the case of works published in more than one volume, containing titlepages with different dates the following rules apply: take the earliest and the latest dates to be found in the set, regardless of volume number, and transcribe as follows:

> *1762–64*

The way in which individual volumes in the set are dated must be specified in a note. Some multivolume sets may be made up with volumes from different printings. It may be possible to link such volumes with the relevant 'unmixed' sets. In especially complex cases, however, it may be necessary to provide a separate record card for each individual volume. In others it may be sufficient to include an explanatory note.

*For the use of 259 $a in addition see above.

In 008 $a m the dates should be transcribed in full, again in chronological order, as follows:

17621764

See above, Information Codes; note that s is changed to *m*.

Works published in parts. The particular kind of part-work with which we are here concerned is that which is made up from a number of parts, each with its own dated titlepage, and issued under a general titlepage. In such cases the date on the general titlepage is transcribed at $c, and any differences on the titlepages to the parts (whether date, edition statement or imprint) should be specified in a 956 note. Where more than ten parts are involved this may need to be summary. The likelihood that other sets bearing the same general titlepage might be similarly eclectic would then be reflected in a general note (500) of the form:

Sets may be made up with parts from various editions.

At 008 $a s transcribe the date from the general titlepage. Each of the parts in sets of this kind should be given a separate entry, with duplicates encoded in the usual way, in accordance with the rule for collections given above.

COLLATION

300 Collation

Rules for transcription within subfields

Subfield mark	Definition	Punctuation generated by computer
$a	Pagination and plates	[Null]
$b	Illustration statement	:
$c	Format	:

Give the number of physical units comprising the work in hand in $a. Record unnumbered pages/leaves/columns within square brackets.

Works in more than one volume. Give the number of volumes, e.g. 3v. If each volume contains its own sequence, do not count the pages. If, however, all the volumes together have only one sequence of pagination, always give it in round brackets after the number of volumes, e.g.:

3v. (xxi, 900 p.)

Works in one volume with more than seven main sequences of page numeration, with or without unnumbered pages. Indicate the number of page sequences. E.g.:

33 pts.

Works in one volume with up to seven page sequences, numbered or not. Count all pages, including those which are unnumbered and those which are blank, so that all leaves containing printed matter are recorded. Leaves which are completely blank should be omitted from the collation, but their presence may be mentioned in the uncoded note area on the verso of the record card. Use roman numbers (preserving upper and lower case forms) only where they are used in the book. E.g.:

[12], 410, [2] p.   *[2], 36; [4], 40; [2], 36 p.*
[36], 24, [14] p.   *[408] p.*
vi, [26], 300, xii p.   *XLV, [1], 292 p.*

Where a roman sequence leads directly into arabic, it is regarded as continuous, e.g.:

pp. i–vi, 7–80 is recorded as *80 p.*

If the page numeration begins after p.1, count back to the page which would have been p.1 had it been numbered. If this page constitutes what could be considered a reasonable place to start the main sequence of pagination (i.e. counting back does not bring you to the middle of the preface, or half-way through the contents list, or some similar absurd place), treat this page as if it had been numbered "1", and record the main sequence as being continuously paginated. Thus, the first numbered page in a book which ends on p. 46 may be "10" on a verso; with four unnumbered preliminary leaves, counting back would mean inferring that the titlepage itself was p. "1"—not unreasonable, so the collation would be simply:

> *46p.*

In a different example, if the first numbered page of a book ending on p. 380 were "12" on a verso, and there were seven unnumbered preliminary leaves, these could very likely include the half-title and titlepage; in which case, counting back from p. 12 would produce a collation:

> *[4], 380p.*

If, in yet another example, in which the first numbered page of a book ending on p. 24 was "8", but there were only two preliminary leaves, counting back would bring you only as far as "3"; in such a case the collation would read:

> *[5], 8–24p.*

Note (a) — It is most common to find that the first numbered page of the main sequence is a verso, numbered "2"; it is *invariably* inferred that the recto of this leaf would have been numbered "1" and the sequence is recorded as continuous, i.e. *not* [1], 2–46p. but 46p. However, in a case such as the last example given above, where the first numbered page is e.g. "8", on a verso, but the sequence cannot be considered as continuous starting from "1", the numbering of the recto of that leaf is *not* inferred. Thus the example given above is recorded as [5], 8–24p. *not* [4], 7–24p.

Note (b) — Again, in this last example, it may be reasonable to infer that the item in question lacks a preliminary leaf, perhaps the half-title or an advertisement leaf; without another copy or reliable secondary source to verify this, the collation should always be recorded as it *is*, with, where appropriate, a 956 note expressed as a query such as the following:

> *Imperfect; wanting the half-title?*

It should not however be automatically assumed that something is missing when an item does not have a p. 1; each case must be considered on its merits. (The way in which the gatherings are signed may help in deciding whether a half-title, etc. is called-for.)

To assist the matching process after the records have been computerised the presence of a half-title, advertisement or errata leaf, or any similar leaf or leaves which could well have been lost or discarded in another copy, without affecting the completeness of the text proper—the presence of these should be mentioned in a 500 footnote. E.g.:

> *With a half-title*
> *With a leaf of advertisements*
> *With one leaf of postscript, and four leaves of errata*

It is not always certain whether these leaves (except in general the half-title) should be found in any one place in the book—the collation in field 300 may help to locate the leaf (or leaves); otherwise its position may best be recorded in a 956 note, as pertaining to the copy, not necessarily to the whole edition. E.g.:

> *The errata leaf is bound after sig. A4*

In some cases the cataloguer may feel doubtful that the 'additional' leaf or leaves are called-for in the whole edition. The *content* of the additional material may clearly imply that the item containing it should be considered as bibliographically distinct from one which does not. In other cases, it is probably better to assume that the item *with* the 'additional' matter is the perfect copy, while those copies which do not have it, have their less-than-perfect condition recorded in a 956 note. N.B. the distinction in phrasing of a note such as:

Imperfect; wanting the half-title
and
Without the leaf of advertisements

The former is categorical (i.e. all copies *should* have a half-title), the second suggests that the advertisement leaf may not in fact have been issued with all copies of that edition. N.B. also that where the library has both perfect and imperfect copies of an item, it is still necessary to give the relevant note in the 500 field to describe the perfect copy, as well as that in 956 which describes the imperfect one(s).

Pages without numeration at the ends of sequences are always recorded in the collation as a total within square brackets. E.g.:

47, [1]p.

means that there is one page at the end without numbering;

vi, [4], 3–205, [5]p.

indicates a preliminary sequence of six pages numbered in lower case roman, followed by four unnumbered pages, then the main sequence numbered in arabic, and five unnumbered pages at the end. The first group of unnumbered pages evidently constitutes a complete unit in this example, as the main sequence is recorded as starting on p. "3", the first *numbered* page. (Were it possible to consider the second of the unnumbered leaves as part of the main sequence, the collation would read vi, [2], 205, [5]p.)

Note that the verso of the last numbered page has no number (as often—it may even be blank)—it therefore counts as one unnumbered page to be added to the final two unnumbered leaves, i.e. a total of [5]. Leaves which are completely blank, whether preliminary, final, or intermediate, are not recorded as part of the collation.

If there is a sequence of unnumbered pages interrupting a numbered sequence record that part of the pagination as follows:

[12], 120, [4], 121–136, [12], 137–156p.

If the book has unusual pagination indicate unnumbered pages as follows:

[3], 5p. (p. 1 occurs unusually on a verso.)

Volumes having foliation rather than, or as well as, pagination should be described as follows:

[8], 163 leaves
[4], 13 leaves, [8], 164p.

18

Volumes numbered in columns should be described as follows:

   [8]p, 1366 columns.

Unnumbered columns, or sequences of columns, are treated as pages. If the paging of a book is duplicated, both pagings are recorded and an explanation is added in the 500 field. E.g.:

   [4], 1–220, 1–220p.

In this case the 500 note should read: *Duplicate pagination.*

If a book is mispaginated in such a way that the final count as printed is incorrect, give the total as printed followed by the corrected total in square brackets. E.g.:

   [4], 337 [i.e. 373], 1p.

Such mispagination, and also, where noticed, that which does not affect the final count should be explained in a 500 note.

Single sheets are recorded as *1 sheet* if printed on one side, as *[2]p.* if printed on both sides and unpaginated, as *2p.* if printed on both sides with pagination.

If the book contains plates (i.e. illustrative matter separately printed and not part of a gathering), record them after the pagination statement as follows:

   , plate(s)   , plate(s) (some fold.)   , table(s)   , fold. table(s)

Note: for books with numbered plates, record as follows:

   [6], 90 plates
   iv, 60 plates

For books consisting largely of unnumbered plates omit the collation statement and give a note in the following form:

   Consisting largely of plates with four numbered/unnumbered pages of letterpress

IMPERFECT BOOKS

It is to be hoped that the collation for a perfect copy will eventually be provided in field 300 for every item in the file. This may derive from another library's report (based on examination of their copy); or in the meantime it may derive from a reliable secondary source, such as Foxon's bibliography of English verse. Any imperfections will then be recorded in a 956 note (see remarks on this field below).

If this information is not available at the time of cataloguing, however, the collation should be recorded as follows:

   pp. 1–36 (p. 36 is clearly not the end of the item in question)
   pp. 7–32, [2] (the item begins with p. 7 which is clearly not the beginning of the work)

If the book is cropped or otherwise mutilated with the loss of the pagination, the collation statement should be enclosed within square brackets. An explanatory note is given, e.g.:

[*56*]*p.* with a 956 note: *Cropped; affecting page numbers 39–56*

In describing an imperfect copy of a multivolume work, record in 300 $a the total number of the volumes if these can be determined from the titlepage or some other reliable source, indicating in 956 the imperfections. E.g.:

300 $a 4v.
956 $b Imperfect; wanting volumes 2 and 3.

Illustration statement. If the book contains illustrative matter which is printed on leaves forming part of a gathering, record thus: *$b ill.*
If the illustrations (whether on plates or text pages) are of a specific kind, these may be signified as follows:

300 $a iv, 40p., plate $b map (contains one plate which is a map)
300 $a 28p., plates $b engr.music (some or all of the plates contain engraved music)
300 $a [12], 400p., plates $b ill., music, ports. (contains both plates and illustrations, including some letterpress music, and some portraits; there is no facility here for specifying which are which)
300 $a 60p. $b ill., map (contains illustrations only, one of which is a map)

Format. Record the bibliographical format at $c in the form of a number (whole or fraction) followed by a degree sign:

$32°, 4°, 1°, \frac{1}{2}°, \frac{1}{4}°, \frac{1}{8}°$

Formats expressed as fractions are used only for single sheet items, and are intended as indications of that proportion of a whole sheet which the item is deemed to represent.

NOTES

500/503/519 Notes

500: General notes

The following information and examples are given for guidance. It is impossible to anticipate and prescribe for every single occasion, but some of the most frequently required forms are given here. Cataloguers should use their discretion in formulating notes for other specific applications, where possible adapting given forms, or using them as a model.

Capitalize as in normal English prose usage. Titles of books quoted in notes are enclosed in single inverted commas; quotations from the text are given in double inverted commas. In footnotes, omissions from within quotations should be indicated by ellipses, but there is no need to indicate that the text continues beyond what has been excerpted.

If more than one footnote is given, separate each by a stop and dash (i.e. . –). Give notes in the following order as far as possible:

Authorship

(a)   Personal:

Anonymous. By Daniel Defoe (For a certain attribution)
Attributed to Daniel Defoe (For a probable attribution)
Sometimes attributed to Daniel Defoe (For a possible attribution)
Preface signed: Archibald McKintosh
Signed at end: a lover of truth, i.e. Archibald McKintosh
A lover of truth = Archibald McKintosh (the pseudonymous statement is quoted from the titlepage)
The author of 'The diaboliad' = William Combe

(b)   Institution responsible for, or concerned with authorship or publication:

Titlepage headed: "Extracted from the Minutes of the Society for the Propagation of the Gospel in Foreign Parts"

Comment: A note on authorship is usually required only in those instances where the information transcribed in the title field is completely inadequate to explain the choice of 100 heading.
(b) is discretionary.

Language:

Parallel Latin and English texts
English text with Latin verse and French prose translations

Comment: The *language statement* is required in this position only when 240 $r does not fully explain the nature of the text.

If the book contains components in various languages, a suitable footnote may be used at discretion, e.g.:

Articles in English, French or German; or *Articles in various languages*

21

Type of work:

A thesis
Verse
An advertisement
A circular letter
*A prospectus for James Killpatrick's translation of Alexander Pope's 'Essay on criticism',
published in 1745*
A slip-song—"Sweet Phillis, well met, the sun is just set,"

Other notes: *A catalogue. An anthology. An autobiography.*

Subject (usually necessary only where the title itself is uninformative or misinformative):

On the Excise Bill
With reference to Robert Walpole
A satire against William Pulteney
The second section relates to the siege of Namur

Summary:

With a summary in English

Additional collation:

A note should be inserted here when necessary to describe physical aspects of the book not explicit in the regular collation:

With a half-title
Titlepage in red and black
With an additional titlepage, engraved
The titlepage is engraved
The titlepage is a cancel
Sig. 02 is a cancel
*'Prolusions' and 'Miscellanea' have separate titlepages dated 1716, and bearing the
statements "The fourth edition" and "The third edition" respectively*
With a final leaf of advertisements
The last six leaves contain advertisements for T. Warner (in cases where the advertisement mentions a name not already included in the imprint or refers to a selection of the names mentioned in the imprint)
With a half-title and a final leaf of advertisements
Last page misnumbered 261; lines misnumbered 1–618
With a 16-page list of subscribers
Pp. iii-xii contain a list of subscribers
Horizontal chain lines
The original sheets have horizontal chain lines; the cancels have vertical chain lines

Publication detail:

A reissue of the edition of 1756, without the plates
*A reissue of Curll's edition of 1712, with a cancel titlepage— The previous issue was entitled
'Court poems'* (this combination should be used to describe, and link, an anonymous reissue of a work previously issued under a different title, also anonymously)
Published in parts
No more published
No more published?
All published of this edition?

Vol. 3 is in two parts
Printed in France
The separate titlepages to vol. 1, 2 bear the imprint "printed for H. Lintot, J. and R. Tonson,
and S. Draper"; those to vol. 3–9 bear the imprint "printed for J. and P. Knapton"
Dated on internal evidence
Printed by Wright on the evidence of the ornaments
Publication date from Foxon

Amended imprint:

A slip bearing the imprint "sold by G. Walsh" has been pasted over the original imprint
The imprint has been overprinted to read, in addition, "sold by G. Walsh"

Contents:

Footnotes listing contents are usually required only in the following cases:

(a)   When the titlepage does not mention additional material, which the cataloguer feels is important (e.g. in helping to determine the status of an edition). E.g.:

   Includes: 'The universal prayer', and 'The dying Christian to his soul'

(b)   When the work is made up from separate pieces, having separate titlepages, and probably (though not necessarily) separate pagination and register (and which may therefore be found issued separately). E.g.:

   Contains three tracts with separate pagination and separate titlepages reading: 'The
   answer of Henry Sacheverell'; and 'The reasons of those lords that entered their protest'

The 'contents' note is not obligatory and should always be used with discretion. It is likely to be useful for smaller collections or selections. It must show the complete contents of the volume; otherwise individual items may be mentioned in a subject note (see above). E.g.:

   Including extracts from the author's diary, May 1754–Jan. 1758

A 'contents' note should seldom be given for a work containing more than ten items, but the exact figure is discretionary.

As an alternative, passages from the book may be quoted between inverted commas, serving as a form of 'contents' note. e.g.:

   "List of the author's unpublished poems": pp. 151–158

503: Bibliographical references

References to the work found in standard bibliographies, etc., are given in a conventional form in field 503, subfield $a. When more than one reference is cited separate each by a semi-colon. E.g.:

   503 $a Foxon P764; Griffith 198

Fingerprint

The fingerprint is given (when required) with a space between each group of four characters, in field 519, subfield $a.

HEADING

100/110 Heading

Rules for choice of heading

Establish and write here the name of the person, institution or government (if any) with prime intellectual responsibility for the work. This is normally clearly the author of the text as shown on the titlepage of the work.

If two authors writing in collaboration are named, enter here only the first, and give an added entry in field 700 for the co-author. This rule also applies to joint corporate authorship (i.e. added entry in the 710 field).

If three authors not writing in collaboration are named, the first-named is given the main entry, the second and third, added entries.

If two or more authors not writing in collaboration are named, but the work has a general or collective title, enter under title only. If there is no general or collective title enter under the first-named only.

Publishers as such, editors, compilers, translators and illustrators are not normally taken as authors; see below, Special Cases.

100 Personal authors

If a work is anonymous and the author's real name is known, make the heading under that name. Give a note of the authorship in the notes area (q.v.).

If a work is anonymous and the author's real name is not known, make no entry in this area.

If the author is using a pseudonym of any kind the following rules apply:

(i) if the author's real name is known, even if he is *always* referred to by one pseudonym, enter the work under his name with the note "XX=   ". Complete a yellow cross-reference card for his pseudonym, leading to his real name and file this in the author-file.

(ii) if the author's real name is not known and cannot be ascertained enter the work under the pseudonym, ensuring that the pseudonymous author statement is given in the title field, or in the note field as appropriate.

This rules applies to all names known to be pseudonymous.

In 967 $c circle the appropriate number as follows:

   1 for pseudonymous works entered under author's real name
   2 for pseudonymous works entered pseudonym
   3 for works entered under initials

If the title indicates the work to be a real dialogue between real persons enter under the first named. If the dialogue is between fictitious persons, and is written by one known author enter under the real author. If the authorship can be ascribed to two persons in dialogue enter under the real name of the first. Dialogues, whether between real or fictitious persons, to which no authorship can be ascribed are entered under title.

110 Corporate headings

A corporate body is an organisation or a group of persons identified by a particular name. As a guide, such a name is likely to be either a specific rather than a general description, consistently capitalized, or preceded by a definite article.

Entry under corporate heading is restricted to works which are published by or for a corporate body and/or which fall into any of the following categories:

(a)   are of an administrative nature, dealing with the corporate body itself (including its policies, operations, finances, resources, library catalogues, inventories, membership lists, staff);

(b)   record the collective thought of the body, (e.g. reports, policy statements, debates);

(c)   record collective activity of a conference, expedition, event, exhibition, etc.;

(d)   or are legal publications of the following types—laws, decrees, regulations, charters, constitutions, treaties, court decisions, bills which have been presented to the body named in the heading.

Special Cases (100 or 110 as appropriate)

Particular law cases. Enter under person prosecuted (criminal cases) or person bringing the action (other cases). If two or more such persons are principally engaged, added entries may be required. Follow the principles for use of field 700/710 outlined below.

Auction Sales. Catalogues or sales are entered under the auctioneer if stated, otherwise the first-named of up to three vendors. If more than three vendors are named enter under title. If this information is lacking enter under the title. Do not count "property of a gentleman" as a statement of a vendor's name.

Prospectuses of books. Enter under the name of the author of the work in question (if stated or known); if no author is named or can be ascertained, enter under title.

Advertisements should be entered under the name of the person(s) or company responsible for their issue. If no person(s) or company can be found, enter under title. Booksellers' catalogues are treated as advertisements.

Rules for form of heading and transcription within subfields

Begin all nouns and proper adjectives in this area with capitals; do not use capitals elsewhere.

100 Personal authors

The entry element ($a) is nearly always the surname, except where the author is consistently known by forename.

Subfield mark	Definition	Punctuation generated by computer
$a	entry element	[null]
$e	roman numerals or titles before forenames	
$h	forename(s)	,
$f	epithet(s)	,
$c	dates	,

110 Corporate authors

Entry is under the name of the corporate body in direct order except for official material, which is entered under the name of the relevant country, city or jurisdiction.

Subfield mark	Definition	Punctuation generated by computer
$a	entry element	[null]
$c	subordinate body [N.B. This subfield can be repeated]	
$d	place addition	,
$c	other addition to name	( )

Rules for indicators

100 Use 0 when entry is under the first element of the name
Use 1 when entry is under the last element of the name i.e. surname
Use 2 when entry is under a middle element of the name i.e. compound surname

110 Use 1 when entry is under the name of a government or other administrative body
Use 2 when entry is under a corporate name in direct order

Do not use indicator 0

Examples

100/0 $a Louis $e XIV
100/0 $a I.B. $f Philomath
100/0 $a Philocriticus
100/0 $a Lover of Truth (note omission of article)
100/1 $a Dalrymple $e Sir $h John $f Bart $c 1726–1810
100/1 $a Jackson $h Joseph $f Instrument-maker
100/2 $a Grasset de Saint-Sauveur $h Jacques
100/2 $a Horatius Flaccus $h Quintus
110/1 $a Great Britain $c Parliament $c House of Commons
110/1 $a Richmond $d Yorkshire
110/1 $a Aberdeen $e Diocese
110/2 $a Church of England $c Convocation $c Province of Canterbury $c Upper House
110/2 $a Royal College of Physicians
110/2 $a Association for preserving Liberty and Property against Republicans and Levellers

COPY NOTES

956 Notes on the copy in hand

Record here, after $b, information which relates solely to the copy in hand, or to a strictly limited number of copies. The most frequent uses will be to describe imperfections and manuscript additions. Other instances are given in the examples below; but as with 500 notes not every need can be anticipated.

Give notes in the following order as far as possible:

Physical characteristics of the copy:

On vellum

Comment: A fine paper issue may be described in 956 as *On fine paper* if the paper stock is the sole difference. Large paper editions, where the gutter margin shows that the formes were unlocked, should be entered separately and a 500 note added thus:

On large paper

Limited edition:

No. 25 of an edition of fifty copies

Comment: Rarely applicable in the accepted modern sense of the term. The volume numeration is given in figures; the number of copies in the edition is spelled out, including the number 'one hundred'. If the volume number is not given, the phrase "Part of . . ." may be used.

Manuscript additions:

MS. notes by the author
MS. notes; by the author?

Comment: Note also the form: *MS. notes; by Joseph Banks?* The word 'few' is not used to describe MS. notes. 'Copious' should be used only when the notes occupy a space equal to at least 10% of the book. MS. is written in capitals, with a single full point after the 'S'.

Other standard notes are: *MS. corrections MS. emendations and corrections by the author MS. additions MS. prices and purchasers' names*

If an additional chapter has been inserted in MS. or missing pages replaced in MS., one of the above notes may be adequate; if not, a fuller note must be given either in this position or after the 'imperfections' note, as appropriate, e.g.: *Imperfect; wanting pp. 29–32, which are supplied in MS.* This form may also be used for imperfections supplied in photocopy: *Imperfect; wanting pp. 29–32, which are supplied in photocopy*

Presentation:

Author's presentation copy

Comment: *Author's presentation copy to the British Museum* and *Author's presentation copy to Joseph Banks* are discretionary according to the degree of interest attaching to the donor or recipient. *Author's presentation copy* should be used when the donor is important but the recipient's name is not known or unlikely to be of interest. Note the combined form: *Author's presentation copy, with annotations, emendations and corrections in his hand*

Previous ownership:

Narcissus Luttrell's copy

Comment: Discretionary, and usually relegated to the uncoded "Provenance" field.

Insertions:

Grangerized or *With newspaper cuttings inserted*

Mention only if substantial or of particular importance. In this category may be considered those changes made, e.g.: to imprints by booksellers, which should be considered *variants* rather than separate publishing ventures. Not an easy matter to determine; when in doubt treat as a distinct issue.

Physical characteristics of copy (not original):

Mounted
Laminated

Imperfections:

Cropped or Mutilated
Cropped, affecting the date in the imprint
The titlepage is slightly mutilated
Imperfect; wanting the half-title

Comment: Mention only if they impair the text or illustrations. In certain cases the term "Without" may be a more appropriate description than "Imperfect; wanting the . . .". There are, predictably, no hard and fast rules. Note also the occasional need to describe here imperfect printing: *The "R" of "Rape" in the title has failed to print*—though this may be true of a whole impression. (See further notes on MS. additions, above.)

If more than one copy has been recorded in 090 (see above page [4]), link these notes to the appropriate copy in the following way:

090 $a 123.a.1 090/1 $a C.146.b.3 090/2 $a 1137.a.2 956/1 $b MS. notes by the author 956/2 $b Imperfect; wanting all after p. 92

This means that 123.a.1 is complete but unannotated; C. 146.b.3 is annotated; 1137.a.2 is imperfect.

SPECIAL CATEGORIES

Treatment of special categories

Almanacs

Catalogue each almanac separately.

Write ALMANAC in the "Heading" box: circle 967 $a v.

If the almanac has a personal name attached to it, however remotely connected with the time and circumstances of authorship, enter the author's name at 100.

In these cases make a uniform title at 240 in the form:

> $a *Almanac. 1762.*
> $a *Kalendar. 1742.*

If there is no name attached to the almanac, make a uniform title at 240 in the form:

> $a *Imperial almanac. 1762.*

The title is a short title most commonly identified with the work (or of the first edition if no title is so identified) and the date is the year covered by the almanac.

If the year covered does not appear in the body of the title it will be necessary to give it in the edition statement.

Directories

Catalogue each directory separately.

Only directories of streets and/or names and trades in places are included as directories: for these write DIRECTORY in the "Heading" box: circle 967 $a d.

Enter under a personal name if one is attached to the directory, i.e. as part of the title, as in *Kent's London directory*, even if that name is the publisher's or printer's.

Directories or lists of members of a society or regiment, etc. are entered under the body concerned.

Lists

"Works to be entered under a corporate heading are those of an administrative nature dealing with . . . its officers and staff, or its resources, e.g.: catalogues, inventories, membership directories" (AACR.21.1B2).

> *A general list of the captains of Her Majesty's Fleet. Admiralty-Office, 1711:*
>
> *110/1 $a Great Britain $c Navy*
> *240/1 $a Lists*
> *245/1 $a A general list . . .*

Proclamations, Bills, etc.

Enter as follows:

110/1 $a Great Britain $c Parliament
240/1 $a Bill. 1766. Jan. 1
110/1 $a Great Britain $c Sovereign, 1760–1820 (George III)
240/1 $a Proclamation. 1776. Feb. 29
110/1 $a Great Britain
240/1 $a Public General Act. 1760/61. 1 Geo 3.c.1

Newspapers and Periodicals (Separate record card)

008
$a m (preprinted) Give here the opening and closing years of the complete run in the form *ml7011785* (no space)
$m p Indicates a periodical

245
$a Give the title of the periodical here as found. E.g.:

Daily Courant
Daily Courant and London Mercury
Daily Courant, or the London Mercury
Daily Courant, incorporating the London Mercury

$g Give the extent of the periodical in this form:

no. 1–663: 5 Jan. 1763–14 Nov. 1792

250
$a Give an edition statement here, and include in 245 $g only those issues which fall into that edition.

300
$c *Format*. No collation required.

500
$a *Notes*. Give here changes of non-entry data, e.g.:

alternative title '. . .' used from no. xx
sub-title '. . .' used from no. xx
drops 'and . . .' from no. xx
publisher changed to '. . .' from no. xx
format changed to '. . .' from no. xx

Give frequency of publication if not apparent from title.

100/110
Few periodicals have authors. Personal authors at 100 can only be assigned when the whole periodical is *written* by one person. An editor's or major contributor's name may be given in 245 or in a note as appropriate.

Periodicals emanating from corporate bodies have an entry under the body at 110 if they report on a body's accounts, or activity, e.g.: "Report . . .". In all other cases the name of the issuing body must be given at 245 or in a note (as appropriate), but no entry is made at 110.

780 Former titles.

> 0 *Continues*
> 1 *Continues in part*
> 2 *Supersedes*
> 3 *Supersedes in part*
> 4 *Formed by union of—and—*
> 5 *Absorbed* ⎫
> 6 *Absorbed in part* ⎬ give number or date after title

785 Later titles.

Write the appropriate number in the second box and the title of the serial in question after $a. (Do not write the words shown against the numbers.)

> 0 *Continued as*
> 1 *Continued in part as*
> 2 *Superseded by*
> 3 *Superseded in part by*
> 4 *Absorbed into*
> 5 *Absorbed in part into*
> 6 *Split into—and—*
> 7 *Merged with—to form—*
> 8 *Changed back to*

N.B.—Do not use this for changes of joint titles, alternative titles and sub-titles: use notes in 500 for these. These links do not go more than one change backwards or forwards: full histories of changes of title and amalgamations, etc. must be sought by going from one reference to another.

956 $b
The first note here will always be of holdings, in the same form as given already under 245 $g:

> *Holdings: no. 1–3: 5–19 Jan. 1763*

(The dates may be omitted if too complex.)

Treaties

Named treaties are entered under that name only if it is generally recognised and the treaty is signed by three or more states.

Other treaties are entered under the name of the first signatory, in the form:

> *110/1 $a Great Britain*
> *240/1 $a Treaties. Spain. 1713. July 2. Protocols, etc. 1715. Aug 3.*

Songs

Single sheet popular verse of which slipsongs and ballads are the most distinctive genres must be accompanied by a transcript of the first line in the 500 field. To facilitate alphabetical filing in the form heading file include the first few words in the heading box.

Prospectuses

Prospectuses should always be catalogued in conjunction with the book to which they refer if it can be found in GK3. If the book cannot be identified, make out a yellow card for the title as given in the prospectus. If the author of the book is given or can be deduced enter his/her name at the top of the bibslip as well as in the 100 field.

Make sure that in the 500 note there is a reference from the prospectus to the work and vice versa.

Advertisements

Attribute authorship in the case of advertisements to the vendor or promoter of the product or event advertised. If no vendor/promoter can be determined enter under title.

ADDED ENTRIES

600/610/645 **Personal or Corporate name subject heading/Title subject heading.**
In the initial stage these fields will not be used.

700/710 **Personal or Corporate name added entry headings.**

General rules for transcription.

In the initial stage, added entries should be given only in the following instances:

(i) When two authors writing in collaboration are named, e.g. for editions of many of the plays by Beaumont and Fletcher, the first-named is given the main entry (100), the second an added entry (700). This rule also applies to joint corporate authorship (110/710).

(ii) When three authors, whether personal or corporate, writing in collaboration are named, the first-named is given the main.entry (100/110) the second and third, added entries (700/710).

(iii) When more than three authors, whether personal or corporate, writing in collaboration are named, the work is entered under title, and the first-named author only is given an added entry (700/710).

(iv) When the titlepage to a work bears the name of a known author, but the attribution is known to be false, the work should be entered under title or under the actual author as appropriate. The author named on the titlepage is given an added entry.

Rules for transcription within subfields.
In the 700 field the same rules apply for transcription as in 100.

Rules for the use of indicators.
First indicator : the same rules apply for the use of first indicator as in the equivalent 100/110 heading.
Second indicator 0: is used for all added entry headings for persons or bodies writing in collaboration (see (i), (ii) and (iii) above).
Second indicator 1: is used for other AACR- required added entry headings, restricted here to cases as in (iv) above.

ADDENDA & CORRIGENDA

Page 4: line 33: FOR three or more language READ three or more languages
Page 5: line 28: DELETE FULL POINT AFTER *Greek*
Page 15: line 13: DELETE FULL POINT AFTER *editions*
Page 22: line 9: DELETE FULL POINTS AFTER *catalogue anthology autobiography*
Page 24: line 9: FOR three authors not writing READ three authors writing
Page 24: line 10: ADD If more than three authors writing in collaboration are named, the work is entered under title and the first-named author only is given an added entry.
Page 25: line 40: ADD $d   further addition to name
Page 28: line 20: FOR *Cropped or Mutilated* READ *Cropped* or *Mutilated*
Page 30: line 21: READ *no. 1 (5 Jan. 1763)—663 (14 Nov. 1792)*
Page 31: line 32: READ *Holdings: no. 1 (5 Jan. 1763)—no. 3 (19 Jan. 1763)*
Page 32: line 31: ADD Where two added entries are required as in (ii) above, the second must be given a repeat indicator (/1) after the first and second indicators. Thus, for a work written by Pope in collaboration with Arbuthnot and Gay.
100/1/0 $a *Pope* $h *Alexander* $f *the Poet*
700/1/0 $a *Arbuthnot* $h *John* $f *M.D.*
700/1/0/1 $a *Gay* $h *John* $f *the Poet*

089 Verified and Unverified Locations

This field is used to record additional locations of the work in hand. The approved library symbol, and the shelf-mark allocated by the holding library, together with the appropriate coding will be added to the master record by the editorial office.

Fourth Year of the French Republic.

1795.

DRESSES

OF THE

REPRESENTATVES OF THE PEOPLE,

MEMBERS OF THE TWO COUNCILS,

AND OF THE

EXECUTIVE DIRECTORY:

ALSO OF THE

MINISTERS, JUDGES, MESSENGERS, USHERS,

AND OTHER PUBLIC OFFICERS, &c. &c.

From the original Drawings given by the Minifter of the Interior to Citizen GRASSET S. SAUVEUR.

The Whole illuftrated by an hiftorical Defcription, tranflated from the French.

PARIS: PRINTED FOR BEROY:

LONDON:

PRINTED FOR E. AND S. HARDING, PRINTSELLERS, NO. 98, PALL-MALL.

1796.

Title	Author	Place	Heading
DRESSES			967 $a a d p s v
* RI *	008 $a s 1796 $b en	$1 eng 049 $a L	$c 1 2 3 $d 1

090 $a 8122.b.134

245 1 0 $a Dresses of the representatves [sic] of the people, members of the two councils, and of the Executive Directory : ... from the original drawings given by the Minister of the Interior to Citizen Grasset S. Sauveur. The whole illustrated by an historical description, translated from the French.

240 3 0 Costumes des représentants du peuple $r English $o 1796

250 $a

260 $a London $b Paris : printed for Dercy : London : printed for E. and S. Harding $c 1796

300 $a [6]p., 12 leaves, plates $b $c 8°

500 $a At head of titlepage : "Fourth year of the French Republic. 1795." — The headlines are in italic

100 $a $h
110 $f

GK3 GRASSET de S. SAUVEUR 519 $a

POINTS TO WATCH

For the purposes of transcription, the title proper is here deemed to start with the word "Dresses"; the words at the head of the titlepage are ignored (in the 245 field) on grounds of the nature of the statement (a date) and typography and layout (italic, above a rule). Instead, they are transcribed in the note field (500). The second note is necessary to distinguish this text from another issue (not described here) in which the headlines are in roman.

Note that the misprint is transcribed *literatim*, and the word [sic] is included after the misprinted word.

The work is a genuine translation, so a uniform entry for the original publication is required in field 240; such titles can usually be taken from the *General Catalogue*, though occasionally other reference works may need to be consulted. The language of the translation is specified in $r (see further, rules for collective and uniform Titles).

Straightforward transcription of the imprint would imply that this item was printed in Paris; in fact, though second in order the word "London" is given prominence typographically and the general appearance is clearly English not French—the imprint is therefore transcribed *verbatim* (with the usual omission of the address) at 260 $b, and London is repeated at $a.

37

Every Man his own Gardener.

Being a New, and much more Complete

GARDENER's KALENDAR,

AND

GENERAL DIRECTOR,

THAN ANY ONE HITHERTO PUBLISHED.

CONTAINING,

Not only an Account of what Work is neceſſary to be done in the KITCHEN and FRUIT GARDEN, PLEASURE GROUND, FLOWER GARDEN and SHRUBBERY; NURSERY, GREEN-HOUSE, and HOT-HOUSE for every Month in the Year, but alſo ample practical Directions for performing the ſaid Work, according to the neweſt and moſt approved Methods now in Practice among the beſt Gardeners.

With complete practical Directions for Forcing all Kinds of choice Plants, Flowers and Fruits, to early Perfection, in Hot-Beds, Hot-Houſes, Hot-Walls, Forcing-Frames, Forcing-Houſes, Vineries, &c.

Alſo particular Directions relative to SOIL and SITUATION, adapted to the different Sorts of Plants and Trees, &c.

And to the Whole are added, complete and uſeful Liſts of

KITCHEN GARDEN PLANTS, FRUIT TREES, FOREST TREES, FLOWERING SHRUBS,	EVERGREENS, ANNUAL, BIENNIAL, and PERENNIAL FIBROUS-ROOTED FLOWERS,	BULBOUS and TUBEROUS-ROOTED FLOWERS, GREEN-HOUSE, and HOT-HOUSE PLANTS,

Proper for Cultivation in the Engliſh Gardens and Plantations, &c. &c.

And, to which, in this Edition, are added, additional Syſtematic General Catalogues of Hardy Herbaceous Perennials and Biennials, and of Hot-Houſe Plants (not in any former Edition) with general Explanations of their Nature and Culture.

By THOMAS MAWE,

(GARDENER TO HIS GRACE THE DUKE OF LEEDS)

JOHN ABERCROMBIE,

Gardener, Newington, Surry; (formerly of Tottenham-court, Middleſex,)

AND OTHER GARDENERS.

THE TWELFTH EDITION,

Corrected, and greatly Enlarged, with conſiderable material new Additions, and wholly new improved in the moſt copious and general Manner in every Department of the Work, rendering it much ſuperior, and more univerſally Inſtructive than any former Edition.

LONDON:

Printed for J. F. and C. RIVINGTON, T. LONGMAN, B. LAW, J. JOHNSON, G. G. J. and J. ROBINSON, T. CADELL, W. GOLDSMITH, R. BALDWIN, J. MURRAY, E. NEWBERY, and W. LOWNDES. 1788.

Title EVERY	Author ABERCROMBIE John	Place	Heading 967 $a a d p s v
* RI *	008 $a s 1788	$b en	$l eng	049 $a L	$c 1 2 3 $d 1

090	$a 1508 / 847 (1)
245	0 0 $a Every man his own gardener. Being a new, and much more complete gardener's kalendar, ... than any one hitherto published. ... By Thomas Mawe, ... John Abercrombie, ... and other gardeners.
240	
250	$a The twelfth edition, corrected, and greatly enlarged, ...
260	$a London $b printed for J. F. and C Rivington, T. Longman, B. Law, J. Johnson, G.G.J. and J. Robinson [and 6 others in London] $c 1788
300	$a [4], 616, [20]p., plate $b $c 12°
500	$a Not in fact by Thomas Mawe, but by John Abercrombie, who signs the preface. – The final ten unpaginated leaves contain an index
100 ~~110~~	1 $a Abercrombie $h John $f Horticulturist
GK3 ABERCROMBIE John	519 $a

POINTS TO WATCH

245 $a
and
250 $a — Note the way in which a very full description of the work on the titlepage has been edited by the cataloguer, to preserve what has been deemed essential, including a part of the information which refers only to this, the twelfth, edition (in 250).

260 $b — Note the abbreviated form of the imprint in this element, while preserving the names of the first five booksellers mentioned.

500 $a — The note field is used here to justify the choice of heading in the 100 field, which is apparently in conflict with the author statement on the titlepage. In these circumstances, Mawe is given an added entry, and his name will be entered in field 700 on the verso of the record card (not illustrated).

A brief explanation is also provided for the content of the twenty unnumbered pages at the end of the book. This is designed to assist the matching process, since the collation for a copy lacking the index would, without comment, not make this imperfection immediately apparent.

A NEW
ESSAY

[By the Pennſylvanian FARMER]

ON THE CONSTITUTIONAL POWER OF

GREAT-BRITAIN

OVER THE COLONIES IN

AMERICA;

WITH THE

RESOLVES

OF THE

COMMITTEE

FOR THE PROVINCE OF

PENNSYLVANIA,

AND THEIR

INSTRUCTIONS

To their REPRESENTATIVES
IN ASSEMBLY.

―――――――――――

PHILADELPHIA
Printed; and London Re-printed for J. ALMON, op-
poſite Burlington Houſe, in Piccadilly. 1774.

Title NEW	Author [DICKINSON J.]	Place	Heading 967 $a a d p s v
* RI *	008 $a s 1774 $b en $l eng 049 $a L		$c ① 2 3 $d 1

090 $a 102. e. 68

245 | 1 | 2 | $a A new essay by the Pennsylvanian farmer on the constitutional power of Great-Britain over the colonies in America ; with the resolves of the committee for the province of Pennsylvania, and their instructions to their representatives in assembly.

240 | 3 | 0 | Essay on the constitutional power of Great-Britain

250 $a

260 $a London $b Philadelphia printed ; and London re-printed for J. Almon $c 1774

300 $a viii, 126, [2]p. $b $c 8°

500 $a The words "by ... farmer" are enclosed in square brackets. – The Pennsylvanian farmer = John Dickinson. – With a final leaf of advertisements

100 | 1 | $a Dickinson $h John $f President of the State of Delaware

GK3 ENGLAND col. 3886 | 519 $a

POINTS TO WATCH

Transcription of the title is complicated by an author statement (such as it is) which is printed in a slightly unusual place, within square brackets. The use of square brackets is to be avoided in field 245, so the title is transcribed as if there were none; their presence and position are the subject of a 500 note. The Pennsylvanian farmer has been identified as John Dickinson; the 100 entry is therefore under the true author. 967 $c 1 is encircled to indicate that the work was published under a pseudonym, but entered under real name.

Note the imprint: "Philadelphia" is given typographical prominence as well as appearing first in order, but it is not the place of origin. The whole (omitting addresses) is transcribed in 260 $b and the true place of origin is repeated in $a.

A note is also provided in the 500 field, explaining the content of the final unpaginated leaf, to assist the matching process.

THE
BEAUTIES
OF THE
ROYAL PALACES:
OR, A
POCKET COMPANION
TO
WINDSOR, KENSINGTON, KEW,
AND
HAMPTON COURT.
ALSO, A
COMPENDIOUS GAZETTEER,
OF THE
TOWNS, VILLAGES, VILLAS,
AND
REMARKABLE PLACES,
WITHIN SIXTEEN MILES OF WINDSOR.
DESCRIBING
Whatever is most Remarkable for Antiquity, Grandeur,
or Rural Beauty;
With Historical and Biographical Remarks.
ILLUSTRATED WITH A MAP.
To which are added,
Short Sketches of the Lives of the most eminent
PAINTERS;
LIKEWISE,
SELECT DESCRIPTIVE POEMS.

WINDSOR:
PRINTED AND SOLD BY C. KNIGHT,
CASTLE-STREET.

Title BEAUTIES	Author	Place WINDSOR	Heading 967 $a a d p s v
* RI *	008 $a s 1798 $b en	$1 eng 049 $a L	$c 1 2 3 $d 1

090 $a 010368 r. 92

245 | 1 | 4 | $a The beauties of the royal palaces : or, a pocket companion to Windsor, Kensington, Kew, and Hampton Court. Also, a compendious gazetteer, . . . To which are added, short sketches of the lives of the most eminent painters ; likewise, select descriptive poems.

240 | 3 | 0 | Délices des châteaux royaux

250 $a

260 $a Windsor $b printed and sold by C. Knight $c [1798]

300 $a [2], iv, 128 ; 42, [66] ; [4], 44 ; 4, 36 p., plates $b map $c 12°

500 $a The 'Guide,' 'Gazetteer,' 'Sketches' and 'Poems' each have separate titlepages ; the 'Guide' is dated 1798, the 'Gazetteer' is of the third edition, 1794, 'Poems' is dated 1794 ; 'Sketches' is a reissue of the sheets previously issued as part of the [1796] edition of 'The beauties of the royal palaces'

100 $a $h
110 $f

GK3 | 519 $a

POINTS TO WATCH

245 $a — Fairly full transcription of the title is required in this instance, to ensure that the contents of the work, as called for on the titlepage, are recorded.

240 $a — Note the use of a uniform title to bring together editions of the same basic work published under different titles—in this instance, the first edition, published in 1785, has a French title (though the text is in English).

300 $a — The rather elaborate record of pagination reflects the made-up nature of the publication.

500 $a — The made-up nature of the work is the subject of further explanation here, including reference to the separate titlepages for the parts, plus evidence for the date of publication which has been assigned in field 260 $c.

Note also that additional record cards are required for those parts of such collections, known to have been (or likely to have been) issued separately.

The following Letter, suggesting a Mode of preserving Potatoes for a long Time, is published by Order of the Society.

MY DEAR SIR,   *Berners-street,* 11 *Jan.* 1800.

IN compliance with your request, expressed at the meeting of the Society for bettering the Condition of the Poor, I herewith send you my simple but effectual mode of preserving Potatoes without fire, sweet and good, for a great length of time.

I have, as yet, only tried it upon small quantities of Potatoes in my own family; and I had intended deferring the publication of any account of it, until I had ascertained, by an apparatus I have ordered to be made, the expense and effects of the operation on a great scale. But your request, and the peculiar circumstances of the present season, added to the existing apprehension that the last year's crop of Potatoes is not calculated for keeping, induce me to give some account of the experiments I have already made; and to express my hope that country gentlemen and farmers may be induced to try, whether, on a bad day, they cannot advantageously employ their poor neighbours, in this mode of preserving from decay, so material an article of food.

The first of the two processes which I have adopted is as follows.— I took three pounds and a half of Potatoes, and had them peeled and rasped, and put them in a coarse cloth between two clean boards in a napkin press, and pressed them into a dry cake, hardly so thick as a very thin cheese. I then placed the cake on a shelf, as I should an oil cake, to dry. There was about a quart of juice expressed from the Potatoes. To this I added the same quantity of cold water; and in about an hour it deposited rather more than sixty grains of very white starch, or flour, fit to make fine pastry,

Title	Author	Place	Heading
SOCIETY	[MILLINGTON L.]		967 $a a d p s v

| * RI * | 008 $a s 1800 | $b en | $l eng | 049 $a L | $c 1 2 3 $d 1 |

090 $a L. 23 c. 4 (68)

245 | 1 | 0 | $a Society for bettering the condition of the poor. The following letter, suggesting a mode of preserving potatoes for a long time, is published by order of the Society.

240 [|]

250 $a

260 $a [London] $b   printed by W Bulmer and Co.

$c [1800]

300 $a   3, [1] p. $b $c 4°

500 $a Letter signed : Langford Millington. — Dated Berners-Street, 11 Jan. 1800. — Printer's name from foot of p. 3

100 | 1 | $a Millington $h Langford
110                               $f

GK3   519 $a

POINTS TO WATCH

The letter is regarded as a personal composition; the Society is not therefore credited with corporate authorship (note the phrase "*published* by order of", and the fact that the letter is signed by an individual).

The date in the address is taken as the date of publication (260 $c), and an explanation provided in the 500 note field (second note).

260 $b includes the printer's name, which is not to be found in the usual imprint position (the work has no titlepage as such). The source of this information is again the subject of a 500 note.

TRACTATUS FOEDERIS

A D

PACEM PUBLICAM

Stabiliendam.

Signatus Londini $\frac{\text{Julii 22.}}{\text{Augusti 2.}}$ 1718.

TREATY of ALLIANCE

For settling the

PUBLICK PEACE.

Signed at *London* $\frac{\text{July 22.}}{\text{August 2.}}$ 1718.

L O N D O N:

Printed by S. Buckley in *Amen Corner.* 1718.

Title	Author	Place	Heading
TRACTATUS	GREAT BRITAIN - TREATIES		967 $a a d p s v

* RI *	008 $a s 1718	$b en	$l eng	049 $a L	$c 1 2 3 $d 1

090 $a 593. d. 21 (20)   090|1 $a 595. f. 22 (2)   090|2 $a 102.h.5

245 | 1 | 0 | $a Tractatus foederis ad pacem publicam stabiliendam. Signatus Londini Julii 22. Augusti 2. 1718. = Treaty of alliance for settling the publick peace. Signed at London July 22. August 2. 1718.

240 | 1 | 0 | $a Treaties, etc. 1718. August 2

250 $a

260 $a London $b printed by S. Buckley

$c 1718

300 $a 76p. $b $c 4°

500 $a Parallel Latin and English texts in two columns

~~100~~ | 1 | $a Great Britain $h
110                               $f

GK3   ENGLAND col. 540   519 $a

POINTS TO WATCH

This example illustrates the method of transcription for a parallel title. Note that the form of date in the title is transcribed as given on the titlepage.

A footnote indicates the nature of the layout of the texts in the work in question.

Note the use of the uniform title field (240) to collect and order this class of material.

Vol. IV.   [45]   Numb. 12

A REVIEW
OF THE
STATE
OF THE
BRITISH NATION.

Saturday, March 8. 1707.

IN our laſt I advanc'd an odd Notion, *at leaſt I expect on firſt Reading, it ſhould be thought ſo*; that in Proſecution of the War in *Poland*, the *Swedes* ſhall be worſted———Indeed I cannot but inſiſt upon it, and that 'tis my Opinion, he will be at laſt obliged to abandon his new King, and the whole Enterprize with no manner of Applauſe, much leſs Advantage.

But becauſe every General, they ſay, is liable to Exception, and this ſeems a new Concluſion, againſt which ſome Difficulties may be rais'd, I ſhall enter into them a ittle.

Two things may bring the *Swede* handſomely off from this War, and if none of them happen, I ſee nothing before him but a tedious unprofitable Enterprize.

Firſt, A Peace with the Czar of *Muſcovy*, and thereby drawing him off from the aſſiſting the new King, he has ſet up in *Poland*. And tho' 'tis true this is poſſible, yet I do not ſee upon what Terms the *Swede* can make a Peace with him on the leaſt Points of Honour, without recovering *Narva*, and the reſt of the Towns on the *Baltick*, which he is poſſeſs'd of. If he leaves them to the *Muſcovite*, he abandons his Honour to the Czar's Victory, and leaves him in Peace, with a Door open to make himſelf formidable to *Europe*, and to himſelf in particular; and what Honour he will get by that, any Man may judge off.

If he will recover thoſe Conqueſts from the Czar, he muſt quit *Poland* to do it; for the Czar has ſo ſtrengthened himſelf there,

that

48

Title	Author	Place	
REVIEW	[DEFoE D.]		NEWSPAPERS #PERIODICALS

# RI #	008 $a m 1707 1712 $b en $l eng $m p		049 $a L

090 $a C. 40. h. i   090|1 $a Burney 5b, 6, 8   090|2 $a 8132. bb. 13 (4)

245 Title | 1 | 2 | $a A review of the state of the British nation.

$g Vol. 4, no. 12 (8 Mar. 1707) — v. 8, no. 211 (29 July 1712)

250 $a

260 $a [London] $b

$c 1707 - 12   300 $c 4°

500 $a Written by Daniel Defoe. — Imprint "printed for the author ; and sold by John Baker " used from v. 7, no. 13 ; changed to "printed for and sold by John Baker " from v. 7, no. 36. — Printed by John Matthews to the end of v. 6. — Issued triweekly

780 | 0 | 0 | Review of the state of the English nation

785 | 0 | 2 | Review

100 | 1 | $a Defoe $h Daniel

110

POINTS TO WATCH

The above entry illustrates the basic principles which apply to the cataloguing of newspapers and periodicals. The titlepage here depicted is not of course intended to represent the source of all information on the record card.

Changes in imprint information are recorded in the 500 field, as is the frequency of publication.

780 records the former title of the periodical, here coded 0 to indicate that the relationship is one of straightforward continuation.

785 records the title by which the periodical was subsequently known, here coded 2 to indicate that as the numeration started afresh with this new title, the former is regarded having been superseded.

Note that the 'Review' is one of the few periodicals considered to have a personal author —hence Defoe is given a 100 entry.

A summary statement of holdings is also given as the first note in 956 $b on the verso of the record card (not illustrated); the form is the same as that in 245 $g.

ALEXANDER POPE

A CATALOGUE OF HIS WORKS
PRINTED BETWEEN 1711 AND 1800
IN ENGLISH

Including editions wholly or
partly in English printed abroad

IN
THE BRITISH LIBRARY

Preface

The following catalogue comprises all relevant eighteenth century editions of the works of Alexander Pope in the collections of the Reference Division of the British Library. It does not include items held by the Lending Division at Boston Spa, though it is anticipated that these will be incorporated in due course. Each item has been recatalogued according to ESTC standards, and a sequence has been established for the file which follows, with certain minor adjustments, the British Library filing rules for complex headings. This sequence has been determined by the use of filing-field 239 (see *Rules* above) and was automatically reproduced by the computer. Thus editions of the complete *Works* are listed first, followed by *Selections*, works and selected works *in one genre, letters,* and finally *single works.*

Because of the complicated publishing history of the early editions of the works, it has been decided to group these, but with separate entries for individual volumes within multi-volume sets as appropriate. By adopting this procedure it should be possible to incorporate within the established sequence the holdings of other libraries possessing sets differently composed. It is well known that for authors such as Pope there are relatively few sets of the early editions of the collected works which may be described as exact duplicates.

Some typographical peculiarities will be immediately obvious: they are, unfortunately, unavoidable since the print-chain available to ESTC at this point lacks certain characters. Thus square brackets, normally used to enclose uniform and collective titles and other supplied information, are here represented by parentheses. Other characters which are not represented include single and double quotation marks, the apostrophe, the hyphen, superscript characters or diacritics, and the digraph AE/ae. These will, at a later date be available.

The inclusion of a certain amount of prescribed punctuation has been unavoidable. This includes the final full point at the end of the title, the dash between title and edition statement and between edition statement and imprint. Where a note ends with a question mark a superfluous full point will also be found. Mechanical justification of line-length also accounts for the occasional odd occurrence of punctuation marks at the beginning of lines.

One further observation concerns added entries: it is proposed to make certain amendments to the computer profile which partly determines the sequence of entries, so that those added entries which are here grouped in a separate sequence at the end will be interfiled at the appropriate point in the alphabetical sequence of single works.

In offering the following catalogue as an exemplification of ESTC principles we trust that we have obeyed a cardinal principle of bibliography: to reveal, if possible, within a sequence of entries a meaningful narrative of the historical progress of an author's works based upon the researches of available scholarship. For the analytical bibliographer, concerned to establish every minute detail in the history of the transmission of a text, it doubtless falls short of expectation: but as a record of one author's work, among thousands, it perhaps has some merit. Enumerative bibliography has always demanded more than its practitioners could give, which is perhaps why every attempt to further it is just a different kind of failure.

M. J. Jannetta
R. C. Alston

POPE, Alexander, the Poet
        (Works.1717-35). The works of Mr. Alexander Pope.. -
        London: printed by W. Bowyer, for Bernard Lintot, 1717.
        (32), 435, (1)p., fold. plate : port. ; 4º.
        With a half-title. Titlepage in red and black. Sig. O2
        is a cancel.
        Griffith 79-81.
C.59.i.20 : Presentation copy from the author to J. Eckersall,
with the autograph of the latter. With two poems added in MS.
C.130.e.5(1) : Presentation copy from the author to R. Graham.
Ashley 4951
Ashley 4950 : On thick paper.
                                                     t005385

POPE, Alexander, the Poet
        (Works.1717-35). The works of Mr. Alexander Pope.. -
        London: printed by W. Bowyer, for Jacob Tonson, and
        Bernard Lintot, 1717. (32), 435, (1)p., fold. plate :
        port. ; 4º.
        Another issue of the Bowyer/Lintot 1717 4º edition, with
        a cancel titlepage.
        Griffith 84,84a.
Ashley 4949
                                                     t005386

POPE, Alexander, the Poet
        (Works.1717-35). The works of Mr. Alexander Pope.. -
        London: printed by W. Bowyer, for Bernard Lintot, 1717.
        (32), 408p., fold. plate : port. ; 2º.
        On large paper; the ornament on the titlepage is
        triangular, containing a lyre with two crossed trumpets.
        With a half-title. Titlepage in red and black. Sig.
        Bb1 is a cancel.
        Griffith 83.
643.m.5 : Imperfect; wanting pp. 13-20 and the folding portrait
of Pope.
Ashley 5234 : Imperfect; wanting the folding portrait of Pope.
                                                     t005387

POPE, Alexander, the Poet
        (Works.1717-35). The works of Mr. Alexander Pope.. -
        London: printed by W. Bowyer, for Bernard Lintot, 1717.
        (32), 408p., fold. plate : port. ; 2º.
        On small paper; the ornament on the titlepage is a
        basket of flowers above two cherub heads. Apparently a
        reimpression of the setting used for the large folio
        edition, partly reset where the decorations were
        removed. Sig. Bb1 is a cancel.
        Griffith 82.
637.k.19
                                                     t005388

POPE, Alexander, the Poet
        (Works.1717-35). The works of Mr. Alexander Pope.. -
        London: printed by W. Bowyer, for Jacob Tonson, and
        Bernard Lintot, 1717. (32), 408p., fold. plate : port. ;
        2º.
        Another issue of the Bowyer/Lintot 1717 small folio
        edition; the titlepage is a cancel(?). With a
        half-title.
        Griffith 85.
11609.k.2
Ashley 4952(1)
                                                     t005389

POPE, Alexander, the Poet
    (Works.1717-35). The works of Mr. Alexander Pope. Volume
    II.. - London: printed by J. Wright, for Lawton
    Gilliver, 1735. (8); (8), 66; 19, (1), 25-33, (2), 8-25,
    (2), 36-72; (4), 56, 65-91, (1); 12, 81 (i.e. 18), 201,
    (1)p. ; 2⁰.
    On small paper. An essay on man has a separate titlepage
    bearing the imprint printed by John Wright, for Lawton
    Gilliver, 1734, and is a reissue of the separately
    published edition of that year; the First satire of the
    second book is also a reissue (without titlepage) of the
    separate small folio edition of 1734. With a
    half-title. Titlepage in red and black.
    Griffith 370.
11609.k.3 : Four leaves, containing the Design of the Essay on
man and the contents of the second book of ethic epistles, have
been misbound before the half-title to the Essay on man.
                                                t005390

POPE, Alexander, the Poet
    (Works.1717-35). The works of Mr. Alexander Pope. Volume
    II.. - London: printed by J. Wright, for Lawton
    Gilliver, 1735. (8); (8), 66; 19, (1), 25-33, (2), 8-25,
    (2), 36-72; (4), 56, 65-91, (1); 12, 81(i.e. 18), 201,
    (1)p. ; 2⁰.
    On large paper. With a half-title. Titlepage in red
    and black.
    Griffith 371.
Ashley 5235 : The two leaves of contents of the second book of
ethic epistles have been misbound before the text of the Essay
on man.
                                                t005391

POPE, Alexander, the Poet
    (Works. 1717-35). The works of Mr. Alexander Pope.
    Volume II.. - London: printed by J. Wright, for Lawton
    Gilliver, 1735. (8), 76; (7), 48-71, (2), 8-27, (2),
    40-78; (2), 87, (1); 14; 19, (1), 219, (1)p. ; 4⁰.
    With a half-title. Titlepage in red and black. The
    sheets of this edition were reissued, possibly in 1739,
    in a number of made-up copies which include, in varying
    combinations, other separately published pieces by Pope
    up to 1738; some copies are on thick paper.
    Griffith 372.
C.59.i.20 : A proof of the suppressed last leaf of the Epitaphs
has been inserted. Without the half-title to Ethic epistles,
the second book.
Ashley 4953 : With an additional sig. C (2 leaves) at the end
of the Epitaphs containing a second epitaph numbered XI, On
James Craggs, Esq; (p. 15), To James Craggs, Esq;, Ode on
solitude, and The dying Christian to his soul.
                                                t005392

POPE, Alexander the Poet
(Works.1717-35). The works of Mr. Alexander Pope. .... -
London: printed by J. Wright, for Lawton Gilliver,
1735(1739?). 2v. ; 4°.
A made-up set consisting of a reissue of the contents of
Works, II, 4°, 1735, together with the sheets of Poems
and imitations, 4°, 1738 (minus titlepage), of The
universal prayer, 2°, 1738 (with reading Incense in last
line), of Sober advice from Horace, 2°, (1734) (minus
titlepage; with reading amise, p. 5, line 3) and with
two additional leaves of Epitaphs. Griffith 514,5 with
which these volumes for the most part correspond, are
described as on thick paper. Publication date from
Griffith.
Griffith 514,5.
C.130.e.5(2,3) : The half-title to vol. II has been transposed
to act as titlepage to the third volume, with the numeral
altered in MS. accordingly.

t005393

POPE, Alexander, the Poet
(Works.1718.Dublin). The works of Mr. Alexander Pope. To
which are added, I. Coopers-Hill. By Sir John Denham.
.... - Dublin: printed by and for George Grierson, 1727.
(4), xxv, (1), 361 (i.e. 401), (1)p. ; 8°.
A reprint, with additions, of Works, Dublin, 1718.
Titlepage in red and black. With an additional
titlepage, also in red and black, reading The works of
Mr. Alexander Pope. According to the London folio
edition. The second edition. To which are added, several
new poems since publishd by the author. Pp. 46, 47, 51,
54, 55, and 401 are misnumbered 44, 45, 49, 52, 53 and
361.
Griffith 193.
1490.k.48

t005394

POPE, Alexander, the Poet
(Works.1718.The Hague). The works of Mr. Alexander
Pope.. - London(i.e. The Hague?): printed by T. J.
(Thomas Johnson) for B. L. (Bernard Lintot?) 8 other
booksellers, 1718. xxviii, 147, (1); 68; 30, (2)p. :
ill., port. ; 8°.
Reprints the contents of Works, 1717. An essay on
criticism, and The rape of the lock, have separate
titlepages dated 1716, and bearing the statement, The
fifth edition. With a final leaf of advertisements.
Probably printed at The Hague by Thomas Johnson. For
Bernard Lintot?.
Griffith 103.
12274.e.12 : The half-title is bound immediately after the
titlepage.

t005395

POPE, Alexander, the Poet
(Works.1718.The Hague). The works of Mr. Alexander
Pope.. - London(i.e. The Hague?): printed by T. J.
(Thomas Johnson) for the company, 1720. (8), xvii-xxxvi,
149, (1), 99, (1)p. : ill., port. ; 8°.
A reprint, with the addition of one piece, of Johnsons
1718 edition, probably printed at The Hague. With a
half-title. Pp. 97-99 contain Popes Verses occasioned
by Mr. Addisons Treatise of medals.
cf. Griffith 126.
11630.aaa.46

                                                t005396

POPE, Alexander, the Poet
(Works.1735-43). The works of Alexander Pope, Esq; Vol.
I. With explanatory notes and additions never before
printed. - London: printed for B. Lintot, 1736. 15, (2),
xviii-xxxix, (4), 20-198p. : ill., port. ; 8°.
Sig. A3 is misprinted A2. Titlepage in red and black.
Griffith 413.
1607/5513(1)

                                                t005397

POPE, Alexander, the Poet
(Works.1735-43). The works of Alexander Pope, Esq; Vol.
I. With explanatory notes and additions never before
printed.. - London: printed for B. Lintot, 1736. 15,
(2), xviii-xxxix, (4), 20-198p. : ill., port. ; 8°.
A different edition from the preceding; the signature
mark A3 is correct. Titlepage in red and black.
Griffith 414.
11609.b.19
636.f.17(1)

                                                t005398

POPE, Alexander, the Poet
(Works.1735-43). The works of Alexander Pope, Esq; Vol.
II.. - London: printed for L. Gilliver, 1735. (8), 58,
(6), 96, (3), 110-170p. ; 8°.
With a half-title, the verso of which bears an
advertisement for the Dunciad. Titlepage in red and
black.
Griffith 388.
12274.f.4 : The half-title is misbound after Sig. A3.

                                                t005399

POPE, Alexander, the Poet
        (Works. 1735-43). The works of Alexander Pope, Esq; Vol.
        II. Containing his epistles and satires.. - London:
        printed for L. Gilliver, 1735. (8), 58, (6), 96, (3),
        110-160(i.e. 170)p. ; 8°.
        A different edition from the preceding. P. 155 is
        misnumbered 145 and this new sequence continues to the
        end. With a half-title, the verso of which is blank.
        Titlepage in red and black.
        Griffith 389.
11609.b.20
                                                        t005400

POPE, Alexander, the Poet
        (Works.1735-43). The works of Alexander Pope, Esq; Vol.
        II. Containing his epistles and satires. - London:
        printed for Lawton Gilliver, 1736. (6), 58, (6), 96,
        (3), 110-160(i.e. 170)p. ; 8°.
        P. 155 is misnumbered 145 and this new sequence
        continues to the end. With a half-title. Titlepage in
        red and black.
        Griffith 430.
1607/5513(2) : Imperfect; wanting the leaf of errata.
C.122.e.31 : With extensive MS. corrections by the author.
Imperfect, wanting the first four leaves, including the
titlepage.
                                                        t005401

POPE, Alexander, the Poet
        (Works.1735-43). The works of Alexander Pope, Esq; Vol.
        II. Containing his epistles, &c.. - London: printed for
        R. Dodsley, and sold by T. Cooper, 1739. (6), 15, (1),
        158; 28, (3); 82-110; (3), 153-159p. ; 8°.
        Titlepage in red and black, with vase ornament. With a
        leaf of Directions to the binder bound immediately after
        the authors address to the reader.
        Griffith 505.
636.f.17(2)
                                                        t005402

POPE, Alexander, the Poet
        (Works.1735-43). The works of Alexander Pope, Esq; Vol.
        II. Containing his epistles, &c.. - London: printed for
        R. Dodsley, and sold by T. Cooper, 1739. (4), 158; (3),
        153-160, (1), 161-168p. ; 8°.
        A different issue from the preceding; the titlepage, in
        red and black, bears a double cornucopia of flowers as
        ornament. The Directions to the binder, congratulatory
        poems, and the imitations of Horace and Donne have been
        omitted from this volume. The last 10 pp. contain three
        additional epitaphs, and six other short pieces.
        Not in Griffith.
686.d.18 : On fine paper.
                                                        t005403

POPE, Alexander, the Poet
        (Works.1735-43). The works of Alexander Pope Esq; Vol.
        III. Consisting of fables, translations, and
        imitations.. - London: printed for H. Lintot, 1736. vii,
        (1), 198, (2)p. ; 8º.
        A different edition from the preceding; p. 9 has a
        dagger in the lower margin. With a half-title.
        Titlepage in red and black.
        Griffith 418.
11609.b.21
636.f.17(3)

                                                        t005404

POPE, Alexander, the Poet
        (Works.1735-43). The works of Alexander Pope, Esq; Vol.
        III. Consisting of fables, translations, and
        imitations.. - London: printed for H. Lintot, 1736. vii,
        (1), 198, (2)p. ; 8º.
        With a half-title, and a final leaf of advertisements.
        Titlepage in red and black. P. 9 has no marginal mark.
        Griffith 417.
1607/5513(3)

                                                        t005405

POPE, Alexander, the Poet
        (Works.1735-43). The works of Alexander Pope, Esq; Vol.
        IV. Containing the Dunciad, with the prolegomena of
        Scriblerus, and notes variorum.. - London: printed for
        L. Gilliver, and J. Clarke, 1736. 258 (i.e. 259), (1)p.
        ; 8º.
        Pp. 31, 144, 218, 257-9 are misnumbered 13, 244, 118,
        256-8. Titlepage in red and black.
        Griffith 431.
1607/5513(4)
11609.b.22

                                                        t005406

POPE, Alexander, the Poet
        (Works.1735-43). The works of Alexander Pope, Esq; Vol.
        IV. Containing the Dunciad, with the prolegomena of
        Scriblerus, and notes variorum.. - London: printed for
        L. Gilliver and J. Clarke, 1736. 258 (i.e. 259), (1)p. ;
        8º.
        A different edition from the preceding; there is no
        comma between Gilliver and and in the imprint; pp. 31,
        144, 218 are correctly numbered, pp. 257-9 are
        misnumbered 256-8. Titlepage in red and black.
        Griffith 432.
1207.c.25(5)
636.f.17(4)

                                                        t005407

POPE, Alexander, the Poet
(Works.1735-43). The works of Alexander Pope, Esq; Vol.
V. Consisting of letters, wherein to those of the
authors own edition, are added all that are genuine from
the former impressions, with some never before printed..
- London: printed for J. Roberts, 1737. (44), 159, (1)p.
; 8°.
Griffith 461.
12274.f.6
                                                          t005408

POPE, Alexander, the Poet
(Works.1735-43). The works of Alexander Pope, Esq; Vol.
V. Containing an authentic edition of his letters.. -
The second edition, corrected. - London: printed for T.
Cooper, 1737. (2), i, (7), 3, (19), 240p. ; 8°.
Titlepage in red and black.
Griffith 472,3.
11609.b.23
10921.a.26 : The titlepage, which reads The letters of
Alexander Pope, Esq; The first part, is a forgery; bound with
The second part.
                                                          t005409

POPE, Alexander, the Poet
(Works.1735-43). The works of Alexander Pope, Esq; Vol
V. Containing an authentic edition of his letters.. -
London: printed for T. Cooper, 1739. (2), ii, (28),
240p. ; 8°.
Titlepage in red and black. There is no full point
between Vol and V on the titlepage.
Griffith 511.
636.f.17(5) : MS. notes by C. W. Dilke.
686.d.22
                                                          t005410

POPE, Alexander, the Poet
(Works.1735-43). The works of Alexander Pope, Esq; Vol.
V. Containing an authentic edition of his letters.. -
London: printed for T. Cooper, 1739. (2),ii, (28), 240p.
; 8°.
A different edition from the preceding; with a full
point between Vol. and V on the titlepage. Titlepage in
red and black.
Griffith 512.
1207.c.25(6)
                                                          t005411

POPE, Alexander, the Poet
       (Works.1735-43). The works of Alexander Pope, Esq; Vol
       VI. Containing the second part of his letters.. - The
       second edition, corrected. - London: printed for T.
       Cooper, 1737. (16), 234p. ; 8°.
       Titlepage in red and black.
       Griffith 472,3.
11609.b.24
10921.a.26 : The titlepage, which reads, The letters of
Alexander Pope, Esq; The second part, is a forgery; bound with
The first part.

                                                    t005412

POPE, Alexander, the Poet
       (Works.1735-43). The works of Alexander Pope, Esq; Vol.
       VI. Containing the second part of his letters.. -
       London: printed for T. Cooper, 1739. (16), 151, (1),
       145-236p. ; 8°.
       Titlepage in red and black. Page numbers 145-152 are
       repeated; p. 236 is correctly numbered.
       Griffith 511.
636.f.17(6) : MS. notes by C. W. Dilke.
686.d.23

                                                    t005413

POPE, Alexander, the Poet
       (Works.1735-43). The works of Alexander Pope, Esq; Vol.
       VI. Containing the second part of his letters.. -
       London: printed for T. Cooper, 1739. (16), 632(i.e.
       236)p. ; 8°.
       A different edition from the preceding; p. 236 is
       misnumbered 632. Titlepage in red and black.
       Griffith 512.
1207.c.25(7)

                                                    t005414

POPE, Alexander, the Poet
       (Works.1735-43). The works of Alexander Pope, Esq; Vol.
       I. Part I.. - London: printed for H. Lintot, 1740(1739).
       15, (2), xviii-xxxix, (4), 20-198p. : ill., port. ; 8°.

       A reprint of the contents of Works, I, 8°, 1736.
       Titlepage in red and black. Publication date from
       Griffith.
       Griffith 510.
1207.c.25(1)
686.d.16 : On fine paper. With an engraved portrait and
vignette inserted.

                                                    t005415

POPE, Alexander, the Poet
        (Works.1735-43). The works of Alexander Pope, Esq; Vol.
        I. Part I.. - London: printed for Henry Lintot, 1743.
        16, (2), xviii-xxxix, (3), 20-198p. : ill., port. ; 8⁰.

        A reprint, with revisions, of Works, I.i, 8⁰,
        1740(1739); there was no reprint of the companion vol.
        I.ii in 1743.
        Griffith 582.
239.h.27
                                                        t005416

POPE, Alexander, the Poet
        (Works.1735-43). The works of Alexander Pope, Esq; Vol.
        I. Part II. Consisting of fables, translations, and
        imitations.. - London: printed for H. Lintot,
        1741(1740). 207, (1)p. ; 8⁰.
        A reprint of the contents of Works, III, 8⁰, 1736. With
        a half-title. Titlepage in red and black. Publication
        date from Griffith.
        Griffith 521.
1207.c.25(2)
686.d.17 : On fine paper.
                                                        t005417

POPE, the Poet, Alexander
        (Works.1735-43). The works of Alexander Pope, Esq; Vol.
        I. Part II. Consisting of fables, translations, and
        imitations.. - London: printed for H. Lintot, and J. and
        R. Tonson, and S. Draper, 1745. 207, (1)p. ; 8⁰.
        Griffith 611.
239.h.28
                                                        t005418

POPE, Alexander, the Poet
        (Works.1735-43). The works of Alexander Pope, Esq; Vol.
        II. Part I. Containing his epistles, &c.. - London:
        printed for R. Dodsley, and sold by T. Cooper, 1740.
        (8), 16, 180, (2)p. ; 8⁰.
        A reprint, with minor changes to the contents, of Works,
        II, 8⁰, 1739. With a half-title. Titlepage in red and
        black. The final leaf contains a note to the reader,
        advising that the epistles and satires are to be found
        in vol. II.ii.
        Griffith 523.
1207.c.25(3)
                                                        t005419

POPE, Alexander, the Poet
(Works.1735-43). The works of Alexander Pope, Esq; Vol.
II. Part. I. Containing his epistles, &c.. - London:
printed for R. Dodsley, and sold by T. Cooper, 1743.
(8), 16, 62, (7), 66-180, (2)p. ; 8°.
With a half-title. Titlepage in red and black. The
final leaf contains a note to the reader advising that
the epistles and satires are to be found in vol. II.
ii.
Griffith 583.
239.h.29

t005420

POPE, Alexander, the Poet
(Works.1735-43). The works of Alexander Pope, Esq; Vol.
II. Part II. Containing imitations of Horace and Dr.
Donne.. - London: printed for R. Dodsley, and sold by T.
Cooper, 1740. 32, (3), 24-187, (1)p. ; 8°.
A reprint, with revised contents, of Works, II.ii, 8°,
1738(1739). With a half-title. Titlepage in red and
black.
Griffith 524.
1207.c.25(4)
686.d.19 : On fine paper.

t005421

POPE, Alexander, the Poet
(Works.1735-43). The works of Alexander Pope, Esq; Vol.
II. Part II. Containing imitations of Horace and Dr.
Donne. - London: printed for R. Dodsley, and sold by T.
Cooper, 1743. 199, (1)p. ; 8°.
With a half-title. Title page in red and black.
Griffith 584.
239.h.30

t005422

POPE, Alexander, the Poet
(Works.1735-43). The works of Alexander Pope Esq; Vol.
III. Part I. Containing the Dunciad, and notes of
Scriblerus.. - London: printed for Henry Lintot, 1742.
256p. ; 8°.
Contains Books I-III only. A reissue of the sheets of
the edition of 1741 (i.e. Griffith 536), with a new
titlepage (Griffith). Titlepage in red and black.
Griffith 545.
686.d.20 : On fine paper.

t005423

POPE, Alexander, the Poet
        (Works.1735-43). The works of Alexander Pope Esq; Vol.
        III. Part I. Containing the Dunciad. Now first published
        according to the complete copy fourd in the year
        MDCCXLI.. - London: printed for R. Dodsley, and sold by
        T. Cooper, 1743. (4), lxxxvii, (1), 163, (1)p. ; 8⁰.
        Contains Books I-III only. With a half-title.
        Titlepage in red and black.
        Griffith 586.
239.h.31
                                                        t005424

POPE, Alexander, the Poet
        (Works.1735-43). The works of Alexander Pope, Esq; Vol.
        III. Part II. Containing the Dunciad, Book IV. And the
        memoirs of Scriblerus. Never before printed.. - London:
        printed for R. Dodsley, and sold by T. Cooper, 1742.
        (8), 82, (2), 261(i.e. 129), (1)p. ; 8⁰.
        With a half-title. Titlepage in red and black. Last
        page misnumbered 261; lines misnumbered 1-618.
        Griffith 566.
1207.c.25(5*)
                                                        t005425

POPE, Alexander, the Poet
        (Works.1735-43). The works of Alexander Pope, Esq; Vol.
        III. Part II. Containing the Dunciad, Book IV. And the
        memoirs of Scriblerus. Never before printed.. - London:
        printed for R. Dodsley, and sold by T. Cooper, 1742.
        (4), 70, 132p. ; 8⁰.
        A different edition from the preceding; the last line of
        the Dunciad is correctly numbered 620. With a
        half-title. Titlepage in red and black. Horizontal
        chain lines.
        Griffith 567.
686.d.21 : On fine paper, with vertical chain lines throughout.
Imperfect; wanting the half-title.
                                                        t005426

POPE, Alexander, the Poet
        (Works.1735-43). The works of Alexander Pope, Esq; Vol.
        III. Part II. Containing the Dunciad, Book IV. And the
        memoirs of Scriblerus. Never before printed.. - London:
        printed for R. Dodsley, and sold by T. Cooper,
        1742(1743). (4), 112, (2), 132p. ; 8⁰.
        A reissue of Griffith 567 (edition E of 1742); sig. B2,
        B4, D1-2, and F2-I6 are cancels. The original sheets
        have horizontal chain lines; the cancels have vertical
        chain lines. With a half-title. Titlepage in red and
        black.
        Griffith 579.
239.h.32 : The appendix to the Dunciad is misbound after the
Memoirs of Scriblerus; pp. 105-6 and 107-8 have been transposed
in binding, as have pp. 109-10 and 111-12. Sig. B4,5 from
Works, III.i, 1743 have been inserted in error.
                                                        t005427

POPE, Alexander, the Poet
(Works.1735-43). The works of Alexander Pope, Esq; Vol.
IV. Part I. Containing an authentic edition of his
letters. - London: printed for T. Cooper, 1742. (2), ii,
(28), 240p. ; 8º.
A reprint of the text of Works, V, 8º, 1739. Titlepage
in red and black.
Griffith 568.
239.h.33

t005428

POPE, Alexander, the Poet
(Works.1735-43). The works of Alexander Pope, Esq; Vol.
IV. Part II. Containing the second part of his letters..
- London: printed for T. Cooper, 1742. (16), 236p. ; 8º

A reprint of the contents of Works, VI, 8º, 1739.
Titlepage in red and black.
Griffith 569.
239.h.34

t005429

POPE, Alexander, the Poet
(Works.1735-43). The works of Alexander Pope, Esq; Vol.
IV. Part III. Containing the third part of Letters.. -
London: printed for R. Dodsley, and sold by T. Cooper,
1742. (16), 232p. ; 8º.
A reprint of the text of Works, VII, 8º, 1741(1742).
Titlepage in red and black, with the date in black.
Vertical chain lines throughout.
Griffith 572.
239.h.35
1207.c.25(8)

t005430

POPE, Alexander, the Poet
(Works.1736). The works of Alexander Pope, Esq; With
explanatory notes and additions rever before printed.
.... - Dublin: London, printed: Dublin, re-printed by
and for G. Faulkner; A. Bradley and T. Moore, 1736. 3v.
; 12º.
A reprint, with additions, of the contents of the London
edition of Works, I-III, 8º, 1735-36.
Griffith 433.
C.108.bb.35 : Without the 8-page list of subscribers.

t005431

POPE, Alexander, the Poet
        (Works.1751). The works of Alexander Pope Esq. In nine
        volumes complete. With his last corrections, additions,
        and improvements; ... Together with the commentaries and
        notes of Mr. Warburton. - London: printed for J. and P.
        Knapton, H. Lintot, J. and R. Tonscn, and S. Draper,
        1751. 9v., plates : ports. ; 8⁰.
        Titlepages in red and black. The separate titlepages to
        vol. 1,2 bear the imprint, printed for H. Lintot, J. and
        R. Tonson, and S. Draper; those to vol. 3-9 bear the
        imprint, printed for J. and P. Knapton.
        Griffith 643-51.
685.e.1-9
G.12850-8 : With MS. notes by John Wilkes. With additional
poems, letters, .etc., inserted in MS., together with
engravings, newspaper and other printed cuttings.
                                                    t005432

POPE, Alexander, the Poet
        (Works.1751). The works of Alexander Pope Esq. In nine
        volumes complete. With his last corrections, additions,
        and improvements. Published by Mr. Warburton. .... -
        London: printed for J. and P. Knapton, H. Lintot, J. and
        R. Tonson, and S. Draper, 1751. 9v., plates : ports. ; 8⁰.
        The small octavo edition. Horizontal chain lines.
        Titlepages in red and black.
        Griffith 653.
12275.e.1
                                                    t005433

POPE, Alexander, the Poet
        (Works.1753). The works of Alexander Pope Esq. In nine
        volumes complete. With his last corrections, additions,
        and improvements; ... Together with the commentary and
        notes of Mr. Warburton.. - London: printed for J. and P.
        Knapton, H. Lintot, J. and R. Tonscn and S. Draper, and
        C. Bathurst, 1753. 9v., plates ; 8⁰.
        Titlepages in red and black. Horizontal chain lines.
012274.g.8
686.d.24 : Imperfect; vol. IX only.
                                                    t005434

POPE, Alexander, the Poet
        (Works.1754). The works of Alexander Pope, Esq. In ten
        volumes complete. With his last corrections, additions,
        and improvements; ... Printed verbatim from the octavo
        edition of Mr. Warburton.. - London: printed for J. and
        P. Knapton, H. Lintot, J. and R. Tonsor, and S. Draper,
        and C. Bathurst, 1754. 10v., plates ; 8⁰.
        Without Warburtons notes. Titlepages in red and black.
        The separate titlepages to Vol. 1,2 bear the imprint,
        printed for H. Lintot, J. and R. Tonson and S. Draper;
        those to vol. 3-10 bear the imprint, printed for J. and
        P. Knapton.
1490.bb.9
                                                    t005435

POPE, Alexander, the Poet
        (Works.1756). The works of Alexander Pope, Esq. In nine
        volumes complete. With his last corrections, additions,
        and improvements; ... printed from the octavo edition of
        Mr. Warburton.. - London: printed for H. Lintot, A.
        Millar, J. and R. Tonson and S. Draper, and C. Bathurst,
        1756. 9v., plates ; 8⁰.
1507/680

                                                        t005436

POPE, Alexander, the Poet
        (Works.1757). The works of Alexander Pope Esq. In nine
        volumes, complete. With his last corrections, additions,
        and improvements; ...Together with the commentary and
        notes of Mr. Warburton.. - London: printed for A.
        Millar, J. and R. Tonson, H. Lintot, and C. Bathurst,
        1757. 9v., plates ; 8⁰.
        Titlepages in red and black.   Horizontal chain lines.
991.g.1-9
                                                        t005437

POPE, Alexander, the Poet
        (Works.1757). The works of Alexander Pope, Esq. In ten
        volumes complete. With his last corrections, additions,
        and improvements; ... printed verbatim from the octavo
        edition of Mr. Warburton.. - London: printed for A.
        Millar; J. and R. Tonson; H. Lintot; and C. Bathurst,
        1757. 10v., plates ; 8⁰.
        Titlepages in red and black.
12274.e.2 : The separate titlepage to vol. 1 is misbound before
the general titlepage.

                                                        t005438

POPE, Alexander, the Poet
        (Works.1760). The works of Alexander Pope Esq. In nine
        volumes, complete. With his last corrections, additions,
        and improvements; ... Together with the commentary and
        notes of Mr. Warburton.. - London: printed for A.
        Millar, J. and R. Tonson, C. Bathurst, R. Baldwin, W.
        Johnston, (and 6 others in London), 1760. 9v., plates ;
        8⁰.
991.h.1-9 : Imperfect; wanting pp. 209-224 of vol. 1.
                                                        t005439

POPE, Alexander, the Poet
        (Works.1762-64). The works of Alexander Pope, Esq. In
        ten volumes complete, with his last corrections,
        additions, and improvements; ... Together with the
        commentary and notes of Mr. Warburton.. - Berlin:
        printed for Fredrick Nicolai, 1762-64. 10v., plates :
        ill., port. ; 8⁰.
        Vol. 3-6 bear the date 1763; vol. 7-10 the date 1764.
        Titlepages in red and black.
11609.a.31-5
                                                        t005440

POPE, Alexander, the Poet
    (Works.1764). The works of Alexander Pope, Esq. In six
    volumes, complete. With his last corrections, additions,
    and improvements; ... Together with the notes of Mr.
    Warburton.. - London: printed for A. Millar, J. and R.
    Tonson, H. Lintot, and C. Bathurst, 1764. 6v., plates :
    port. ; 8⁰.
    Titlepages in red and black.
991.g.10-15

                                                    t005441

POPE, Alexander, the Poet
    (Works.1764). The works of Alexander Pope, Esq. In six
    volumes complete. With his last corrections, additions,
    and improvements; ... printed verbatim from the octavo
    edition of Mr. Warburton.. - London: printed for A.
    Millar, J. and R. Tonson, C. Bathurst, H. Woodfall, R.
    Baldwin (and 7 others in London), 1764. 6v., plates ; 12⁰.
1607/4208 : Imprimatur leaf in vol. 1 slightly mutilated.
                                                    t005442

POPE, Alexander, the Poet
    (Works.1764). The works of Alexander Pope, Esq. .... -
    Edinburgh: printed for J. Balfour, 1764. 6v., plates :
    port. ; 12⁰.
12274.e.3
                                                    t005443

POPE, Alexander, the Poet
    (Works.1764). The works of Alexander Pope, Esq; In four
    volumes, complete. .... - Edinburgh: printed in the
    year, 1764. 4v., plate : port. ; 12⁰.
11609.aa.27-30
                                                    t005444

POPE, Alexander, the Poet
    (Works.1764). The works of Alexander Pope, Esq. In ten
    volumes complete. With his last corrections, additions,
    and improvements. Together with all his notes, ...
    printed verbatim from the octavo edition of Mr.
    Warburton.. - Dublin: printed by J. Potts; and J.
    Williams, 1764. 10v., plates ; 12⁰.
    Titlepages in red and black.
1606/1520
                                                    t005445

POPE, Alexander, the Poet
        (Works.1766). The works of Alexander Pope Esq. In nine
        volumes, complete. With his last corrections, additions,
        and improvements: .... - London: printed for A. Millar,
        J. and R. Tonson, C. Bathurst, H. Woodfall, R. Baldwin
        (and 6 others in London), 1766. 8v., plates ; 8°
        Titlepages in red and black.
11411.ff.12 : The titlepage to vol. 1 is bound before the
general titlepage.
239.k.43-7
                                                        t005446

POPE, Alexander, the Poet
        (Works.1767). The works of Alexander Pope, Esq. In six
        volumes, complete. With his last corrections, additions,
        and improvements; together with all his notes. -
        Edinburgh: printed by A. Donaldson, and sold at his
        shops in London and Edinburgh, 1767. 6v., plates : port.
        ; 12°
11609.cc.1-6
                                                        t005447

POPE, Alexander, the Poet
        (Works.1769). The works of Alexander Pope, Esq.
        complete. With his last corrections, additions, and
        improvements: together with the commentary and notes of
        his editor. A new edition, in five volumes. To which is
        annexed the life of the author, ... By Owen Ruffhead,
        Esq.. - London: printed for C. Bathurst, H. Woodfall, W.
        Strahan, J. and F. Rivington, W. Johnston (and 8 others
        in London), 1769. 5v., plates : ports. ; 4°
        The fifth volume, containing Ruffheads Life of Alexander
        Pope, has no general titlepage or half-title for the
        Works. A sixth volume, intended to complete Ruffheads
        edition, was published in 1807.
77.l.3-8
                                                        t005448

POPE, Alexander, the Poet
        (Works.1769-70). The works of Alexander Pope, Esq. In
        nine volumes, complete. With his last corrections,
        additions, and improvements: together with the
        commentaries and notes of his editor.. - Dublin: printed
        for G. Faulkner, and A. Bradley, 1769-70. 8v. ; 12°
        Vol. 2-9 bear the imprint, printed for George Faulkner
        and Hulton Bradley. Vol. 5 is dated 1770.
12269.aa.6
                                                        t005449

POPE, Alexander, the Poet
(Works.1770). The works of Alexander Pope Esq. In nine
volumes, complete. With his last corrections, additions,
and improvements: together with the commentary and notes
of his editor.. - London: printed for C. Bathurst, W.
Strahan, J. and F. Rivington, R. Baldwin, W. Johnston
(and 7 others in London), 1770. 9v., plates ; 8⁰.
11609.d.7-15

t005450

POPE, Alexander, the Poet
(Works.1770). The works of Alexander Pope, Esq; In eight
volumes. With his last corrections, additions, and
improvements. Together with all his notes.. - London:
printed for S. Crowder, C. Ware, and T. Payne, 1770. 8v.
; 18⁰.
1606/1938

t005451

POPE, Alexander, the Poet
(Works.1770). The works of Alexander Pope, Esq;
complete. With his last corrections, additions, and
improvements: .... - A new edition, in six volumes. ....
- Dublin: printed for J. Potts, and J. Williams, 1770.
6v., plates ; 12⁰.
1487.ee.18

t005452

POPE, Alexander, the Poet
(Works.1770). The works of Alexander Pope, Esq; In eight
volumes. With his last corrections, additions, and
improvements. Together with all his notes.. - Edinburgh:
printed by and for Martin & Wotherspoon, 1770. 8v. ; 12⁰.
1606/1540

t005453

POPE, Alexander, the Poet
(Works.1772). The works of Alexander Pope, Esq; In six
volumes, complete. With his last corrections, additions,
and improvements; together with all his notes.. -
London: printed in the year, 1772. 6v., plates : port. ;
12⁰.
1507/679

t005454

POPE, Alexander, the Poet
(Works.1776). The works of Alexander Pope, Esq. In six
volumes complete. With his last corrections, additions,
and improvements ... printed verbatim from the octavo
edition of Mr. Warburton.. - London: printed for C.
Bathurst, W. Strahan, J. & F. Rivington, R. Baldwin, T.
Caslon (and 7 others in London), 1776. 6v., plates.
12274.e.4

t005455

POPE, Alexander, the Poet
(Works.1777). (The works of Alexander Pope, Esq; In
eight volumes. With his last corrections, additions, and
improvements. Together with all his notes.). - (London):
(printed for J. Buckland, and T. Longman), (1777). 8v. ;
12⁰
1484.bbb.6 : Imperfect; vol. 3,4 only, and wanting pp. 51-58,
231-244 of vol. 4.

t005456

POPE, Alexander, the Poet
(Works.1777). The works of Alexander Pope, Esq; In six
volumes, complete. With his last corrections, additions,
and improvements; together with all his notes.. -
London: printed for J. Gardner, R. Gray, and P.
Anderson, Edinr., 1777. 6v. ; 12⁰
1607/4225

t005457

POPE, Alexander, the Poet
(Works.1778). The works of Alexander Pope, Esq. In four
volumes complete. With his last corrections, additions,
and improvements. Carefully collated and compared with
former editions: together with notes from the various
critics and commentators.. - London: printed for the
Editor, and sold by J. Werman, 1778. 4v., plates ; 8⁰
11609.dd.1-4

t005458

POPE, Alexander, the Poet
(Works.1787-88). The works of Alexander Pope, Esq. In
six volumes complete. With his last corrections,
additions, and improvements; ... printed verbatim from
the octavo edition of Mr. Warburton. - London: printed
for C. Bathurst, J. Rivington & Sons, B. White, T.
Longman, B. Law (and 8 others in London), 1787-88. 6v.,
plates ; 12⁰
Vol. 2-4 are dated 1787.
11612.df.7

t005459

POPE, Alexander, the Poet
(Works.1789). The works of Alexander Pope, Esq; .... -
Edinburgh: printed by James Donaldson, 1789. 6v., plates
: port. ; 12⁰
11613.a.1

t005460

POPE, Alexander, the Poet
        (Works.1794). The works of Alexander Pope, Esq. With
        remarks and illustrations. By Gilbert Wakefield, ... -
        Warrington: printed for the author by W. Eyres, and sold
        by Payne; Egerton; Shepperson and Reynolds; and
        Kearsley, London, 1794. (4), xxiii, 368, (4)p. ; 8⁰.
        No more published of this edition. With one leaf of
        corrections and additions, and a final leaf of
        advertisements.
991.h.27
G.12882
                                                        t005461

POPE, Alexander, the Poet
        (Works.1795). The works of Alexander Pope, Esq. In eight
        volumes, complete, with his last corrections, additions,
        and improvements; together with all his notes.. -
        London: printed for W. Cavil, T. Martin, T. French, and
        J. Wren, 1795. 8v., plates ; 12⁰.
1606/1522 : Imperfect; wanting pp. 229-(256) of vol. 1.
                                                        t005462

POPE, Alexander, the Poet
        (Works.1797). The works of Alexander Pope, Esq. In nine
        volumes, complete. With notes and illustrations by
        Joseph Warton, D.D. and others. .... - London: printed
        for B. Law, J. Johnson, C. Dilly, G. G. and J. Robinson,
        J. Nichols (and 13 others in London), 1797. 9v., plates
        : ports. ; 8⁰.
685.e.10-18
79.e.2-10
G.12859-67
                                                        t005463

POPE, Alexander, the Poet
        (Works. Supplements). A supplement to the works of
        Alexander Pope Esq. Containing such poems, letters, &c.
        as are omitted in the edition published by the Reverend
        Dr. Warburton. To which is added, a key to the letters..
        - London: printed for M. Cooper, 1757. (2), v, (3),
        206p. ; 8⁰.
12274.e.17 : MS. notes by C. W. Dilke.
                                                        t005464

POPE, Alexander, the Poet
    (Works. Supplements). Additions to the works of
    Alexander Pope, Esq. Together with many original poems
    and letters, of cotemporary writers, never before
    published. In two volumes. .... - London: printed for H.
    Baldwin, T. Longman, R. Baldwin, G. Robinson, T. Caslon
    (and 2 others in London), 1776. 2v. ; 8⁰.
    Edited by William Cocke? or George Steevens?.
636.f.18 : MS. notes by C. W. Dilke.
C.23.e.16
239.k.48 : MS. notes by Horace Walpole, Earl of Orford. A
cutting from the St. Jamess Chronicle of 27 July 1782 is
inserted at the end.

POPE, Alexander, the Poet
    (Works. Supplements). Additions to the works of
    Alexander Pope, Esq. Together with many original poems
    and letters, of cotemporary writers. Never before
    published. In two volumes. .... - Dublin: printed for W.
    Watson, J. Potts, J. Williams, W. Colles, W. Wilson (and
    7 others in Dublin), 1776. 2v. ; 12⁰.
    Edited by William Cooke? or George Steevens?.
1507/501

POPE, Alexander, the Poet
    (Selections). The works of Mr. Alexander Pope, in prose.
    Vol. II.. - London: printed (by John Wright) for J. and
    P. Knapton, C. Bathurst, and R. Dodsley, 1741. vi, (10),
    108, 85-173, (1); (3), 300-312; (4), 70, (2); (3),
    190-243; (1), 260-266; (1), 256-280; (3), 244-257, (1)p.
    ; 2⁰.
    On large paper. With a half-title, repeating the title
    and adding: Containing the rest of his letters, with the
    Memoirs of Scriblerus ... and other tracts ....
    Titlepage in red and black. The Scriblerus material has
    a separate titlepage reading Tracts of Martinus
    Scriblerus: and other miscellaneous pieces, and bearing
    the imprint, London: printed for Benjamin Motte and
    Charles Bathurst, Lawton Gilliver and John Clarke, 1737.
     Printed by Wright on the evidence of the ornaments.
    The first volume, of which this is the companion, was
    published in 1737 with the title, Letters of Mr.
    Alexander Pope, ... and is entered below under Letters.
    Griffith 530.
834.bb.4(2)
Ashley 5228

POPE, Alexander, the Poet
        (Selections). The works of Mr. Alexander Pope, in prose.
        Vol. II.. - London: printed (by J. Wright) for J. and P.
        Knapton, C. Bathurst, and R. Dodsley, 1741. vi, (10),
        115, (1); 89-182; (3), 326-339, (1); 75, (3); (5),
        208-270; (1), 182-88; (1), 278-304, (3), 266-179(i.e.
        279), (1)p. ; 4º.
        With a half-title, repeating the title and adding:
        Containing the rest of his letters, with the Memoirs of
        Scriblerus ... and other tracts. Titlepage in red and
        black. Contains the nine leaves of Thoughts on various
        subjects originally printed to form part of the first
        volume of prose works, Letters of Mr. Alexander Pope,
        ..., 1737. Pp. 269-279 in the final section misnumbered
        169-179.
        Griffith 531.
Ashley 4945 : The sheets containing the Memoirs of Scriblerus
and the Essay on the origine of sciences have been transposed
in binding.
                                                    t005468

POPE, Alexander, the Poet
        (Selections). The beauties of Pope, or, useful and
        entertaining passages selected from the works of that
        admired author; as well as from his translation of
        Homers Iliad and Odyssey, &c. .... - London: printed for
        G. Kearsley, 1796. 2v. ; 12º.
1075.l.15
                                                    t005469

POPE, Alexander, the Poet
        (Poems). The poetical works of Alexander Pope, Esq. ....
        - Glasgow: printed by Robert and Andrew Foulis, 1773.
        4v. ; 12º.
        Gaskell 560.
238.a.48-51
                                                    t005470

POPE, Alexander, the Poet
        (Poems). The poetical works of Alex. Pope, Esq. With his
        last corrections, additions, and improvements. From the
        text of Dr. Warburton. In four volumes. Vol. I.. -
        Edinburg: at the Apollo Press, by the Martins,
        1776(1777). 250, (2),. plates ; 12º.
        In: Bells edition. The poets of Great Britain complete,
        from Chaucer to Churchill. Colophon dated: Oct. 9th
        1776; engraved portrait and titlepage dated 1777. With
        the volume number in the direction line.
1066.bb.20(1)
                                                    t005471

POPE, Alexander, the Poet
(Poems). The poetical works of Alex. Pope, Esq. With his
last corrections, additions, and improvements. From the
text of Dr. Warburton. In four volumes. Vol. I.. -
Edinburg: at the Apollo Press, by the Martins,
1776(1778). (2), 250, (2)p., plates ; 12º
In: Bells edition. The poets of Great Britain complete,
from Chaucer to Churchill. Colophon dated: Oct. 9th,
1776; engraved titlepage dated 1777; portrait dated
1778. Without the volume number in the direction line.
1506/368(1)

t005472

POPE, Alexander, the Poet
(Poems). The poetical works of Alex. Pope, Esq. With his
last corrections, additions, and improvements. From the
text of Dr. Warburton. In four volumes. Vol. II.. -
Edinburg: at the Apollo Press, by the Martins,
1776(1777). 249, (3)p.,plate ; 12º
In: Bells edition. The poets of Great Britain complete,
from Chaucer to Churchill. Colophon dated: Nov. 27,
1776; engraved titlepage dated 1777. With the volume
number in the direction line.
1066.bb.20(2)

t005473

POPE, Alexander, the Poet
(Poems). The poetical works of Alex. Pope, Esq. With his
last corrections, additions, and improvements. From the
text of Dr. Warburton. In four volumes. Vol. II.. -
Edinburg: at the Apollo Press, by the Martins,
1776(1777). (2), 249, (3)p., plate ; 12º
In: Bells edition. The poets of Great Britain complete,
from Chaucer to Churchill. Colophon dated: Nov. 27,
1776; engraved titlepage dated 1777. Without the volume
number in the direction line.
1506/368(2)

t005474

POPE, Alexander, the Poet
(Poems). The poetical works of Alex. Pope, Esq. With his
last corrections, additions and improvements. From the
text of Dr. Warburton. In four volumes. Vol. III.. -
Edinburg: at the Apollo Press, by the Martins,
1776(1777). 255, (7)p., plate ; 12º
In: Bells edition. The poets of Great Britain complete,
from Chaucer to Churchill. Colophon dated: Dec. 17,
1776; engraved titlepage dated 1777. The verso of p.
255 is blank; the last 3 leaves contain a list of
contents. With the volume number in the direction
line.
1066.b.21(1)
1506/368(3) : A variant, with the Contents printed on the verso
of p. 255, and on 2 additional, unpaginated leaves; pagination:
255, (5)p. Imperfect; wanting the engraved titlepage.

t005475

POPE, Alexander, the Poet
    (Poems). The poetical works of Alex. Pope, Esq. With his
    last corrections, additions, and improvements. From the
    text of Dr. Warburton. In four volumes. Vol. IV.. -
    Edinburg: at the Apollo Press, by the Martins,
    1776(1777). 214, (2)p., plate ; 12⁰
    In: Bells edition. The poets of Great Britain complete
    from Chaucer to Churchill. Colophon dated: Dec. 23,
    1776; engraved titlepage dated 1777. With the volume
    number in the direction line.
1066.b.21(2)

                                                    t005476

POPE, Alexander, the Poet
    (Poems). The poetical works of Alex. Pope, Esq. With his
    last corrections, additions, and improvements. From the
    text of Dr. Warburton. In four volumes. Vol. IV.. - at
    the Apollo Press, by the Martins, 1776(1778). (2), 214,
    (2)p., plate ; 12⁰
    In: Bells edition. The poets of Great Britain complete,
    from Chaucer to Churchill. Colophon dated: Dec. 23,
    1776; engraved titlepage dated 1778.
1506/368(4)

                                                    t005477

POPE, Alexander, the Poet
    (Poems). The poems of Alexander Pope, Esq. In three
    volumes. .... - London: printed in the year, 1779. 3v. ;
    8⁰
11609.b.29-31

                                                    t005479

POPE, Alexander, the Poet
    (Poems). The poetical works of Alexander Pope, Esq. In
    three volumes. .... - Glasgow: printed by Andrew Foulis,
    1785. 3v. ; 2⁰
    With a 4-page list of subscribers.
    Gaskell 678.
1505/352 : Bound in two volumes. Imperfect; wanting the list of
subscribers.
75.i.2,3

                                                    t005478

POPE, Alexander, the Poet
    (Poems). The poetical works of Alexander Pope, with his
    last corrections, additions, and improvements. From the
    text of Dr. Warburton. With the life of the author.
    Cookes pocket edition. ... Embellished with superb
    engravings.. - London: printed for C. Cooke, (1800).
    3v., plates ; 12⁰
    The plate illustrating Winter is dated August, 1800.
1606/1944
                                                    t005480

POPE, Alexander, the Poet
(Poems. Selected poems). A miscellany on taste. By Mr.
Pope, &c. Viz. I. Of taste in architecture. ... II. Of
Mr. Popes taste in divinity, ... III. Of Mr. Popes taste
of Shakespeare. IV.His satire on Mrs. P-y. V. Mr.
Congreves fine epistle on retirement and taste .... -
London: printed; and sold by G. Lawton; T. Osborn; and
J. Hughes, 1732. (4), 45, (1)p. ; 8⁰
Edited by Matthew Concanen, the elder?.
Griffith 266; Guerinot, p. 207ff.
T.1056(15) : Imperfect; wanting the frontispiece.
12274.h.2(8)

t005481

POPE, Alexander, the Poet
(Poems. Selected poems). Ethic epistles, satires, &c.
With the authors notes. Written by Mr. Pope.. -
London(i.e. The Hague?): printed (by T. Johnson) for the
Company, 1735. (4), 184p. ; 12⁰
Apparently a reprint, with some changes, of the contents
of Works, II, 1735, small folio. Probably printed by T.
Johnson at the Hague.
Griffith 391.
11633.aa.56(1)

t005482

POPE, Alexander, the Poet
(Poems. Selected poems). Satires of Dr. John Donne, Dean
of St. Pauls. Done into modern English by Mr. Pope.. -
Dublin: London: printed. And, Dublin re-printed by
George Faulkner, 1736. pp. 131-170 ; 8⁰
Presumably intended to form part of a larger collection.
 Pp. 163-170 contain the epitaphs.
Griffith 434.
C.136.aa.1(2)

t005483

POPE, Alexander, the Poet
(Poems. Selected poems). Poems, and imitations of
Horace. By Mr. Pope. Now first collected together.. -
London: printed for J. and P. Knapton, L. Gilliver, J.
Brindley, and R. Dodsley, 1738(1739). (2), 39 (1); 81,
(1); 8; 23(i.e. 25), (1)p. ; 4⁰
P. 25 of Dialogue II is misnumbered 23. The sheets
containing the Latin texts and the imitations of
Epistles I.i, I.vi, II.i, II.ii, and Odes I.iv were
issued in 1738 with the title Epistles of Horace
imitated. Copies may have groups bound in different
orders. Also issued as part of made-up sets of the
Works, possibly in 1739.
Griffith 504.
641.l.17(2) : On thick paper.

t005484

POPE, Alexander, the Poet
        (Poems. Selected poems). Epistles to several persons.. -
        (London), (1744). (4), 96p. ; 4⁰.
        Anonymous. By Alexander Pope. This edition was
        suppressed; the second epistle contains for the first
        time the character of Atossa, now generally thought to
        refer to Katherine, Duchess of Buckingham. Title taken
        from half-title.
        Griffith 591.
C.59.e.1(2)
                                                            t005485

POPE, Alexander, the Poet
        (Poems. Selected poems). Four ethic epistles. By
        Alexander Pope, Esq;. - Glasgow: printed by R. Urie, for
        Daniel Baxter, 1750. 64p. ; 8⁰.
        Containing the epistles To Sir Richard Temple, Lord
        Viscount Cobham, To a lady, To the Right Honourable
        Allen Lord Bathurst, and To Richard Boyle, Earl of
        Burlington.
        Not in Griffith.
1607/4229
                                                            t005486

POPE, Alexander, the Poet
        (Poems. Selected poems). Epistles. By Alexander Pope,
        Esq; to which is subjoined, The messiah, a sacred
        eclogue, and Eloisa to Abelard, by the same author.. -
        Aberdeen: printed and sold by F. Douglas and W. Murray,
        1754. (4), 60p. ; 12⁰.
        Contains seven epistles, with the three other works.
        Gathered in 2s and 4s.
11630.a.14
                                                            t005487

POPE, Alexander, the Poet
        (Poems. Selected poems). The essay on man, Universal
        prayer, and Eloisa to Abelard, three celebrated poems.
        By Alexander Pope, Esq;. - London: printed and sold by
        Thomas Palmer, (1755?). (4), 52p. ; 8⁰.
11655.ff.80
                                                            t005488

POPE, Alexander, the Poet
        (Poems. Selected poems). A collection of essays,
        epistles and odes. ... By Alexander Pope, Esq;. -
        London: printed for T. Daniel, W. Thompson, and J.
        Steele, and A. Todd, 1758. (4), 215, (1)p., plate :
        port. ; 12⁰
1568/4585
                                                            t005489

POPE, Alexander, the Poet
      (Poems. Selected poems). A collection of essays,
      epistles and odes. ... By Alexander Pope, Esq;. -
      London: printed for J. James, 1762. (4), 55, (1); 69,
      (1); 25, (4), 28-30; 26; 25, (1)p. ; 8º.
      Arranged in five sections; the Essay on man has a
      separate titlepage; the other four sections, together
      with a number of the individual pieces have divisional
      titles. A reprint of the contents of the edition of
      1758.
1506/369

                                                           t005490

POPE, Alexander, the Poet
      (Poems. Selected poems). Popes poetical beauties;
      selected.. - A new edition. - London: printed for W.
      Lane, 1784. (2), 69, (1); 25, (4), 28-30; 26; 25, (1);
      55, (1)p. ; 8º.
      A reissue of the sheets of J. Jamess 1762 edition of A
      collection of essays, epistles and odes, with a cancel
      titlepage.
991.g.29(1,2) : The section containing the Essay on man has
been bound at the end of the volume.

                                                           t005491

POPE, Alexander, the Poet
      (Poems. Selected poems). Pastorals. By Alexander Pope..
      - Manchester: printed by G. Nicholson and Co. Sold by T.
      Knott; and Champante 8 Whitrow, London, 1793. 14p. ; 24º.
      In: The literary miscellany; or, elegant selections of
      the most admired fugitive pieces, Manchester, 1794.
1493.t.44

                                                           t010219

POPE, Alexander, the Poet
      (Poems. Selected poems. Polyglot). Traduction des
      eclogues de Pope, et de son ode sur la musique, en vers
      francois. ... Par M. de F. de B.. - Paris: chez J. G.
      Merigot le jeune, 1789. xxiv, 123, (3)p. ; 8º
      Dedication signed: De Rocquigny de Bulonde. Parallel
      French and English text of each pastoral is followed by
      a Latin verse translation.
1609/3950

                                                           t005492

POPE, Alexander, the Poet
      (Poems. Selected poems. French). Les principes de la
      morale et du gout, traduits de langlois de M. Pope, par
      M. lAbbe du Resnel.. - Nouvelle edition augmentee de La
      boucle de cheveux enlevee ... mis en vers. - Londres,
      1750. (4), xlviii, 248p. ; 12º
      Half-title: Oeuvres de M. Pope, traduites en vers
      francois.
11609.a.30

                                                           t005493

POPE, Alexander, the Poet
(Poems. Selected poems. French and English). Les
pastorales dAlexandre Pope, avec son Discours sur la
poesie pastorale, et Le poeme sur la forest de Windsor,
traduits de langlois.. - Paris: chez David le jeune,
1753. (12), 165, (3)p. ; 12⁰.
Dedication signed: De Lustrac. Parallel French prose
translation and original text. Privilege du Roi dated:
13 Avril 1753.
1487.a.2 : With a few MS. corrections to the English text.

t005494

POPE, Alexander, the Poet
(Poems. Selected poems. Latin). A. Popii excerpta
quaedam: viz. Tentamen de homine. Tentamen de
criticismo. Eloisa Abelardo ... Latine reddidit Jac.
Kirkpatrick, M.D.. - Londini: typis J. Purser, 1749.
(4), xii, (2), 122p. ; 4⁰.
With a 2-page list of subscribers.
Foxon, p. 403.
11630.c.2(3) : Titlepage cropped at foot, affecting the
imprint.

t005496

POPE, Alexander, the Poet
(Poems. Selected poems. Latin and English). Bucolica
Alexandri Popii, (quatuor anni temporum inscripta
titulis) Latine reddita: interprete S. Barrett, M.A.
.... - Londini: excudebat E. Cave; prostant nec non apud
R. & J. Tonson & S. Draper; R. Fletcher, & S. Parker,
Oxon. & J. Thurlbourn, Cantab., 1746. (4), 43, (1)p. ; 4⁰.

Latin verse translation with the original text. With
engraved headpieces for each season, by Boitard.
Foxon B88; Griffith 616.
11630.c.5(10) : Cropped.
11630.f.44 : A variant, without the engravings.

t005495

POPE, Alexander, the Poet
        (Letters. 1735). Letters of Mr. Wycherley 8 Mr. Pope,
        from the year 1704 to 1710. (Letters of Sir William
        Trumbull, Mr. Steele, Mr. Addison, and Mr. Pope.). -
        (London), (1735). 2v. ; 8º.
        Without titlepages and without the prefatory address To
        the reader; the title is taken from the drop-head on p.
        1.   Consisting in part of remaindered sheets of J.
        Roberts 1729 edition of The posthumous works of William
        Wycherley, Esq., edited by Pope. Sherburn, apparently
        following Griffith and Dearing, lists this as the first
        of at least four variant issues, ... all of which
        contain considerable parts printed from the same setting
        of type.
        Griffith 374.
12274.h.18 : Pp. 115-164 containing Letters of Mr. Pope to Mr.
Gay have been misbound before Sig. A1 in the second volume. MS.
notes.
                                                        t005497

POPE, Alexander, the Poet
        (Letters. 1735). Letters of Mr. Pope and several eminent
        persons. In the years 1705, 8c. to 1717.. - London:
        printed for J. Roberts, (1735). 2v. ; 8º.
        Another issue of the sheets of the preceding, with the
        addition of a titlepage to vol. 1, an address To the
        reader, and a leaf of errata; the letters to Jervas,
        Digby and Blount are omitted, as are also those to Gay
        and Lord Burlington, and a letter from Arbuthnot.
        Griffith 375.
12274.h.15 : MS. notes by C. W. Dilke. The leaf of errata is
bound after the preface.
                                                        t005498

POPE, Alexander, the Poet
        (Letters. 1735). Letters of Mr. Pope , and several
        eminent persons, from the year 1705, to 1711. Vol. I. -
        London: printed and sold by the booksellers of London
        and Westminster, 1735. 2v. ; 8º.
        Another issue of the sheets of the Roberts edition with
        a cancel titlepage; the first leaf of the preface is
        also a cancel, incorporating an additional paragraph.
        The excisions made in the Roberts edition are here
        restored, using sheets from the same printing as in the
        first edition.
        Griffith 378.
12274.h.16 : Copious MS. notes and emendations by C. W. Dilke.
In this copy the preface has been reset throughout, and
occupies sig. A, as described in Griffith 381; the text,
however, is as described in Griffith 378.
                                                        t005499

POPE, Alexander, the Poet
        (Letters. 1735). Letters of Mr. Pope, and several
        eminent persons, from the year 1705, to 1711. Vol. I.. -
        London: printed and sold by the booksellers of London
        and Westminster, 1735. 2v. ; 8⁰.
        Another issue of the preceding; sig. B in vol. 1 is,
        however, a whole sheet, reprinted and substituted for
        *B, B, *C.
        Griffith 380.
    12274.h.11
                                                    t005500

POPE, Alexander, the Poet
        (Letters. 1735). Letters of Mr. Pope, and several
        eminent persons, from the year 1705, to 1711. .... -
        London: printed and sold by the booksellers of London
        and Westminster, 1735. 2v. ; 8⁰.
        A different edition from the preceding; in vol. 2, which
        has a separate titlepage, the letter of 19 Jan. 1716
        from Trumbull is on sig. P*1. Sig. B in vol. 1 is
        reissued from the preceding; sig. P-T, X and Y in vol. 2
        are supplied by the sheets witheld from the Roberts
        edition (Griffith 375).
        Griffith 381.
    12274.h.17 : MS. notes by C. W. Dilke.
    12274.h.14
                                                    t005501

POPE, Alexander, the Poet
        (Letters. 1735). Letters of Mr. Pope, and several
        eminent persons, from the year 1705, to 1711.. - London:
        printed and sold by the booksellers of London and
        Westminster, 1735. 2v. ; 8⁰.
        Another issue; sig. L-Q reprint P* and P-T of the
        preceding, and sig. X-Y have been reset.
        Griffith 383.
    12274.h.12 : A variant? Sig. B in vol. 1 is a different setting
    from that in the preceding; no volume no. in the direction line
    to p. 1.
                                                    t005502

POPE, Alexander, the Poet
        (Letters. 1735). Letters of Mr Pope, and several eminent
        persons, from the year 1705, to 1735. Vol. I.. - London:
        printed for T. Cooper, 1735. xxxi, (1), 216, 221-340p.,
        plate : port. ; 12⁰.
        The pagination leaps from 216 to 221; text is apparently
        complete. Pp. iii-xxxi contain A narrative of the
        method. Vol. 2 is without a separate titlepage;
        pagination and register are continuous.
        Griffith 396.
    10921.aa.17
                                                    t005503

POPE, Alexander, the Poet
        (Letters. 1735). Letters of Mr Pope, and several eminent
        persons, from the year 1705, to 1735. Vol. I.. - London:
        printed for T. Cooper, 1735. xxxi, (2), 10-216, 221-345,
        (1)p., plate : ports. ; 12º
        Another issue of the text of the preceding Cooper
        edition, with a new frontispiece; one leaf has been
        substituted and three leaves added at the end,
        containing two additional letters. These four leaves
        have vertical chain lines.
        Griffith 397.
12274.e.15
12274.e.16 : Imperfect; wanting the plate.
                                                    t005504

POPE, Alexander, the Poet
        (Letters. 1735). Letters of Mr. Pope, and several
        eminent persons. From the year 1705. to 1735. N.B. This
        edition contains more letters, and more correctly
        printed, than any other extant.. - London: printed; and
        sold by the booksellers of London and Westminster, 1735.
        (2), vi, 266; (2), 22p. : ill., port. ; 12º
        The second sequence of pagination contains A narrative
        of the method. P. 145 is misnumbered 345.
        Griffith 400.
12274.e.14 : MS. notes by C. W. Dilke; A narrative of the
method is bound before the letters.
Ashley 1317 : Without A narrative of the method.
Ashley 1318 : Imperfect; wanting all except A narrative of the
method.
                                                    t005505

POPE, Alexander, the Poet
        (Letters. 1735). Letters of Mr. Pope, and several
        eminent persons. From the year 1705, to 1735. N.B. This
        edition contains more letters, and more correctly
        printed, than any other extant.. - London: printed for
        J. Smith; and sold by the booksellers of London and
        Westminster, 1735. 266, 22p. ; 12º
        The second sequence of 22p. contains A narrative of the
        method.
        Griffith 408.
12274.e.13
                                                    t005506

POPE, Alexander, the Poet
    (Letters. 1735-37). Mr. Popes literary correspondence
    for thirty years; from 1704 to 1734. Being, a collection
    of letters, which passed between him and several eminent
    persons. Volume the first.. - London: printed for E.
    Curll, 1735. (8), 128, 155, (1), 161-316p., plates :
    ports. ; 8º
    In the second sequence of pagination, there is a break
    between pp. 155 and 161, and pp. 177-184 are misnumbered
    169-176; the text is apparently complete. A reprint of
    the text of the Roberts edition of (1735) entered
    above.
    Griffith 376.
12274.i.12 : The first sequence, pp. 1-128, has been misbound
between pp. 232 and 233 of the second sequence. MS. notes by C.
W. Dilke; a note on the front free end-paper is signed: Orrery,
1735.
12274.i.14 : The first sequence, pp. 1-128, has been misbound
between pp. 232 and 233 of the second sequence. MS.notes by C.
W. Dilke; interleaved. Without the portrait of Bolingbroke.
Ashley 3776 : With the frontispiece portrait of Pope only.
                                                    t005507

POPE, Alexander, the Poet
    (Letters. 1735-37). Mr. Popes literary correspondence.
    Volume the second. With letters to, and from, Lord
    Somers. Lord Harrington. .... - London: printed for E.
    Curll, 1735. xvi, xvi, 48; 79,(1); 160; 92, (4)p.,
    plates : ports. ; 8º
    Griffith 386.
12274.i.12 : MS. notes by C. W. Dilke.
Ashley 3777 : Without the portrait of Pope.
                                                    t005508

POPE, Alexander, the Poet
    (Letters. 1735-37). Mr. Popes literary correspondence.
    Volume the second. With letters to, and from, Lord
    Somers. Lord Harrington. .... - The second edition. -
    London: printed for E. Curll, 1735. xxxii, (2), 228p. :
    ill., ports. ; 12º
    Griffith 403.
10921.aa.18 : Imperfect; wanting the frontispiece portrait of
Pope and that of Atterbury.
                                                    t005509

POPE, Alexander, the Poet
(Letters. 1735-37). Mr. Popes literary correspondence.
Volume the third. With letters to, and, from the Duke of
Shrewsberry, Lord Lansdowne, ... - London: printed for
E. Curll, 1735. xxxii, 241, 46; (2), 66; (2), 30p.
plates : ports. ; 8º.
Includes: Impartial memorials of the life and writings
of Thomas Hearne, M.A., with a separate titlepage (dated
1736), pagination and register; and, A short memorial
and character of ... Mary Dutchess of Ormonde, with
separate pagination and register.
Griffith 402.
12274.i.12
Ashley 3778

t005510

POPE, Alexander, the Poet
(Letters. 1735-37). Mr. Popes literary correspondence.
Volume the fourth. With letters, &c. to and from, Mr.
Addison. Bishop Atterbury. ... To which are added,
Muscovian letters.. - London: printed for E. Curll,
1736. vii, (1), 152; (5), 52-62; 48; xii, 190p., plates
: ports. ; 8º.
Contains neither letters to nor from Pope; the Muscovian
letters were also issued separately. Some copies
contain a 4-page catalogue of new books issued by
Curll.
Griffith 415.
Ashley 3779

t005511

POPE, Alexander, the Poet
(Letters. 1735-37). Mr. Popes literary correspondence.
Volume the fifth. With letters of Lord Bolingbroke. Lord
Lansdowne. .... - London: printed for E. Curll, 1737.
(2), ii, (2), 66, (1), 66-242(i.e. 252); (4), ii, (2),
xii, 86p., plates : ports. ; 8º.
Includes: The works of William Walsh, Esq; In prose and
verse, with a separate titlepage dated 1736. Pp. 237-8,
240 and 252 are misnumbered 273, 240, 140 and 242. The
sheets of the first part of the volume were also issued
with an additional titlepage, reading, New letters of
Mr. Alexander Pope. What constitutes a sixth volume in
the series was published by Curll in 1741 with the title
Dean Swifts literary correspondence.
Griffith 462.
Ashley 3780

t005512

PCPE, Alexander, the Poet
   (Letters. 1737). Letters of Mr. Alexander Pope, and
   several of his friends.. - London: printed by J. Wright
   for J. Knapton, L. Gilliver, J. Brindley, and R.
   Dodsley, 1737. (37), 10-222, 215-332p. ; 4°
   Half-title: The works of Mr. Alexander Pope, in prose.
   Titlepage in red and black. The authorized text. A
   second volume, published in 1741 with the title, The
   works of Mr. Alexander Pope, in prose. Vol. II, is
   entered above under Selections.
   Griffith 454.
831.k.15
12270.k.11
Ashley 4943 : Cn fine paper. Bound in this vclume are the 9
leaves, also fine paper, containing Thoughts on various
subjects, originally printed to form part of this book, but
withheld until 1741 when they were included in the 4° Works, in
prose, vol. 2.
Ashley 4944

                                             t005513

POPE, Alexander, the Poet
   (Letters. 1737). Letters of Mr. Alexander Pope, and
   several of his friends.. - London: printed by J. Wright
   for J. Knapton, L. Gilliver, J. Brindley, and R.
   Dodsley, 1737. (37), 10-196, 189-307, (1)p. ; 2°
   On large paper. Half-title: The works cf Mr. Alexander
   Pope, in prose. Titlepage in red and black. Oblong
   engraved tail-piece on sig. D1r.
   Griffith 456.
834.bb.4(1) : The half-title is bound after the titlepage.
Ashley 5227

                                             t005514

POPE, Alexander, the Poet
   (Letters. 1737). Letters of Mr. Alexander Pope, and
   several of his friends.. - London: printed by J. Wright
   for J. Knapton, L. Gilliver, J. Brindley and R. Dodsley,
   1737. (37), 10-196, 189-307, (1)p. ; 2°
   Another issue, on small paper. Half-title: The works of
   Mr. Alexander Pope, in prose. Titlepage in black only.
   Tail-piece on sig. D1r: large oval, urn with scroll
   work.
   Griffith 457.
 831.k.16
                                             t005515

POPE, Alexander, the Poet
    (Letters. 1737). New letters of Mr Alexander Pope, and
    several of his friends.. - London: printed, Anno
    Reformationis, 1737. (4), ii, (2), 66, 66-242(i.e. 252),
    (2), 16p., plate : port. ; 8º.
    Apparently another issue of the sheets of the first part
    of vol. 5 of Curlls edition of Mr. Popes literary
    correspondence, with the original titlepage left
    uncancelled. Includes a leaf of advertisements after
    the dedication, a 16-page list of Books printed for E.
    Curll, and, following p. 252, a leaf headed
    Advertisement, signed and dated at end: E. Curll, June
    8, 1737.
    Griffith 429 (collation differs).
12274.i.12 : With a leaf of MS. notes by C. W. Dilke inserted.
                                                    t005516

POPE, Alexander, the Poet
    (Letters. 1748). Letters and and from Alexander Pope,
    Esq; and others.. - London: printed in the year, 1748.
    (26), 351, (1)p. ; 12º.
    The verso of Sig. A4 in the prelims. is numbered 2.
    Griffith 633.
12274.f.7
                                                    t005517

POPE, Alexander, the Poet
    (Letters. 1751). A collection of letters, never before
    printed: written by Alexander Pope, Esq; and other
    ingenious gentlemen, to the late Aaron Hill, Esq;. -
    London: printed for W. Owen, 1751. (4), 88p. ; 12º.
    The leaf following the titlepage contains Proposals for
    printing by subscription, ... the works of the late
    Aaron Hill,, dated May 1. 1751.
    Griffith 642.
10920.c.22
1085.k.22 : Imperfect; wanting the leaf of Proposals.
                                                    t005518

POPE, Alexander, the Poet
    (Letters. 1751). A collection of letters, never before
    printed: written by Alexander Pope, Esq: and other
    ingenious gentlemen. To the late Aaron Hill, Esq;. -
    Dublin: printed by Richard James, 1751. 75, (1)p. ; 12º.
    Not in Griffith.
1083.f.6
                                                    t005519

POPE, Alexander, the Poet
        (Letters. 1769). Letters of the late Alexander Pope,
        Esq. To a lady. Never before published.. - London:
        printed for J. Dodsley, 1769. 87, (1)p. ; 8⁰.
        With a half-title.
10920.bbb.8
Ashley 1320

                                                    t005520

POPE, Alexander, the Poet
        A blast upon bays; or, a new lick at the the Laureat.
        Containing, remarks upon a late tatling performance,
        entitled, A letter from Mr. Cibber to Mr. Pope, &c.. -
        London: printed for T. Robbins, 1742. (2), 26p. ; 8⁰.

        Attributed to Alexander Pope. Dated at end: July 29,
        1742.
641.h.5(4)
116.i.20
Ashley 3782

                                                    t005521

POPE, Alexander, the Poet
        Bounce to Fop. An heroick epistle from a dog at
        Twickenham to a dog at court. By Dr. S-t.. - London:
        Dublin, printed, London, reprinted for T. Cooper, 1736.
        11, (1)p. ; 2⁰.
        With a half-title. It is generally agreed that the
        original idea was Swifts, but that the writing is
        largely by Pope (Foxon).
        Foxon B326; Teerink 976.
11602.i.16(6)
Ashley 5067

                                                    t005522

POPE, Alexander, the Poet
        Bounce to Fop. An heroick epistle from a dog at
        Twickenham to a dog at court. By Dr. S-t.. - The second
        edition. - London: Dublin, printed, London, reprinted
        for T. Cooper, 1736. 11, (1)p. ; 2⁰.
        With a half-title. A reimpression (Foxon). It is
        generally agreed that the original idea was Swifts, but
        that the writing is largely by Pope (Foxon).
        Foxon B327.
11646.w.15

                                                    t005523

POPE, Alexander, the Poet
    The character of Katharine, late Duchess of
    Buckinghamshire and Normanby. By the late Mr. Pope.. —
    London: printed for M. Cooper, 1746. 7, (1)p. ; 2⁰
    Pope claimed to have revised, but not written this work
    (Correspondence, ed. Sherburn, V, 460).
    Griffith 617.
Ashley 4947
Ashley 4948 : On fine paper.

                                            t005524

POPE, Alexander, the Poet
    A clue to the comedy of the Non-juror. With some hints
    of consequence relating to that play. In a letter to N.
    Rowe, Esq; .... — London: printed for E. Curll, 1718.
    25, (3)p. ; 8⁰
    Attributed to Alexander Pope. With a half-title
    reading: A letter to Mr. Rowe ..., and a final leaf of
    advertisements. Catchword p. 17: the; p. 8, line 6 from
    bottom: in the Hind and Panther.
    Griffith Add. 90a.
1343.e.3
164.i.70 : Imperfect; wanting the half-title.

                                            t005525

POPE, Alexander, the Poet
    (Clue to the comedy of the Non-juror). The plot
    discoverd: or, a clue to the comedy of the Non-juror.
    With some hints of consequence relating to that play. In
    a letter to N. Rowe, Esq; .... — The second edition. —
    London: printed for E. Curll, 1718. 25, (3)p. ; 8⁰
    Attributed to Alexander Pope. Partly reimpressed,
    partly reset, with a new titlepage, and half-title
    reading A clue to the Non-juror. Catchword p. 17: but;
    p. 8, line 6 from bottom: in Mr. Drydens Hind and
    Panther.
    Griffith Add. 90b.
11775.bbb.11

                                            t005526

POPE, Alexander, the Poet
    The court ballad. By Mr. Pope. To the tune of, To all
    you ladies now at land, &c.. — (London): printed for R.
    Burleigh, in Amen-Corner, (1717). 2p. ; 1/2⁰
    Foxon P762; Griffith 67.
Ashley 4931 : Some of the blanks have been completed in MS.
                                            t005527

POPE, Alexander, the Poet
        The court ballad. By Mr. Pope. To the tune of, To all
        you ladies now at land, &c.. - The second edition,
        corrected. - (London): printed for A. Smith in Cornhill,
        (1717). 2p. ; 1/2⁰
        A reimpression (of the edition printed for R. Burleigh),
        with at least one textual revision; the imprint and
        advertisement are reset (Foxon).
        Foxon P763; Griffith 69.
12273.m.1(5)
                                                        t005528

POPE, Alexander, the Poet
        The discovery: or, the squire turnd ferret. An excellent
        new ballad. To the tune of High boys! up go we; Chevy
        Chase; or what you please.. - Westminster: printed by A.
        Campbell, for T. Warner, and sold by the booksellers,
        1727 (1726). 8p. ; 2⁰
        Ascribed to Alexander Pope, in collaboration with
        William Pulteney, by Spence on Popes authority.
        Publication date from Twickenham edition. On the
        imposture of Mary Toft.
        Foxon D328.
643.1.24(49) : With a folding engraved plate by William Hogarth
inserted.
163.n.13
                                                        t005529

POPE, Alexander, the Poet
        The discovery: or, the squire turnd ferret. An excellent
        new ballad. To the tune of High boys! up go we; Chevy
        Chase; or what you please.. - The second edition. -
        Westminster: printed by A. Campbell; for T. Warner, and
        sold by the booksellers, 1727 (1726). 8p. ; 2⁰
        Apparently a reimpression (Foxon). Ascribed to
        Alexander Pope, in collaboration with William Pulteney,
        by Spence on Popes authority. Publication date from
        Twickenham edition.
        Foxon D329.
C.116.i.4(30)
1178.h.4(14)
                                                        t005530

POPE, Alexander, the Poet
        The discovery: or, the squire turnd ferret. An excellent
        new ballad. To the tune of High boys! up go we; Chevy
        Chase; or what you please.. - The third edition. -
        Westminster: printed by A. Campbell, for T. Warner, and
        sold by the booksellers, 1727. 8p. ; 2⁰
        Apparently a reimpression (Foxon). Ascribed to
        Alexander Pope, in collaboration with William Pulteney,
        by Spence on Popes authority.
        Foxon D330.
1850.c.10(60)
                                                        t005531

POPE, Alexander, the Poet
(Discovery: or, the squire turnd ferret). The squire
turnd ferret. An excellent new ballad. To the tune of
Hey boys! up go we; Chevy Chase, or what you please. -
Westminster: printed by A. Campbell, for T. Warner: sold
by the booksellers of London and Westminster, 1727. 1
sheet ; 1/2⁰
Printed in two columns. Ascribed to Alexander Pope, in
collaboration with William Pulteney, by Spence on Popes
authority.
Not in Foxon.
C.117.g.1(14)

t005532

POPE, Alexander, the Poet
Duke upon duke, an excellent new play-house ballad. Set
to musick by Mr. Holdecombe.. - (London): (printed for
A. Moor, and sold by the booksellers), 1720. (2), 4p. ;
2⁰
With typeset music at head of p. 1. The order of
editions has not been determined (Foxon). A good part
of this ballad is ascribed to Pope by Spence on Popes
authority. A MS. note by Maurice Johnson on the BL copy
of the 1723 edition attributes the work to James Craggs,
and revision and correction to Thomas Tickell.
Foxon D502.
1876.f.1(94) : Imperfect; wanting the titlepage.

t005533

POPE, Alexander, the Poet
Duke upon duke. An excellent new play-house ballad. Set
to musick by Mr. Holdecombe. - (London): (printed by F.
Clifton), (1720). (2)p. ; 1/2⁰
Crude woodcut music at head. Printed in two columns.
Imprint information from Foxon. A good part of this
ballad is ascribed to Pope by Spence on Popes
authority.
Foxon D504.
C.116.i.4(52) : Mutilated.

t005534

POPE, Alexander, the Poet
(Duke upon duke). An excellent old ballad, called Pride
will have a fall, as set forth in the true and
delectable history of the deadly strife between the
Dukes of Guise and Lancastere .... - (London): printed
for J. Blare on London-Bridge, (1720?). 1 sheet ; 1/2⁰

The imprint is false. A reprint of Duke upon duke, a
good part of which is ascribed to Pope by Spence on
Popes authority. Printed in four columns.
Foxon D505.
1871.f.3(25) : Date in MS.: 14 Aug. 1720.

t005535

POPE, Alexander, the Poet
        Duke upon duke, an excellent new play-house ballad. Set
        to musick by Mr. Holdecombe.. - London: printed for A.
        Moor, and sold by the booksellers, 1723. (2), 4p. ; 2º.
        A new edition of Foxon D502. Typeset music at head of
        p. 1. A good part of this ballad is ascribed to Pope by
        Spence on Popes authority.
        Foxon D507.
C.175.dd.12(3) : Maurice Johnsons copy, with a note in his hand
attributing the work to James Craggs, and revision and
correction to Thomas Tickell.
                                                    t005536

POPE, Alexander, the Poet
        The Dunciad. An heroic poem. In three books.. - London:
        Dublin, printed, London re-printed for A. Dodd, 1728.
        (2), viii, (2), 51, (1)p. : ill. ; 12º.
        Anonymous. By Alexander Pope. There was no earlier
        Dublin edition.
        Foxon P764; Griffith 198.
C.59.ff.13(4) : Uncut.
Ashley 1304 : Uncut.
                                                    t005537

POPE, Alexander, the Poet
        The Dunciad. An heroic poem. In three books.. - London:
        Dublin, printed, London re-printed for A. Dodd, 1728.
        (2), viii, (2), 51, (1)p. : ill. ; 8º.
        Anonymous. By Alexander Pope. A reimpression with
        changed format.
        Foxon P765; Griffith 199.
C.59.ff.12(1)
Ashley 1303
                                                    t005538

POPE, Alexander, the Poet
        The Dunciad. An heroic poem. In three books.. - The
        second edition. - London: Dublin printed; London
        re-printed for A. Dodd, 1728. (2), viii, (2), 51, (1)p.
        : ill. ; 12º.
        Anonymous. By Alexander Pope. A reimpression of the
        first edition, with sheet B and most of C reset.
        Foxon P766; Griffith 201,2.
C.125.dd.25(1) : Imperfect; wanting sig. A6.
Ashley 1306 : Uncut.
Ashley 1305 : A variant, with Dublin mis-spelt Dudlin in the
imprint.
                                                    t005539

POPE, Alexander, the Poet
The Dunciad. An heroic poem. In three books.. - The
third edition. - London: Dublin, printed; London,
reprinted for A. Dodd, 1728. (2), viii, (2), 51, (1)p. :
ill. .; 12º
Anonymous. By Alexander Pope. Press-figures iv-3, 2-2,
24-3, 26-4. Apparently a reimpression with sheets E, F
and part of D reset (Foxon).
Foxon P767; Griffith 203.
Ashley 1307 : A1 supplied (Foxon).

t005540

POPE, Alexander, the Poet
The Dunciad. An heroic poem. In three books.. - The
third edition. - London: Dublin, printed; London,
reprinted for A. Dodd, 1728. (2), viii, (2), 51, (1)p. :
ill. ; 12º
Anonymous. By Alexander Pope. Press figures iv-2, 2-4,
26-4, 48-4. Apparently a reimpression with corrections
(Foxon).
Foxon P768; Griffith 204.
Ashley 1308

t005541

POPE, Alexander, the Poet
The Dunciad. An heroic poem. In three books.. -
London(i.e. Edinburgh?): Dublin, printed, London
reprinted for A. Dodd, 1728. viii, 51, (1)p., plate ; 12º
Anonymous. By Alexander Pope. A piracy of the first
edition known as the Gold chains edition from a misprint
in line 76 (Foxon).
Foxon P769; Griffith 200.
Ashley 1310

t005542

POPE, Alexander, the Poet
The Dunciad. An heroic poem. In three books. Written by
Mr. Pope.. - Dublin: London: printed, and Dublin
re-printed by and for G. Faulkner, J. Hoey, J. Leathley,
E. Hamilton, P. Crampton, and T. Benson, 1728. 47, (1)p.
; 8º
Foxon P770; Griffith 206.
12274.e.1(1)
Ashley 1309

t005543

POPE, Alexander, the Poet
        The Dunciad, variorum. With the prolegomena of
        Scriblerus.. - London: printed (by John Wright) for A.
        Dod, 1729. (2), 16, (2), 6, 9-29, (3), 124p. ; 4⁰.
        Anonymous. By Alexander Pope. The titlepage is
        engraved; sig. K1,2 are cancels. Printers name from
        Foxon.
        Foxon P771; Griffith 211.
    11633.g.56

                                                    t005544

POPE, Alexander, the Poet
        The Dunciad, variorum. With the prolegomena of
        Scriblerus.. - London: printed for A. Dod, 1729. (2),
        16, (2), 6, 9-29, (3), cxxiv, (2)p. ; 4⁰.
        Anonymous. By Alexander Pope. The titlepage is
        engraved. A reissue of the preceding, with an added
        leaf, headed Addenda. M. Scriblerus lectori, at end.
        Foxon P773; Griffith 212.
    642.k.2(1) : The added leaf is bound between pp. 84-85.
    Ashley 3773

                                                    t005545

POPE, Alexander, the Poet
        The Dunciad, variorum. With the prolegomena of
        Scriblerus.. - London: printed for A. Dob, 1729. (2),
        xxxvii, (3), 80, xxx, (6)p. ; 8⁰.
        Anonymous. By Alexander Pope. The titlepage is
        engraved. A piracy, published by James Watson, printer,
        Thomas Astley, John Clarke, and John Stagg,
        booksellers.
        Foxon P774; Griffith 216.
    11659.bb.48(2) : Imperfect; wanting the titlepage.

                                                    t005546

POPE, Alexander, the Poet
        The Dunciad, variorum. With the prolegomena of
        Scriblerus.. - London: printed for A. Dob, 1729. (2),
        xxxvii, (3), 80, xxx, (8)p. ; 8⁰.
        Anonymous. By Alexander Pope. A reissue of the Watson
        piracy (Foxon P774), with a leaf of Addenda, sig. f1,
        inserted. The titlepage is engraved.
        Foxon P775; Griffith 217.
    12274.i.11 : The leaf of addenda is bound after p. 80.
    11632.df.41 : Imperfect; wanting the last two leaves of the
    index.
    11657.g.42 : Imperfect; wanting the titlepage.

                                                    t005547

POPE, Alexander, the Poet
        The Dunciad. With notes variorum, and the prolegomena of
        Scriblerus.. - London: printed for Lawton Gilliver,
        1729. 24, (2), 19-ccxxxii, (2)p. : ill. ; 8°.
        Anonymous. By Alexander Pope. With the owl
        frontispiece. Sig. Bb3 is a cancel.
        Foxon P779; Griffith 218.
12274.i.9 : With the half-title printed on the recto of the
frontispiece.
12274.i.8 : With the half-title printed on the recto of the
frontispiece. With a 10-page catalogue of Gillivers books,
dated 1728, bound at end. Sig. Bb3 is not a cancel in this
copy.
C.131.d.25 : Not intended for publication? The titlepage,
printed in red and black and bearing the imprint 'Printed for
A. Dod', has been slit for cancellation. With the ass
frontispiece, no cancel Bb3 or errata leaf (Foxon P776).
                                                    t005548

POPE, Alexander, the Poet
        The Dunciad. With notes variorum, and the prolegomena of
        Scriblerus.. - London: printed for Lawton Gilliver,
        1729. 24, (2), 19-ccxxxii, (2)p. ; 8°.
        Anonymous. By Alexander Pope. A different issue from
        the preceding, having both the owl and the ass
        frontispieces.
        Foxon P780; Griffith 219.
G.19019 : The owl frontispiece is bound between pp. 50-51; the
errata leaf is bound between pp.190-191. The recto of the ass
frontispiece is blank.
Ashley 1311 : The owl frontispiece is bound between pp.86-87.
The recto of the ass frontispiece is blank.
                                                    t005549

POPE, Alexander, the Poet
        The Dunciad. With notes variorum, and the prolegomena of
        Scriblerus.. - The second edition, with some additional
        notes. - London: printed for Lawton Gilliver, 1729. 24,
        (2), 19-232, 6, (4)p. : ill. ; 8°.
        Anonymous. By Alexander Pope. Sig. D3, E2 and P3 are
        cancels. Griffith 222-227, treating copies with some
        uncancelled leaves and without 2E1 as variants (Foxon).
        Titlepage printed in red and black.
        Foxon P781; Griffith 224-7.
991.h.26 : Without the final leaf of additional errata.
Ashley 1312
                                                    t005550

POPE, Alexander, the Poet
      The Dunciad, variorum. With the prolegomena of
      Scriblerus.. - Dublin: London: printed and reprinted,
      for the booksellers in Dublin, 1729. (4), 192,
      185-105(i.e. 205), (1)p. ; 12⁰
      Anonymous. By Alexander Pope. Another issue of Griffith
      221, with a letterpress titlepage in addition to the
      engraved one. P. 205 is misnumbered 105.
      Foxon P784; Griffith 222.
12274.f.3
11630.b.43
1607/4324(1) : Imperfect; wanting the engraved titlepage.
                                                   t005551

POPE, Alexander, the Poet
      The Dunciad. With notes variorum, and the prolegomena of
      Scriblerus. Written in the year, 1727.. - London:
      printed for Lawton Gilliver, (1735). 263, (1)p., plate ;
      8⁰
      Anonymous. By Alexander Pope. P. 23 is misnumbered 22.
      Foxon P785; Griffith 392,4.
12274.e.11 : With the owl frontispiece.
11633.aa.36 : With the owl frontispiece.
                                                 t005552

POPE, Alexander, the Poet
      The Dunciad. An heroic poem. To Dr. Jonathan Swift. With
      the prolegomena of Scriblerus, and notes variorum.. -
      London: printed for Lawton Gilliver, 1736(1735). 263,
      (1)p., plate ; 8⁰
      Anonymous. By Alexander Pope. A reissue of the Gilliver
      (1735) edition; the titlepage, printed in red and black,
      and sig. C7 are cancels. Publication date from
      Griffith.
      Foxon P786; Griffith 405.
12274.f.5
                                                 t005553

POPE, Alexander, the Poet
      (Dunciad). The new Dunciad: as it was found in the year
      1741. With the illustrations of Scriblerus, and notes
      variorum.. - London: printed for T. Cooper, 1742. (8),
      39, (1)p. ; 4⁰
      Anonymous. By Alexander Pope. With a half-title.
      Foxon P787; Griffith 546,7.
11642.h.43(3)
11630.e.3(11)
Ashley 4934
                                                 t005554

POPE, Alexander, the Poet
   (Dunciad). The new Dunciad: as it was found in the year
   MDCCXLI. With the illustraticns of Scriblerus, and notes
   variorum.. - London: printed for T. Cooper, 1742. (8),
   44p. ; 4º.
   Anonymous. By Alexander Pope. With a half-title.
   Foxon P789; Griffith 549.
11630.f.17
11632.g.61(1) : Imperfect; wanting the half-title.

                                             t005555

POPE, Alexander, the Poet
   (Dunciad). The new Dunciad: as it was found in the year
   1741. With the illustraticns of Scriblerus. And notes
   variorum,. - London: printed for J. H. Hubbard, 1742.
   36p. ; 8º.
   Anonymous. By Alexander Pope. In most copies the date
   (in the imprint) appears as MDCCXLIII, with the second I
   very faint; it might possibly be a raised space
   (Foxon).
   Foxon P791; Griffith 548.
T.1057(1)

                                             t005556

PCPE, Alexander, the Poet
   (Dunciad). The new Dunciad: as it was found in the year
   1741. With the illustraticns of Scriblerus, and notes
   variorum.. - London(i.e. Edinburgh): printed for T.
   Cooper, 1742. (4), 36p. ; 8º.
   Anonymous. By Alexander Pope. A piracy; the imprint is
   false.
   Foxon P793; Griffith 551.
1633.e.11

                                             t005557

POPE, Alexander, the Poet
   (Dunciad). The new Dunciad: as it was found in the year
   1741. With the illustraticns of Scriblerus, and notes
   variorum.. - Dublin: re-printed by and for George
   Faulkner, 1742. 51, (1)p. ; 8º.
   Anonymous. By Alexander Pope. A reprint of the first
   quarto edition.
   Foxon P794; Griffith 552.
11633.cc.2(7)

                                             t005558

POPE, Alexander the Poet
    (Dunciad). The new Dunciad: as it was found in the year
    1741. With the illustrations of Scriblerus, and notes
    variorum.. - Dublin: printed by A. Reilly; for G. Ewing,
    1742. 58p. ; 12⁰.
    Anonymous. By Alexander Pope. Reissued as part of
    Ewings 1744 edition of The Dunciad in four books.
    Foxon P795; Griffith 553.
1607/4324(2)
11774.aaa.10(2)

                                               t005559

POPE, Alexander, the Poet
    The Dunciad, in four books. Printed according to the
    complete copy found in the year 1742. With the
    prolegomena of Scriblerus, and notes variorum. To which
    are added, several notes now first publishd, ... -
    London: printed for M. Cooper, 1743. vi, (4), ix-x, 235,
    (13)p. ; 4⁰.
    Anonymous. By Alexander Pope. With a half-title;
    binding of preliminaries varies. Sig. X3 is a cancel.
    Foxon P796,7; Griffith 578.
641.l.17(1) : On fine paper; sig. X3 is not cancelled.
Ashley 3774(2)

                                               t005560

POPE, Alexander, the Poet
    The Dunciad, as it is now changed by Mr. Pope. In four
    books.. - Dublin: printed for Philip Bowes,
    MDCCXLIII(1744). (2), 49, (1)p. ; 12⁰.
    The date in the imprint is followed by what is perhaps a
    damaged piece of type, perhaps a V. Without the
    prolegomena and notes variorum.
    Foxon P798; not in Griffth.
1607/5245

                                               t005561

POPE, Alexander, the Poet
    The Dunciad, in four books. Printed according to the
    complete copy found in the year 1742. With the
    prolegomena of Scriblerus, and notes variorum. To which
    are added, several notes now first publishd, ... -
    Dublin: London printed, and Dublin re-printed for G. and
    A. Ewing, 1744. 196, (3), 8-97, (15)p. ; 12⁰.
    Anonymous. By Alexander Pope. The text of Book 4 is
    reissued from Reillys edition of The new Dunciad, 1742.
    Foxon P799; Griffith 605a.
 1488.f.41

                                               t005562

POPE, Alexander, the Poet
    The Dunciad, complete in four books, according to Mr.
    Popes last improvements. With several additions now
    first printed, ... Published by Mr. Warburton.. -
    London: printed for J. and P. Knapton, 1749. (7),
    xxii-xxxviii, 163, (3), 78, (1), lxviii-lxxxvii, (1)p.,
    plate ; 8⁰
    Anonymous. By Alexander Pope. Sheets a, b, d, e and B-L
    are reissued from the octavo edition of Popes Works
    1743; B1, 6, 8, D4-6, E2, 5, B4-5 are cancels as in that
    edition (Foxon). Titlepage in red and black.
    Foxon P800; Griffith 639.
12274.f.1
                                                    t005563

POPE, Alexander, the Poet
    The Dunciad. By Alexander Pope. From the text of Dr.
    Warburton. With advertisements, prefaces, ... - London:
    printed for J. Bell, 1788. (3), 6-214, (2)p. ; 12⁰
11658.e.50 : Imperfect; wanting the half-title?.
                                                    t005564

POPE, Alexander, the Poet
    (Elegy to the memory of an unfortunate lady. Latin).
    Elegeia Popi in memoriam infelicis nymphae, in latinum
    versum reddita.. - Londini: impensis M. Fletcher, in
    Oxon, & M. Cooper, 1744. (2), 5, (1)p. ; 2⁰
    Foxon E34; Griffith, p. 477.
11630.g.32
                                                    t005565

POPE, Alexander, the Poet
    Eloisa to Abelard. Written by Mr. Pope.. - The second
    edition. - London: printed for Bernard Lintot,
    1720(1719). 63, (1)p. : ill. ; 8⁰
    Includes also Popes Verses to the memory of an
    unfortunate lady, with poems by other authors.
    Foxon P801; Griffith 109.
1465.f.26
991.h.25(3)
C.59.ff.13(3)
                                                    t005566

POPE, Alexander, the Poet
    Eloisa to Abelard. By Alexander Pope.. - Manchester:
    printed by G. Nicholson and Co. Sold by T. Knott; and
    Champante & Whitrow, London, 1794. 12p. ; 24⁰
    In: The literary miscellany; or, elegant selections of
    the most admired fugitive pieces, Manchester, 1794.
1493.t.44
                                                    t010220

POPE, Alexander, the Poet
An epistle from Mr. Pope, to Dr. Arbuthnot.. - London:
printed by J. Wright for Lawton Gilliver, 1734(1735).
(4), 30(i.e. 20)p. ; 2⁰
The last page is misnumbered 30.
Foxon P802; Griffith 352.
644.m.14(5)
1484.m.7(11)
C.131.h.1(4*)
162.n.24
Ashley 5221

t005567

POPE, Alexander, the Poet
An epistle from Mr. Pope to Dr. Arbuthnot.. -
London(i.e. Edinburgh): printed by J. Wright for Lawton
Gilliver, 1734(1735). 27, (1)p. ; 8⁰
The imprint is false; Printed by Ruddiman on the
evidence of the ornaments (Foxon). Publication date
from Foxon.
Foxon P803; Griffith 353.
11630.bbb.42(4)
993.e.51(4)

t005568

POPE, Alexander, the Poet
An epistle from Mr. Pope, to Dr. Arbuthnot.. - Dublin:
London: printed. And, Dublin re-printed by George
Faulkner, 1735. (4), 20p. ; 8⁰
Foxon P804; Griffith 354.
11630.aaa.45(10)

t005569

POPE, Alexander, the Poet
An essay on criticism.. - London: printed for W. Lewis;
and sold by W. Taylor, T. Osborn, and J. Graves, 1711.
(2), 43, (3)p. ; 4⁰
Anonymous. By Alexander Pope. With a half-title and a
final leaf of advertisements.
Foxon P806; Griffith 2.
Cup.402.f.4 : Uncut; half-title mutilated.
161.m.24 : Imperfect; wanting the advertisement leaf. Luttrells
MS. date on titlepage: 17 May.
Ashley 3765 : Imperfect; wanting the half-title and
advertisement leaf.
C.57.i.49 : Imperfect; wanting the half-title and advertisement
leaf.

t005570

POPE, Alexander, the Poet
An essay on criticism. - Dublin: printed by A. Rhames,
for George Grierson, (1711?). 36p. ; 12º
Anonymous. By Alexander Pope. Pp. 33-36 contain John
Philips The splendid shilling.
Foxon P809; Griffith Add.27a.
1488.de.46(5) : Imperfect; wanting pp. 29-32.

t005571

POPE, Alexander, the Poet
An essay on criticism. Written by Mr. Pope.. - The
second edition. - London: printed for W. Lewis,
1713(1712). (4), 36p. ; 8º
With a half-title. Publication date from Foxon.
Foxon P810; Griffith 8.
11631.bbb.45

t005572

POPE, Alexander, the Poet
An essay on criticism. Written by Mr. Pope.. - The third
edition. - London: printed for W. Lewis, 1713. 35, (1)p.
; 12º
With a half-title. Titlepage in red and black.
Foxon P811; Griffith 26.
1346.d.31

t005573

POPE, Alexander, the Poet
An essay on criticism. Written by Mr. Pope.. - The
fourth edition. - London: printed for W. Lewis, 1713.
35, (1)p. ; 12º
Apparently a press-variant title of the preceding;
certainly from the same setting of type (Foxon). With a
half-title. Titlepage in red and black.
Foxon P812; Griffith 27.
11886.d.9(1)

t005574

POPE, Alexander, the Poet
An essay on criticism. Written by Mr. Pope.. - The fifth
edition. - London: printed for Bernard Lintot, 1716. 35,
(1)p. ; 12º
With a half-title.
Foxon P813; Griffith 71.
1346.d.33(3)

t005575

POPE, Alexander, the Poet
An essay on criticism. Written by Mr. Pope.. - The fifth
edition. - London(i.e. The Hague): printed for T.
Johnson, 1716. 68p. ; 8°.
Contains also: The temple of fame: a vision, with a
separate titlepage dated: 1716; Windsor-Forest; and Ode
for musick on St. Cecilias Day. In: The works of Mr.
Alexander Pope, printed by Johnson for B.L., 1718.
Griffith 63.
12274.e.12

t005576

PCPE, Alexander, the Poet
An essay on criticism. Written in the year 1709.. -
Dublin: London, printed: Dublin, re-printed, for George
Grierson, 1717. 34p. ; 8°.
Anonymous. By Alexander Pope. Also issued in Griersons
reprint of Popes Works, 1718 (Foxon).
Foxon P815; cf. Griffith 102.
832.b.15(2)

t005577

POPE, Alexander, the Poet
An essay on criticism. Written by Mr. Pope.. - The sixth
edition, corrected. - London: printed for Bernard
Lintot, 1719. 48p. : ill. ; 8°.
Foxon P816; Griffith 107.
11634.b.3

t005579

PCPE, Alexander, the Poet
An essay on criticism. Written by Mr. Pope.. - The
seventh edition, corrected. - London: printed for
Bernard Lintot, 1722(1721). 48p. : ill. ; 8°.
Publication date from Foxon.
Foxon P817; Griffith 129.
991.h.25(1)

t005578

POPE, Alexander, the Poet
An essay on criticism. Written in the year MDCCIX. With
the commentary and notes of W. Warburton, A. M.. -
(London): (printed for M. Cooper), (1744). (4), 60p. ; 4°.

Anonymous. By Alexander Pope. Title taken from
half-title. Imprint details from Foxon. Issued with An
essay on man 1743(1744).
Foxon P819; Griffith 590.
643.k.4(1)
C.59.e.1(3)
Ashley 3774(1*)
642.k.2(3)

t005580

POPE, Alexander, the Poet
An essay on criticism. By Alexander Pope, Esq; With
notes by Mr. Warburton.. - London: printed for William
Owen, 1751. (2), 89, (1)p. ; 8⁰
Horizontal chain lines.
Griffith 654.
11631.b.54(2) : Half-title bound following the titlepage.
t005581

POPE, Alexander, the Poet
An essay on criticism. By Alexander Pope, Esq. Written
in the year MDCCIX.. - Glasgow: printed by R. Urie,
1754. 60, (2)p. ; 8⁰
With a final leaf of advertisements.
1480.r.25
t005582

POPE, Alexander, the Poet
(Essay on criticism. French and English). Essais sur la
critique et sur l'homme par M. Pope. Ouvrage traduit de
langlois en francois. - Nouvelle edition. - Londres:
chez Guillaume Darres, et Claude Du Bosc, (imprime chez
G. Smith), 1741. 193, (7)p. ; 4⁰
French prose translations, by Etienne de Silhouette,
with the original English texts. With a postscript.
Printers name from colophon.
Griffith 539.
83.l.22 : Large paper copy (Griffith).
t005583

POPE, Alexander, the Poet
(Essay on criticism. German and English). Versuch uber
die Critik aus dem Englischen des Herrn Pope. Nebst
einem Versuche einer Critik uber die deutschen Dichter,
... von M. Gottfried Ephraim Muller.. - Dressden: bey
George Conrad Walther, 1745. (12), 164p. ; 8⁰
Parallel English text and German verse translation.
1160.f.1(2)
t005584

POPE, Alexander, the Poet
(Essay on criticism. Latin). Celeberrimi Popii Tentamen
de modis criticis scripta dijudicandi. Latine tentatum.
Jac. Killpatrick.. - Londini: typis Joh. Purser;
prostant apud R. Dodsley; & Jac. Robinson, (1745). (2),
x, (2), 41, (1)p. ; 8⁰
Preface dated at end: Cal: Julii, A. C. 1745.
Translated by James Kirkpatrick (formerly Killpatrick).
A prospectus for this work is entered below.
Foxon K88; Griffith pp. 485-6.
11633.df.3
t005585

POPE, Alexander, the Poet
   (Essay on criticism. Latin). Tentamen de re critica.
   Anglice prius celeberrimo Alexandro Pope, latine nunc
   emittente Ushero Gahagan. .... - Londini: prostant apud
   M. Cooper; apud J. Hinton, 1747. (4), xv, (1), 88p. ; 8⁰.
   Listed in the Gentlemans Magazine cf January 1749 (p.
   48) and possibly published for the first time in that
   year. Pp. 57-88 contain A letter to the author from a
   friend, with notes on the foregoing translation, signed:
   J. C.
   Foxon G6; Griffith p. 511.
11633.df.2
                                                        t005586

PCPE, Alexander, the Poet
   (Essay on criticism. Prospectus. Latin). Mr. Popes Essay
   on criticism being translated into Latin verse, ... This
   translation, with a Latin dedication prefixd, will be
   printed in a well-sizd letter, on fine paper, in large
   8vo. at 1s. 6d. Which easy subscription will be taken,
   at Mr. Dodsleys ... Georges Coffee-house, ...; and at
   Mr. Pursers, ... - (London?), (1745?). 1 sheet ; 1/4⁰.
   A prospectus for James Kirkpatricks (formerly
   Killpatrick) translation of Alexander Popes Essay on
   criticism, published in 1745. With specimens. Probably
   printed by John Purser.
833.e.16(4) : Mounted.
                                                        t005587

POPE, Alexander, the Poet
   (Essay on criticism. Latin and English). Alexandri Pope
   De arte critica liber. Essay on criticism. Poema
   anglicum carmine latino reddere tentavit Jo. Jac.
   Collenbusch, ... - Dessaviae: in Taberna Libraria
   Eruditorum, 1782. xvi, 79, (1), xvii-xxivp. ; 8⁰.
   Pp. xvii-xxiv contain corrections and emendations.
11631.bbb.49
                                                        t005588

POPE, Alexander, the Poet
   (Essay on man. Epistle 1). An essay on man. Addressd to
   a friend. Part I.. - London: printed for J. Wilford,
   (1733). 19, (1)p. ; 2⁰.
   Anonymous. By Alexander Pope.
   Foxon P822; Griffith 294.
C.59.h.9(2)
Ashley 5212
                                                        t005589

POPE, Alexander, the Poet
(Essay on man. Epistle 1). An essay on man. Addressd to
a friend. Part I.. - London: printed for J. Wilford,
(1733). 20p. ; 2⁰.
Anonymous. By Alexander Pope. Pp.1-6 ... are
reimpressed; the remainder is from standing type revised
and rearranged (Foxon).
Foxon P823,4; Griffith 304.
Ashley 5211 : A made-up copy; all leaves apart from the title
apparently removed from copy at 644.m.14(2).
644.m.14(2) : Imperfect; wanting all except the titlepage.
Ashley 4935 : On fine paper.

t005590

POPE, Alexander, the Poet
(Essay on man. Epistle 1). An essay on man. In epistles
to a friend. The second edition. Part I.. - London:
printed for J. Wilford, 1733. 21, (1)p. ; 4⁰.
Anonymous. By Alexander Pope. With a half-title. A
reimpression of the preceding, with pp. 7-8 reset.
Foxon P825,6; Griffith 305.
1346.i.25 : Imperfect; wanting the half-title.
11630.e.5(16) : Imperfect; wanting the titlepage and the
half-title.
Ashley 5213 : On fine paper.

t005591

POPE, Alexander, the Poet
(Essay on man. Epistle 1). An essay on man. In epistles
to a friend. Epistle I. Corrected by the author.. -
London: printed for J. Wilford, (1733). (2), 17, (1)p. ;
2⁰.
Anonymous. By Alexander Pope. Pp. 8, 12 are misnumbered
4, 11.
Foxon P827; Griffith 307.
12273.m.1(3)
Ashley 5214

t005592

POPE, Alexander, the Poet
(Essay on man. Epistle 1). An essay on man. Addressd to
a friend. Part I.. - Dublin: printed by S. Powell, for
George Risk, George Ewing, and William Smith, 1733. 19,
(1)p. ; 8⁰.
Anonymous. By Alexander Pope.
Foxon P830; Griffith 297.
11630.aaa.45(6)

t005593

POPE, Alexander, the Poet
        (Essay on man. Epistle 1). An essay on man. Addressd to
        a friend. Part I.. - The second edition. - Dublin:
        printed by S. Powell, for George Risk, George Ewing, and
        William Smith, 1734. 19, (1)p. ; 8⁰
        Anonymous. By Alexander Pope.
        Foxon P831; Griffith 349.
11631.aa.47(1)
                                                    t005594

POPE, Alexander, the Poet
        (Essay on man. Epistle 2). An essay on man. In epistles
        to a friend. Epistle II.. - London: printed for J.
        Wilford, (1733). (2), 18p. ; 2⁰
        Anonymous. By Alexander Pope. With a half-title,
        bearing rules. The lines are numbered (erroneously).
        Foxon P833; Griffith 300.
C.59.h.9(2)
12273.m.1(3) : Imperfect; wanting the half-title.
Ashley 4935
Ashley 5215
                                                    t005595

POPE, Alexander, the Poet
        (Essay on man. Epistle 2). An essay on man. In epistles
        to a friend. Epistle II.. - London: printed for J.
        Wilford, (1733). (2), 18p. ; 2⁰
        Anonymous. By Alexander Pope. Lines unnumbered except
        for 175 on p. 13; printers flowers instead of rules on
        half-title. Titlepage ornament: a pedestalled platter
        of fruit and flowers.
        Foxon P834; Griffith 311.
Ashley 5216
                                                    t005596

POPE, Alexander, the Poet
        (Essay on man. Epistle 2). An essay on man. In epistles
        to a friend. Epistle II.. - Dublin: London: printed.
        Dublin, re-printed, by and for George Faulkner, 1733.
        18, (2)p. ; 8⁰
        Anonymous. By Alexander Pope. With a final leaf of
        advertisements.
        Foxon 837; Griffith 302.
11630.aaa.45(7) : A variant; p. 18 is misnumbered 15.
                                                    t005597

POPE, Alexander, the Poet
        (Essay on man. Epistle 2). An essay on man. In epistles
        to a friend. Epistle II.. - The second edition. -
        Dublin: printed by S. Powell, for George Risk, George
        Ewing and William Smith, 1734. 16p. ; 8⁰
        Anonymous. By Alexander Pope.
        Foxon P838; Griffith 350.
11631.aa.47(1)
                                                    t005598

POPE, Alexander, the Poet
        (Essay on man. Epistle 2). An essay on man. In epistles
        to a friend. Epistle II.. - London: printed for J.
        Wilford, (1734). (2), 18p. ; 2º
        Anonymous. By Alexander Pope. Probably printed in 1734
        or 1735. Lines unnumbered; rules on half-title.
        Titlepage ornament: a bear holding crossed clubs.
        Foxon P839; Griffith 313.
Ashley 5217

                                                        t005599

POPE, Alexander, the Poet
        (Essay on man. Epistle 3). An essay on man. Addressd to
        a friend. In epistles to a friend. Epistle III.. -
        London: printed for J. Wilford, (1733). 20p. ; 2º
        Anonymous. By Alexander Pope. With a half-title.
        2-line advertisement on p. 20; lines misnumbered as
        323.
        Foxon P840; Griffith 308.
644.m.14(2)
12273.m.1(3)
C.59.h.9(2)
Ashley 4935
Ashley 5218 : Imperfect; wanting the half-title.

                                                        t005600

POPE, Alexander, the Poet
        (Essay on man. Epistle 3). An essay on man. In epistles
        to a friend. Epistle III.. - Dublin: printed by S.
        Powell, for George Risk, George Ewing, and William
        Smith, 1733. 20p. ; 8º
        Anonymous. By Alexander Pope. With a half-title.
        Foxon P843; Griffith 310.
11630.aaa.45(3)
11631.aa.47(1*)

                                                        t005602

POPE, Alexander, the Poet
        (Essay on man. Epistle 3). An essay on man. In epistles
        to a friend. Epistle III.. - London: printed for J.
        Wilford, (1734). 20p. ; 2º
        Anonymous. By Alexander Pope. Probably printed in 1734
        or 1735. With a half-title. One line advertisement on
        p. 20; penultimate line correctly numbered 315.
        Titlepage ornament: a bird with outspread wings.
        Foxon P844; Griffith 315.
Ashley 5219

                                                        t005601

POPE, Alexander, the Poet
        (Essay on man. Epistle 3. Latin and English). . –
        Oxonii: e Typographeo Clarendoniano, impensis Jacobi
        Fletcher. Prostant apud J. & J. Rivington, M. Cooper, &
        W. Owen, London, 1752. (8), 19, (1)p. ; 4º.
        The third epistle only. Verse translation, with the
        English text printed as footnotes.
11658.h.23

                                                        t005603

POPE, Alexander, the Poet
        (Essay on man. Epistle 4). An essay on man. In epistles
        to a friend. Epistle IV.. – London: printed for J.
        Wilford, (1734). (4), 18, (2)p. ; 2º.
        Anonymous. By Alexander Pope. With a final leaf of
        advertisements. P. 17 is misnumbered 71.
        Foxon P845; Griffith 331.
12273.m.1(3)
644.m.14(2)
C.59.h.9(2)
Ashley 4935
Ashley 5220

                                                        t005604

POPE, Alexander, the Poet
        (Essay on man. Epistle 4). An essay on man. In epistles
        to a friend. Epistle IV.. – Dublin: London: printed. And
        re-printed in Dublin, by George Faulkner, 1734. 22,
        (2)p. ; 8º.
        Anonymous. By Alexander Pope. With a final leaf of
        advertisements.
        Foxon P84; Griffith 334.
11631.aa.47(1**)
11631.a.63(1)

                                                        t005605

POPE, Alexander, the Poet
        (Essay on man. Epistle 4). An essay on man. In epistles
        to a friend. Epistle IV.. – The second edition. –
        Dublin: printed by S. Powell, for George Risk, George
        Ewing, and William Smith, 1734. 23, (1)p. ; 8º.
        Anonymous. By Alexander Pope.
        Foxon P848; Griffith 351.
11630.aaa.45(9)

                                                        t005606

POPE, Alexander, the Poet
      An essay on man, being the first book of ethic epistles.
      To Henry St. John, L. Bolingbroke.. - London: printed by
      John Wright, for Lawton Gilliver, 1734. (8), 74p. ; 4º.
      Anonymous. By Alexander Pope. Titlepage in red and
      black. With a half-title. P. 54 is misnumbered 45;
      sig. I2 is a cancel.
      Foxon P852; Griffith 336.
1486.d.3
                                                t005607

POPE, Alexander, the Poet
      An essay on man, being the first book of ethic epistles.
      To Henry St. John, Lord Bolingbroke.. - Dublin: London,
      printed: and, re-printed in Dublin, by George Faulkner,
      1734. 64p. ; 8º.
      Anonymous. By Alexander Pope..
      Foxon P854; Griffith Add.351b.
1607/3627 : Sig. B1 and B2, pp. (9-12), misbound between pp. 16
and 17.
                                              t005608

POPE, Alexander, the Poet
      An essay on man. Addressd to a friend. .... -
      London(i.e. Edinburgh): printed for J. Wilford,
      1733(1734). 80p. ; 8º.
      Anonymous. By Alexander Pope. The imprint is false;
      printed by Ruddiman on the evidence of the ornaments.
      Each epistle has a separate titlepage, the first three
      being dated 1733; pagination and register are
      continuous. Publication date inferred from that of
      Epistle 4. Each epistle may have been issued
      separately, and is so treated by Foxon.
      Foxon P828, 835, 841, 846; Griffith 296, 301, 309, 333.
011641.ee.130
                                              t005609

POPE, Alexander, the Poet
      An essay on man. In four epistles to a friend. Corrected
      by the author.. - The seventh edition. - London: printed
      for J. Witford(sic), 1736. 38p. ; 12º.
      Anonymous. By Alexander Pope. A pirated edition. No
      watermark.
      Foxon P858; Griffith 420.
11805.bb.40(1)
                                            t005610

POPE, Alexander, the Poet
        An essay on man. In four epistles to a friend. Corrected
        by the author.. - The seventh edition. - London: printed
        for J. Witford(sic), 1736. 48p., plate ; 12⁰
        Anonymous. By Alexander Pope. A pirated edition
        possibly printed later than 1736, and in Dublin.
        Includes: Verses on the death of Dr. Swift.
        Foxon P859; not in Griffith; Teerink 775.
1607/4620

                                                              t005611

POPE, Alexander, the Poet
        An essay on man: being the first book of ethic epistles
        to H. St. John L. Bolingbroke. With the commentary and
        notes of W. Warburton, A.M.. - London: printed by W.
        Bowyer for M. Cooper, 1743(1744). (6), 111, (1)p. ; 4⁰
        Anonymous. By Alexander Pope. With a half-title.
        Publication date from Griffith.
        Foxon P865; Griffith 589.
Ashley 3774(1)
642.k.2(2) : Imperfect; wanting the half-title, titlepage and
the leaf of Design.

                                                              t005612

POPE, Alexander, the Poet
        An essay on man. By Alexander Pope Esq. Enlarged and
        improved by the author. With notes by William Warburton,
        M.A.. - London: printed for John and Paul Knapton, 1745.
        xxviii, 66, (2)p., plate ; 8⁰
        Titlepage in red and black. With a final leaf of
        advertisements. Price Eighteen pence on the titlepage.
        Includes: The universal prayer.
        Foxon P867.
1471.df.21

                                                              t005613

POPE, Alexander, the Poet
        An essay on man. By Alexander Pope Esq. Enlarged and
        improved by the author. With notes by William Warburton,
        M.A.. - London: printed for John and Paul Knapton, 1745.
        xxviii, 66, (2)p., plate ; 8⁰
        Titlepage in red and black. With a final leaf of
        advertisements. A different edition from the preceding;
        price Eighteen-pence on the titlepage. Includes: The
        universal prayer.
        Foxon P868; Griffith 607.
11632.aaa.39 : MS. notes by Michael Lort.

                                                              t005614

POPE, Alexander, the Poet
        An essay on man. By Alexander Pope, Esq; Enlarged and
        improved by the author. With notes by, William
        Warburton, A.M.. - Dublin: printed by George Faulkner,
        1745. 94, (2)p., plate ; 12º.
        With a final leaf of advertisements.   Includes: The
        universal prayer.
        Foxon P870; not in Griffith.
1607/4236

                                                        t005615

POPE, Alexander, the Poet
        An essay on man. By Alexander Pope Esq. Enlarged and
        improved by the author. With notes by Mr. Warburton.. -
        London: printed for John and Paul Knapton, 1746. xxviii,
        67, (1)p., plate ; 8º.
        Titlepage in red and black.   Includes: The universal
        prayer.
        Foxon P871; Griffith 620.
11632.aaa.40

                                                        t005616

POPE, Alexander, the Poet
        An essay on man. By Alexander Pope Esq. Enlarged and
        improved by the author. With notes by Mr. Warburton. -
        London: printed for John and Paul Knapton, 1748. xxviii,
        67, (1)p., plate ; 8º.
        Titlepage in red and black.   Includes: The universal
        prayer.
        Foxon P872; not in Griffith.
11634.b.13
1484.bbb.13 : MS. pagination supplied on p. 61 and,
incorrectly, on p. 62.

                                                        t005617

POPE, Alexander, the Poet
        A(n) essay on man. By Alexander Pope Esq. Enlarged and
        improved by the author. With the commentary and notes of
        Mr. Warburton.. - London: printed for J. and P. Knapton,
        1748. vi, 165, (1)p., plate ; 8º.
        Titlepage in red and black.   Part of the titlepage has
        failed to print.   Includes: The universal prayer.
        Foxon P873; Griffith 631.
11631.c.36 : A made-up copy.

                                                        t005618

POPE, Alexander, the Poet
        An essay on man. By Alexander Pope, Esq; Enlarged and
        improved by the author. With notes by William Warburton,
        A.M.. - Dublin: printed by George Faulkner, 1749. 96p.,
        plate ; 12º.
        Includes: The universal prayer.
        Foxon P874; Griffith 637.
1490.r.24

                                                        t005619

POPE, Alexander, the Poet
An essay on man. Being the first book of ethic epistles
to H. St. John L. Bolingbroke. With the commentary and
notes of Mr. Warburton.. - London: printed for J. and P.
Knapton, 1743(1749?). (2), 111, (1)p. ; 4⁰
Anonymous. By Alexander Pope. Another issue of the text
of the edition printed by W. Bowyer for M. Cooper,
1743(1744), with a cancel titlepage, but without the
half-title or the preliminary leaf containing the
Design.
Not in Foxon: cf. P865(note); not in Griffith.
C.59.e.1(1)

t005620

POPE, Alexander, the Poet
An essay on man. In four epistles to a friend. Corrected
by the author.. - A new edition. - London(i.e. Dublin?):
printed for, and sold by the booksellers, in town and
country, (1750?). 47, (1)p. : ill. ; 8⁰
Anonymous. By Alexander Pope. Possibly much later than
1750. The engraved frontispiece closely resembles that
in the 1771 Dublin edition. Includes: Verses on the
death of Dr. Swift by Swift.
Foxon P864; Griffith 412; Teerink 1607.
11631.bb.25 : MS. ownership note dated 1775.

t005621

POPE, Alexander, the Poet
An essay on man. By Alexander Pope Esq. Enlarged and
improved by the author. With the notes of Mr.
Warburton.. - London: printed for J. and P. Knapton,
1751. xvi, 104p., plate ; 8⁰
Titlepage in red and black. Includes: The universal
prayer.
Griffith 656.
11631.aaa.30

t005622

POPE, Alexander, the Poet
An essay on man. In four epistles. By Alexander Pope
Esq;. - Glasgow: printed and sold by R. & A. Foulis,
1751. (8), 51, (5)p. ; 8⁰
Pp. 41-48 misnumbered 49-56. Includes: The universal
prayer.
Griffith 657; Gaskell 210.
11632.aa.37

t005623

POPE, Alexander, the Poet
An essay on man. In four epistles. By Alexander Pope,
Esq;. - Glasgow: printed by William Duncan, Junior,
1751. (8), 51, (5)p. ; 8⁰
Includes: The universal prayer.
Not in Griffith.
1607/4228

t005624

POPE, Alexander, the Poet
An essay on man. By Alexander Pope Esq. Enlarged and
improved by the author. Together with his MS. additions
and variations, as in the last edition of his works.
With the notes of Mr. Warburton.. - London: printed for
J. and P. Knapton, 1753. xvi, 124p., plate ; 8⁰
Titlepage in red and black. Horizontal chain lines.
Includes: The universal prayer and The dying Christian
to his soul.
11631.b.54(1)

t005625

POPE, Alexander, the Poet
An essay on man. In four epistles. By Alexander Pope
Esq;. - Glasgow: printed by Robert and Andrew Foulis,
and sold by them and Andrew Stalker, 1754. 63, (1)p. ; 8⁰
Includes: The universal prayer.
Gaskell 275.
11630.aaa.44

t005626

POPE, Alexander, the Poet
An essay on man. By Alexander Pope, Esq. Enlarged and
improved by the author. With notes by William Warburton,
A.M.. - Dublin: printed by George Faulkner, 1755. 96p.,
plate ; 12⁰
P. 79 misnumbered 97. Includes: The universal prayer.
1484.ee.2(1)

t005627

POPE, Alexander, the Poet
An essay on man. In four epistles. By Alexander Pope
Esq.. - Glasgow: printed by William Duncan junior, 1755.
(2), 2, (4), 51, (5)p. ; 8⁰
Pp. 41-48 misnumbered 49-56, as in the 1751 Foulis Press
edition. Includes: The universal prayer.
11601.aa.60(1)

t005628

POPE, Alexander, the Poet
An essay on man. By Alexander Pope, Esq. Enlarged and
improved by the author. Together with his MS. additions
and variations, as in the last edition of his works.
With the notes of Mr. Warburton.. - London: printed for
J. and R. Tonson, and A. Millar, 1758. (2), xvi, 124p. :
ill. ; 8⁰
Titlepage in red and black. Horizontal chain lines.
Includes: The universal prayer and The dying Christian
to his soul.
11643.b.28

t005629

POPE, Alexander, the Poet
An essay on man. By Alexander Pope, Esq. Enlarged and
improved by the author. Together with his MS. additions
and variations as in the last edition of his works. With
the notes of William, Lord Bishop of Gloucester.. –
London: printed for A. Millar, and J. and R. Tonson,
1763. (2), xvi, 124p. : ill. ; 8⁰.
Titlepage in red and black. Includes: The universal
prayer and The dying Christian to his soul.
1486.aa.8

t005630

POPE, Alexander, the Poet
An essay on man. In four epistles. By Alexander Pope,
Esq;. – London: printed and sold by the booksellers in
town and country, (1766?). 60p. ; 12⁰
A pirated edition, possibly printed in Scotland, ca.
1766. Includes: The universal prayer.
Foxon P863; Griffith 612.
1608/5624(2)

t005631

POPE, Alexander, the Poet
An essay on man. By Alexander Pope, Esq. Enlarged and
improved by the author. Together with his MS. additions
and variations as in the last edition of his works. With
the notes of William, Lord Bishop of Gloucester.. –
London: printed for A. Millar, and J. and R. Tonson,
1767. (2), xvi, 124p. : ill. ; 8⁰
Titlepage in red and black. Includes: The universal
prayer and The dying Christian to his soul.
11658.a.76(3)

t005632

POPE, Alexander, the Poet
An essay on man. By Alexander Pope, Esq. Enlarged and
improved by the author. Together with his MS. additions
and variations as in the last edition of his works. With
the notes of William, Lord Bishop of Gloucester.. –
London: printed for W. Strahan; and T. Cadell, 1771.
(2), xvi, 124p. : ill. ; 8⁰
Titlepage in red and black. Horizontal chain lines.
Includes: The universal prayer and The dying Christian
to his soul.
991.g.35

t005633

POPE, Alexander, the Poet
An essay on man. In four epistles to a friend. Enlarged
and improved by the author.. – A new edition. – Dublin:
printed in the year, 1771. viii, 47, (1)p. : ill. ; 8⁰.

Anonymous. By Alexander Pope. Includes: The universal
prayer and The dying Christian to his soul.
11630.bbb.26(1)

t005634

POPE, Alexander, the Poet
An essay on man. By Alexander Pope, Esq; Enlarged and
improved by the author. Together with his MS. additions
and variations as in the last edition of his works. With
the notes of William, Lord Bishop of Gloucester.. -
London: printed for W. Strahan; and T. Cadell, 1774.
(2), xvi, 124p. : ill. ; 8⁰
Titlepage in red and black. Horizontal chain lines.
Includes: The universal prayer and The dying Christian
to his soul.
012611.e.43(2) : Imperfect; wanting the engraved frontispiece
and pp. 123-124, containing The dying Christian ...; titlepage
and sig. A3 are mutilated.

t005635

POPE, Alexander, the Poet
An essay on man. By Alexander Pope, Esq; Enlarged and
improved by the author. Together with his MS. additions
and variations as in the last edition of his works. With
the notes of William, Lord Bishop of Gloucester.. -
London: printed for W. Strahan; and T. Cadell, 1777.
(2), xvi, 124p. : ill. ; 8⁰
Titlepage in red and black. Horizontal chain lines.
Includes: The universal prayer and The dying Christian
to his soul.
1607/4195

t005636

POPE, Alexander, the Poet
An essay on man, by Alexander Pope, Esq; Enlarged and
improved by the author. With notes, critical and
explanatory.. - London: printed for J. Coote, 1778. 48p.
; 12⁰
Only a selection from Warburtons notes is given.
Includes: The universal prayer and The dying Christian
to his soul.
11602.e.1(4) : Sig. A2 is misbound after A4.

t005637

POPE, Alexander, the Poet
An essay on man. By Alexander Pope, Esq; Enlarged and
improved by the author. Together with his MS. additions
and variations as in the last edition of his works. With
the notes of William, Lord Bishop of Gloucester.. -
London: printed for A. Strahan; and T. Cadell, 1786.
xvi, 124, (2)p. : ill. ; 8⁰
Titlepage in red and black. Horizontal chain lines.
Includes: The universal prayer and The dying Christian
to his soul.
1608/4276

t005638

POPE, Alexander, the Poet
        Alexander Popes Essay on man and Universal prayer with
        notes.. - Copenhagen: printed for F. C. Pelt av N.
        Moller and Son, 1789. 79, (1)p. ; 8°
1608/4346
                                                        t005639

POPE, Alexander, the Poet
        An essay on man. By Alexander Pope, Esq. Enlarged and
        improved by the author. Printed from the last elegant
        quarto edition. With notes by William Warburton, M.A.. -
        Dublin: printed by George Perrin, 1791. 147, (1)p.,
        plate ; 12°
        Includes: The universal prayer.
1507/677
                                                        t005640

POPE, Alexander, the Poet
        An essay on man, in four epistles, to Henry St John, Ld.
        Bolingbroke, by Alexander Pope, Esq. Written in the year
        1732.. - Perth: printed by R. Morison, junior, for R.
        Morison and Son, Perth; G. Mudie, Edinburgh; W. Coke,
        Leith; Brash and Reid, Glasgow; and J. Burnet, Aberdeen,
        1792. (2), 84p. ; 12°
        Includes: The universal prayer and the text of letters
        exchanged between Pope and Louis Racine.
11631.a.39.
                                                        t005641

POPE, Alexander, the Poet
        An essay on man: in four epistles. To H. St John, L.
        Bolingbroke. By Alex. Pope, Esq.. - Newcastle upon Tyne:
        printed by and for S. Hodgson, 1795. (4), 44p. ; 18°
11631.a.40(1)
                                                        t005642

POPE, Alexander, the Poet
        An essay on man, by Alexander Pope. With notes, critical
        and explanatory.. - London: printed and sold by Darton
        and Harvey, 1796. (16), 96p., plate ; 8°
11631.aaa.31
                                                        t005643

POPE, Alexander, the Poet
An essay on man. By Alexander Pope, Esq.. - A new
edition. To which is prefixed A critical essay, by J.
Aikin, M.D.. - London: printed for T. Cadell, Jun. and
W. Davies (successors to Mr. Cadell), 1796(1797). (4),
142, (2)p., plates ; 8°.
With a half-title and final leaf of advertisements. The
engraved plates are dated March 1, 1797. Includes: The
universal prayer and The dying Christian to his soul.
991.g.27(1)
238.f.39

t005644

POPE, Alexander, the Poet
An essay on man: in four epistles to H. St. John, Lord
Bolingbroke. To which is added, The universal prayer. By
Alexander Pope, Esq.. - Worcester, Massachusetts:
printed by Thomas, Son & Thomas, sold by them, and the
booksellers in Boston, 1797. 59, (1)p. ; 12°.
Evans 32702.
1507/106

t005645

POPE, Alexander, the Poet
An essay on man. By Alexander Pope. Inscribed to Henry
Saint-John, Lord Bolingbroke.. - Cornish edition. -
Helston: printed at the Stannary Press, by Thomas
Flindell, 1798. 120p. ; 4°.
With a half-title. Includes: The universal prayer and
The dying Christian to his soul.
1465.e.32

t005646

POPE, Alexander, the Poet
(Essay on man. English prose). An essay on man. Together
with The universal prayer, and The dying Christian to
his soul. By Alexander Pope, Esq; Translated into prose,
after the manner of the Rev. Mr. Hervey, ... By T.
Robert, A.M. To which is prefixed the life of the
author.. - London: sold by R. Thompson, (1761?). (2),
66, 118p., plate ; 12°.
The date is taken from the engraved portrait
frontispiece, publishd by Jo Wood, 1761 which has been
inserted in the BL copy. The life of Alexander Pope,
Esq; occupies the first group of 66 pages, of which p.
22 is misnumbered 2.
11632.de.3

t005647

POPE, Alexander, the Poet
(Essay on man. Polyglot). Essai sur lhomme, poeme
philosophique par Alexandre Pope, en cinq langues,
savoir; anglois, latin, italien, francois & allemand.. -
Amsterdam: chez Zacharie Chatelain, 1762. (8), 347,
(1)p., plate ; 8⁰.
Latin verse translation by J. J. G. Am-Ende; Italian
verse by A.-F. Adami; French verse by J. F. du Resnel du
Bellay and German verse by H. C. Kretsch.
1162.f.29

t005648

POPE, Alexander, the Poet
(Essay on man. Polyglot). Saggio sopra luomo poema
filosofico di Alessandro Pope in tre lingue inglese,
francese, e italiana nuova edizione notabilmente
accrescinta, e ornata di figure.. - Napoli: a spese di
Domenico Terres, 1768. XXXV, (1), 320, (2), 123-144(i.e.
344)p., plates : ill., port. ; 8⁰.
With Il tempio della fama in Italian only, and other
poems, not by Pope, translated from the French. French
prose version of the Essay on man is by E. de
Silhouette; the Italian verse translation by A.-F.
Adami. The original text is given parallel with the
French. Titlepage in red and black. Includes an
engraved frontispiece. Sig. X mispaginated.
1485.r.22 : The plates are bound in at the beginning of the
English/French text of each epistle of the Essay on man.
1609/3008 : The plates are bound in at the beginning of the
Italian translation of each epistle of the Essay on man.

t005649

POPE, Alexander, the Poet
(Essay on man. Polyglot). Essai sur lhomme, poeme
philosophique par Alexandre Pope, en cinq langues,
savoir: anglois, latin, italien, francois & allemand.. -
Nouvelle edition. - Strasbourg: chez Armand Konig (de
limprimerie de Jonas Lorenz), 1772. (8), 351, (1)p. :
ill. ; 8⁰.
Latin verse translation by J. J. G. Am-Ende; Italian
verse by G. Castiglioni; French verse by J. F. du Resnel
du Bellay; German verse by H. C. Kretsch and French
prose by E. de Silhouette. Printers name from
colophon.
991.g.28 : The half-title to the Essay on man in English has
been misbound before the publishers advertisement to the
reader.

t005650

POPE, Alexander, the Poet
        (Essay on man. French). Essai sur lhomme. Par M. Pope.
        Traduit de langlois en francois, Editior revue par le
        traducteur.. - Londres: chez Pierre Dunoyer. A
        Amsterdam, chez Jean Frederic Bernard, 1736. xxxvi,
        112p. ; 12⁰
        Prose translation by Etienne de Silhouette.
240.e.23(1)

                                        t005651

POPE, Alexander, the Poet
        (Essay on man. French and English). Essai sur lhomme,
        par Monsieur Alexandre Pope. Traduction francoise en
        prose, par Mr. S****. Nouvelle edition, avec loriginal
        anglois; ornee de figures en taille-douce.. - Lausanne &
        Geneve: chez Marc-Michel Bousquet & Compagnie, 1745.
        xxiv, 116p., plates : ill., port. ; 4⁰
        Mr. S**** = Etienne de Silhouette. Parallel English and
        French texts. Titlepage in red and black.
1347.l.43
84.k.7 : BL catalogue describes this as a large paper copy.
                                        t005652

POPE, Alexander, the Poet
        (Essay on man. French and English). Essai sur lhomme,
        par Monsieur Alexandre Pope. Traduction francoise en
        prose, par Mr. S****. Nouvelle edition. Avec loriginal
        anglois; ornee de figures en taille-douce.. - Lausanne:
        chez Marc Chapuis, 1762. xxiv, 116p., plates : ill.,
        port. ; 4⁰
        Mr. S**** = Etienne de Silhouette. Parallel English and
        French texts. Titlepage in red and black.
11631.g.45

                                        t005653

POPE, Alexander, the Poet
        (Essay on man. German and English). Hrn. B. H. Brockes,
        Lti, ... aus dem Englischen ubersetzter Versuch vom
        Menschen, des Herrn Alexander Pope, Esq. nebst
        verschiedenen andern Uebersetzungen und einigen
        Gedichten. Nebst einer Vorrede und einem Anhange von
        Briefen, worinnen die Einwurfe des Hrn. C... wider den
        Essay on man beantwortet werden, aus der History of the
        Works of the Learned ubersetzet von B. J. Zinck.. -
        Hamburg: verlegts Christian Herold, 1740. (30), 318p.,
        plate : port. ; 8⁰
        Parallel English text and German verse translation.
        Hrn. C... = J. P. de Crousaz.
1160.b.11(2)
                                        t005654

POPE, Alexander, the Poet
(Essay on man. German and English). Essay on man. Der
Mensch ein philosophiches Gedichte von Alexander Pope.
Deutsche Uebersetzung. Mit der englandischen Urschrift
nach der letzen vermehrten Ausgabe.. - Altenburg: in der
Richterischen Buchhandlung, 1759. (18), 203, (1)p. ; 4⁰.
Parallel English text and German verse translation by H.
C. Kretsch. With engraved head- and tailpieces.
Includes: The universal prayer, Messiah and The dying
Christian to his soul.
11631.g.1

t005655

POPE, Alexander, the Poet
(Essay on man. German and English). Alexander Popes
Versuch am Menschen in vier Briefen an Herrn St. John
Lord Bolingbroke aus dem Englischen ubersetzt von Johann
Jakob Harder ... Herausgegeben von Herrn Klotz.. -
Halle: bei Joh. Jac. Curt, 1772. (16), 79, (1)p. ; 8⁰.
Parallel English text and German verse translation.
Translators address dated at end: 15. Merz, 1771.
1164.h.30

t005656

POPE, Alexander, the Poet
(Essay on man. German and English). Versuch uber den
Menschen. Von Alexander Pope, Esq. Nebst dessen
Allgemeinem Gebothe. Nach dem englischen Originale
getreu in deutsche Prosa ubersetzt. = An essay on man
.... - Zweite Auflage. - Wien: bei Rudolph Sammer, 1798.
(4), 139, (1)p. ; 12⁰.
Parallel English and German texts.
11659.a.37 : Printed on blue paper.

t005657

POPE, Alexander, the Poet
(Essay on man. Italian). Saggio sopra luomo di
Alessandro Pope tradotto dallinglese e diretto a** T****
B***. - Londra: a spese di Antonio Graziosi, 1765. 92p.
; 8⁰.
Italian prose translation.
1608/3220

t005658

POPE, Alexander, the Poet
    (Essay on man. Italian and English). Saggio sulluomc del
    Sig. Alessandro Pope tradotto dallinglese dal Sig. Gio.
    Castiglioni .... - Berna: a spese della Soc. Letter.
    appreso Abr. Wagner figlic, 1760. LXXXVIII, 192p. ; 8⁰.

    Parallel English text and Italian verse translation.
    Includes: Alcune traduzicni di Petronio and Poesie
    diverse del traduttore. Translators dedication dated:
    Utrecht 8. Gennajo 1759.
11631.aaa.59

                                                    t005659

POPE, Alexander, the Poet
    The first epistle of the first bock of Horace imitated.
    By Mr. Pope. - London: printed for R. Dcdsley, and sold
    by T. Cooper, 1737(1738). (2), 21(i.e. 19), 1p. ; 2⁰.
    Price 1s. on titlepage; pp. 18-19 misnumbered 20-21.
    Publication date frcm Foxcn. Parallel Latin and English
    texts.
    Foxon P877; Griffith 480.
644.m.14(8)
162.n.41
C.57.g.7(4) : Imperfect; wanting the titlepage.
Ashley 5224

                                                    t005660

POPE, Alexander, the Poet
    The first epistle of the first book of Horace imitated.
    By Mr. Pope.. - London: printed for R. Dodsley, and sold
    by T. Cooper, 1737(i.e. 1738). (2), 19, (1)p. ; 2⁰.
    Pric 1s. on titlepage; pp. 18-19 correctly numbered.
    Apparently reset except for sheet E and part of F
    (Foxon). Publication date from Griffith. Parallel
    Latin and English texts.
    Foxon P878; Griffith 481.
1486.g.14

                                                    t005661

POPE, Alexander, the Poet
    The first epistle of the first book of Horace imitated.
    By Mr. Pope.. - Dublin: re-printed by Gec. Faulkner,
    1738. 19, (1)p. ; 8⁰.
    Parallel Latin and English texts.
    Foxon P880; Griffith 483.
C.136.aa.1(11)

                                                    t005662

POPE, Alexander, the Poet
      The first epistle of the second book of Horace,
      imitated.. - London: printed for T. Cooper, 1737. iv,
      23, (1)p. ; 2º
      Anonymous. By Alexander Pope. Catchword on p. 21:
      37Charles.
      Foxon P881; Griffith 458, 467.
835.m.29
Ashley 5226 : A variant, with catchword 38Charles on p. 21.
                                                    t005663

POPE, Alexander, the Poet
      (First epistle of the second book of Horace, imitated).
      The second book of the epistles of Horace. Imitated by
      Mr. Pope.. - London: printed for T. Cooper, 1737. (2),
      iv, 23, (1)p. ; 2º
      Another issue, with sig. A1 changed to a half-title,
      reading Epistles of Horace, imitated, and a general
      titlepage added; probably intended to accompany Dodsleys
      1737 edition of the second epistle (Foxon P955-7).
      Catchword on p. 21 38Charles.
      Foxon P882; Griffith 458,467.
644.m.14(10) : On fine paper.
                                                    t005664

POPE, Alexander, the Poet
      The first epistle of the second book of Horace,
      imitated.. - London: printed for T. Cooper, 1737. iv,
      23, (1)p. ; 2º
      Anonymous. By Alexander Pope. Catchword on p. 21:
      28Charles. Largely reset (Foxon).
      Foxon P883.
1485.dd.1
                                                    t005665

POPE, Alexander, the Poet
      The first satire of the second book of Horace, imitated
      in a dialogue between Alexander Pope of Twickenham in
      Com. Midd. Esq; on the one part, and his learned council
      on the other.. - London: printed by L. G.(Lawton
      Gilliver) and sold by A. Dodd, E. Nutt, and by the
      booksellers of London and Westminster, 1733. 19, (1)p. ;
      2º
      No price on titlepage; no comma after Pope; press-figure
      15-1. Parallel Latin and English texts.
      Foxon P886; Griffith 288.
644.m.14(7)
162.n.38
Ashley 5206
                                                    t005666

POPE, Alexander, the Poet
   The first satire of the second book of Horace, imitated
   in a dialogue between Alexander Pope, of Twickenham in
   Com. Midd. Esq; on the one part, and his learned council
   on the other.. - London: printed by L. G. (Lawton
   Gilliver) and sold by A. Dodd, E. Nutt, and by the
   booksellers of London and Westminster, 1733. 19, (1)p. ;
   2⁰.
   No price on titlepage; comma after Pope; no
   press-figure. Sheet A is reset, together with part of
   pp. 9,10 (Foxon). Parallel Latin and English texts.
   Foxon P887; Griffith 290,1.
Ashley 5207
C.59.h.9(5) : A variant; incorrect catchword In on p. 13
corrected to Whether.
Ashley 5208 : A variant; incorrect catchword In on p. 13
corrected to Whether.

                                                    t005667

POPE, Alexander, the Poet
   The first satire of the second book of Horace, imitated
   in a dialogue between Alexander Pope, of Twickenham in
   Com. Midd. Esq; on the one part, and his learned council
   on the other.. - London: printed by L. G. (Lawton
   Gilliver) and sold by A. Dodd; E. Nutt; and by the
   booksellers of London and Westminster, 1733. 19, (1)p. ;
   2⁰.
   A reimpression: Price One Shilling added to titlepage;
   catchword Whether on p. 13. Parallel Latin and English
   texts.
   Foxon P888; Griffith 292.
Ashley 5209
1484.m.7(9) : Imperfect; wanting the titlepage.

                                                    t005668

POPE, Alexander, the Poet
   The first satire of the second book of Horace, imitated
   in a dialogue between Alexander Pope, of Twickenham in
   Com. Midd. Esq; on the one part, and his learned council
   on the other.. - London: printed by L. G. (Lawton
   Gilliver) and sold by A. Dodd; E. Nutt, and by the
   booksellers of London and Westminster, 1733. 19, (1)p. ;
   2⁰.
   Reset throughout ... On p. 9, line 2, Laureat lacks the
   final e, present in all other folio printings (Foxon).
   Parallel Latin and English texts.
   Foxon P889; Griffith 293.
Ashley 5210

                                                    t005669

POPE, Alexander, the Poet
The first satire of the second book of Horace, imitated
in a dialogue between Alexander Pope of Twickenham in
Com. Midd. Esq; on the one part, and his learned council
on the other.. - London(i.e. Edinburgh): printed by L.
G. and sold by A. Dodd; E. Nutt; and by the booksellers
of London and Westminster, 1733. Pp. (1), 26-43, (1) ; 8⁰.
The imprint is false; Printed by Ruddiman on the
evidence of the ornaments. Pagination and signatures are
intended to follow the Edinburgh piracy of Of the use of
riches (Foxon). Parallel Latin and English texts.
Foxon P890; Griffith 289.
993.e.51(2)

t005670

POPE, Alexander, the Poet
The first satire of the second book of Horace, imitated
in a dialogue between Alexander Pope, of Twickenham, in
Com. Midd. Esq; on the one part, and his learned council
on the other.. - Dublin: London: printed. Dublin,
re-printed by and for George Faulkner, 1733. 24p. ; 8⁰.
Pp. 21 4 contain an advertisement for Faulkners edition
of Swifts works, dated March 2, 1733. Parallel Latin
and English texts.
Foxon P891; Griffith 298.
11601.ccc.38(12)

t005671

POPE, Alexander, the Poet
The first satire of the second book of Horace, imitated
in dialogue between Alexander Pope of Twickenham, in Com
Mid Esq; and his learned council. To which is added, the
second satire of the same book. By the same hand. Never
before printed.. - London: printed for I. G. (Lawton
Gilliver), 1734. (2), 40p. ; 4⁰.
Issued in various formats; the order of printing has not
been determined (Foxon). Parallel Latin and English
texts.
Foxon P893; Griffith 341.
12273.m.1(4)
11630.c.10(6) : Cropped.
11642.h.43(1)

t005672

POPE, Alexander, the Poet
The first satire of the second book of Horace, imitated
in dialogue between Alexander Pope of Twickenham, in Com
Mid Esq; and his learned council. To which is added, the
second satire of the same book. By the same hand. Never
before printed.. - London: printed for L. G. (Lawton
Gilliver), 1734. (2), 36p. ; 2º.
Another impression, in folio. The second satire, B2-I2,
was also issued separately (Foxon). Parallel Latin and
English texts.
Foxon P884; Griffith 343.
1489.f.40
Ashley 4937

t005673

POPE, Alexander, the Poet
A full and true account of a horrid and barbarous
revenge by poison, on the body of Mr. Edmund Curll,
bookseller; with a faithful copy of his last will and
testament. Publishd by an eye witness.. - (London): sold
by J. Roberts, J. Morphew, R. Burleigh, J. Baker, and S.
Popping, (1716). 6p. ; 2º.
An eye witness = Alexander Pope. Horizontal chain
lines. See also: A further account of the most
deplorable condition of Mr. Edmund Curll.
Griffith 52.
C.59.i.5
Ashley 4932

t005674

POPE, Alexander, the Poet
A further account of the most deplorable condition of
Mr. Edmund Curll, bookseller. Since his being poisond on
the 28th of March. To be publishd weekly.. - London:
printed, and sold by all the publishers, mercuries, and
hawkers, within the bills of mortality, 1716. 22p. ; 8º.
Anonymous. By Alexander Pope. A sequel to A full and
true account of a horrid and barbarous revenge by
poison, on the body of Mr. Edmund Curll. With a
half-title.
Griffith 56.
Ashley 1298

t005675

POPE, Alexander, the Poet
Gods revenge against punning. Shewing the miserable
fates of persons addicted to this crying sin, in court
and town.. - London: printed for J. Roberts, 1716. 2p. ;
1/2⁰.
Signed at end: J. Baker, Knight, sometimes identified as
Alexander Pope. Imprint reads: at the Oxford-Arms in in
Warwick-Lane.
Griffith 60.
C.70.h.4
Ashley 4933 : A variant, with the imprint corrected, and partly
reset.
t005676

POPE, Alexander, the Poet
Horace his ode to Venus. Lib. IV. Ode I. Imitated by Mr.
Pope.. - London: printed for J. Wright, and sold by J.
Roberts, 1737. (2), 7, (1)p. ; 2⁰.
Parallel Latin and English texts.
Foxon P896; Griffith 443.
644.m.14(14)
Ashley 4942
t005677

POPE, Alexander, the Poet
The impertinent, or a visit to the court. A satyr. By an
eminent hand.. - London: printed for John Wileord (sic),
1733. 16p. ; 4⁰.
An eminent hand = Alexander Pope. With a half-title.
Foxon P898; Griffith 317.
Ashley 3775
840.k.3(1) : Imperfect; wanting the half-title.
t005678

POPE, Alexander, the Poet
The impertinent: or, a visit to the court. A satyr. By
Mr. Pope.. - The second edition. - London: printed for
E. Hill, 1737. (4), 15, (1)p. ; 2⁰.
Sig. A2 contains added verses To the author of the
following satire.
Foxon P899; Griffith 463.
11630.h.40
t005679

POPE, Alexander, the Poet
The impertinent: or, a visit to the court. A satyr. By
Mr. Pope.. - The third edition. - London: printed for E.
Hill, 1737. 14p. ; 2⁰.
Without the added verses.
Foxon P900; Griffith 465.
11630.h.39
Ashley 5690
t005680

POPE, Alexander, the Poet
        The impertinent: or, a visit to the court. A satyr. By
        Mr. Pope.. - The second edition. - Dublin: London:
        printed. Dublin: re-printed by and for George Faulkner,
        1737. 20p. ; 8⁰
        Foxon P902; Griffith 464.
C.136.aa.1(21)

                                                    t005681

POPE, Alexander, the Poet
        A key to the lock. Or, a treatise proving, beyond all
        contradiction, the dangerous tendency of a late poem,
        entituled, The rape of the lock, to government and
        religion. By Esdras Barnivelt, apoth.. - London: printed
        for J. Roberts, 1715. 32p. ; 8⁰
        Esdras Barnivelt = Alexander Pope.
        Griffith 37.
994.c.42
Ashley 3767

                                                    t005682

POPE, Alexander, the Poet
        A key to the lock. Or, a treatise proving, beyond all
        contradiction, the dangerous tendency of a late poem,
        entituled, The rape of the lock. To government and
        religion. By Esdras Barnivelt, apoth.. - The second
        edition. To which are added commendatory copies of
        verses, ... - London: printed for J. Roberts, 1715.
        32p. ; 8⁰
        Esdras Barnivelt = Alexander Pope.
        Griffith 38.
11840.ccc.12
                                                    t005683

POPE, Alexander, the Poet
        A key to the lock. Or, a treatise, proving, beyond all
        contradiction, the dangerous tendency of a late poem,
        entituled, The rape of the lock, to government and
        religion. By Esdras Barnivelt, apoth.. - The third
        edition. To which are added commendatory copies of
        verses, ... - London: printed for J. Roberts, 1718.
        32p. ; 8⁰
        Esdras Barnivelt = Alexander Pope.
        Griffith 101.
12274.h.3(2)
                                                    t005684

POPE, Alexander, the Poet
A key to the lock: or, a treatise proving, beyond all
contradiction, the dangerous tendency of a late poem,
entituled, The rape of the lock, to government and
religion. By Esdras Barnivelt, apoth.. - The fourth
edition. To which are added, commerdatory copies of
verses, ... - (London?): printed in the year, 1723.
32p. ; 8⁰.
Esdras Barnivelt = Alexander Pope.
Griffith 141.
11634.b.5(2)

t005685

POPE, Alexander, the Poet
(Memoirs of Martinus Scriblerus). Memoirs of the
extraordinary life, works, and discoveries of Martinus
Scriblerus. By Mr. Pope.. - Dublin: printed by and for
George Faulkner, 1741. (2), 12, 165, (1)p. ; 12⁰.
P. 165 bears the statement The end of the first book.
All published.
Griffith 538.
12330.bb.31

t005686

POPE, Alexander, the Poet
(Memoirs of Martinus Scriblerus. French). Histoire de
Martinus Scriblerus, de ses ouvrages & de ses
decouvertes; traduite de langlois de monsieur Pope.. -
Londres(i.e. Paris?): chez Paul Knapton, 1755. xxiv,
324p. ; 12⁰.
Translator identified in LAnnee Litteraire (1755, I,
359) as M. Larcher, i.e. Pierre Henri Larcher.
Cup.407.bb.15

t005687

POPE, Alexander, the Poet
Messiah, a sacred eclogue, in imitation of Virgils
Pollio. By Alexander Pope, Esq;. - (London?): printed
for the proprietors, and sold by all the booksellers,
1766. 12p. ; 12⁰.
With a half-title. Possibly printed in Scotland.
1609/5624(1)

t005688

POPE, Alexander, the Poet
        (Messiah. Greek and English). Ecloga sacra Alexandri
        Pope, vulgo Messia dicta, Graece reddita. Accedit etiam
        Graece inscriptio sepulchralis ex celeberrima elegia
        Thomae Gray. Curante Johanne Plumptre, A.M. .... -
        (Worcester?): veneunt apud bibliopolas Cxcniae,
        Cantabrigiae, Etonae; T. Smart et T. Holl, Wigorniae; R.
        Faulder, F. et C. Rivingtcn, Londini, 1795. (4), 19,
        (1)p. ; 4⁰.
        Translated by John Plumptre. Parallel English and Greek
        texts.
    78.h.11
                                                    t005689

POPE, Alexander, the Poet
        (Messiah. Greek and English). Ecloga sacra Alexandri
        Pope, vulgo Messia dicta, Graece reddita. Accedit etiam
        Graece inscriptio sepulchralis ex celeberrima Thomae
        Gray. Curante Johanne Plumptre, A.M. .... - Editio
        altera, emendata. - (Worcester?): veneunt apud
        bibliopolas Oxoniae, Cantabrigiae, Etonae: T. Smart et
        T. Holl, Vigorniae; R. Faulder, F. et C. Rivington,
        Londini, 1796. (4), 19, (1)p. ; 4⁰.
        Translated by John Plumptre. Parallel English and Greek
        texts. Dedication dated: Aprilis die 20ma 1795.
    641.l.21(6) : Translators presentaticn copy to Dr. Burney, with
    an autograph letter dated January 16th 1796, inserted.
                                                    t005690

PCPE, Alexander, the Poet
        (Messiah. Latin and English). Messias. Idyllium sacrum.
        Per Alexandrum Pope, anglice conscriptum. Latine
        redditum.. - Wolverhamptcr: typis, J. Smart, 1784. (5),
        4-8, 4-8, (1)p. ; 8⁰.
        The translator identified in the dedication as C.
        Billinge. Parallel English and Latin texts; duplicate
        pagination. Horizontal chain lines.
    11633.c.8(2)
                                                    t005691

POPE, Alexander, the Poet
        The narrative of Dr. Robert Norris, concerning the
        strange and deplcrable frenzy of Mr. John Denn--- an
        officer of the custcm-house: being an exact account of
        all that past betwixt the said patient and the doctor
        .... - London: printed for J. Morphew, 1713. 24p. ; 8⁰.
        Signed and dated at end: Robert Norris, M.D. July the
        30th. Attributed to Alexander Pope. Half-title: Dr.
        Norriss narrative concerning the frenzy of Mr. John
        Denn-- .... A satire against John Dennis.
        Griffith 23.
    Ashley 1294
    1076.g.43 : Cropped, affectirg the imprint. Imperfect; wanting
    the half-title.
                                                    t005692

POPE, Alexander, the Poet
        A narrative of the method by which the private letters
        of Mr. Pope have been procurd and publishd by Edmund
        Curll, bookseller. NB. The original papers, in Curls own
        hand, may be seen at T. Coopers.. - London: printed for
        T. Cooper, 1735. (4), 36p. ; 12⁰
        Attributed to Alexander Pope. With a half-title.
        Griffith 382.
Cup.403.tt.12
                                                                t005693

POPE, Alexander, the Poet
        Ode for musick.. - London: printed for Bernard Lintott,
        1713. (4), 8p. ; 2⁰
        Half-title: Mr. Popes Ode on St. Cecilias Day.
        Foxon P904; Griffith 20.
643.l.26(5)
Ashley 4919
                                                                t005694

POPE, Alexander, the Poet
        Ode for musick on St. Cecilias Day. Written by Mr.
        Pope.. - The third edition. - London: printed for
        Bernard Lintot, 1719. (2), 12, (2)p. : ill. ; 8⁰
        With a final leaf of advertisements.
        Foxon P905; Griffith 110.
11634.b.4
                                                                t005695

POPE, Alexander, the Poet
        Ode for musick on St. Cecilias Day. Written by Mr.
        Pope.. - The fourth edition. - London: printed for
        Bernard Lintot, 1722. (2), 12, (2)p. : ill. ; 8⁰
        Probably published in 1721. With a final leaf of
        advertisements.
        Foxon P906; Griffith 136.
991.h.25(4) : Imperfect; wanting the leaf of advertisements.
                                                                t005696

POPE, Alexander, the Poet
        (Ode for musick). An ode composd for the publick
        commencement, at Cambridge: on Monday July the 6th.
        1730. At the musick-act. The words by Alexander Pope
        Esq; the musick by Maurice Greene, Doctor in Musick.. -
        (Cambridge), (1730). 4p. ; 8⁰
        Another edition of Popes Ode for musick on St. Cecilias
        Day, probably intended to be issued as part of
        Quaestiones, una cum carminibus, 1730; sometimes, as
        here, found separately. The words only.
        Griffith 240; cf. Foxon P907(note).
837.h.39
                                                                t005697

POPE, Alexander, the Poet
      (Ode for musick. Latin and English). Carmen cl.
      Alexandri Pope in S. Caeciliam latine redditum a
      Christophero Smart, ... - Cantabrigiae: typis
      academicis excudebat J. Bentham, impensis authoris,
      1743. (2), 13, (1)p. ; 2⁰
      Parallel English and Latin texts.
      Foxon S490; Griffith 581.
11409.k.1
837.l.4(17)

                                                t005698

POPE, Alexander, the Poet
      (Ode for musick. Latin and English). Carmen cl.
      Alexandri Pope in S. Caeciliam latine redditum a
      Christophero Smart.. - Editio altera. To which is added
      Ode for musick on Saint Cecilias Day, by Christopher
      Smart, ... - Cambridge: printed by J. Bentham, and sold
      by R. Dodsley, London, 1746. (2), 37, (1)p. ; 4⁰
      The final leaf contains an advertisement for a Latin
      version of the Essay on criticism, etc., by the same
      translator. Parallel English and Latin texts.
      Foxon S491; Griffith 618.
11602.gg.24(11)

                                                t005699

POPE, Alexander, the Poet
      (Of false taste). An epistle to the Right Honourable
      Richard Earl of Burlington. Occasiond by his publishing
      Palladios designs of the baths, arches, theatres, 8c. of
      ancient Rome. By Mr. Pope.. - London: printed for L.
      Gilliver, 1731. 14, (2)p. ; 2⁰
      Half-title: Of taste, ... Price 1s. on titlepage; ten
      books advertised on recto of final leaf. P. 6, line 13
      reads: Oft have have you ....
      Foxon P908; Griffith 259.
162.n.18
Ashley 5203

                                                t005700

POPE, Alexander, the Poet
      (Of false taste). An epistle to the Right Honourable
      Richard Earl of Burlington. Occasiond by his publishing
      Palladios designs of the baths, arches, theatres, 8c. of
      ancient Rome. By Mr. Pope.. - London: printed for L.
      Gilliver, 1731. 14, (2)p. ; 2⁰
      Half-title: Of taste, ... Price 1s. on titlepage; ten
      books advertised on recto of final leaf. P. 6, line 13
      reads: Oft have you .... On large and fine paper.
      cf. Foxon P909.
1485.f.3

                                                t005701

POPE, Alexander, the Poet
        (Of false taste). An epistle to the Right Honourable
        Richard Earl of Burlington. Occasiond by his publishing
        Palladios designs of the baths, arches, theatres, &c. of
        ancient Rome. By Mr. Pope.. - London: printed for L.
        Gilliver, 1731. 14, (2)p. ; 2⁰.
        With a half-title; twelve books advertised on recto of
        final leaf. A reimpression with sheet B reset; Todds B
        edition.
        Foxon P910.
12273.m.1(1) : Imperfect; wanting the half-title and the final
leaf of advertisements. MS. notes.
                                                    t005702

POPE, Alexander, the Poet
        (Of false taste). Of false taste. An epistle to the
        Right Honourable Richard Earl of Burlington. Occasiond
        by his publishing Palladios designs of the baths,
        arches, theatres, &c. of ancient Rome. By Mr. Pope.. -
        The third edition. - London: printed for L. Gilliver,
        1731(1732). 14, (2)p. ; 2⁰.
        With a final leaf of advertisements. A reimpression of
        the second edition; p. 11, line 19 reads Cielings.
        Todds D edition. Publication date from Twickenham
        edition.
        Foxon P912; Griffith 267.
C.59.h.9(3)
162.n.19 : With a copy of Hogarths engraving, The gate of
Burlington House, inserted.
                                                    t005703

POPE, Alexander, the Poet
        (Of false taste). Of false taste. An epistle to the
        Right Honourable Richard Earl of Burlington. Occasiond
        by his publishing Palladios designs of the baths,
        arches, theatres, &c. of ancient Rome. By Mr. Pope.. -
        The third edition. - London: printed for L. Gilliver,
        1731. 14, (2)p. ; 2⁰.
        A different edition from the preceding; p. 11, line 19
        reads Ceilings. Todds E edition. With a final leaf of
        advertisements.
        Foxon P913.
Ashley 5204
                                                    t005704

POPE, Alexander, the Poet
        (Of false taste). Of taste, an epistle to the Right
        Honourable Richard, Earl of Burlington. Occasiond by his
        publishing Palladios designs of the baths, arches,
        theatres, &c. of ancient Rome.. - (Edinburgh), 1732. 15,
        (1)p. ; 8⁰.
        Printed in Edinburgh on the evidence of the ornaments
        (Foxon).
        Foxon P915; Griffith 264.
11630.bbb.42(1)
                                                    t005705

POPE, Alexander, the Poet
(Of false taste). Of taste. An epistle to the Right
Honourable Richard Earl of Burlington. Occasiond by his
publishing Palladios designs of the baths, arches,
theatres, &c. of ancient Rome.. - Dublin: London:
printed. And, Dublin re-printed by George Faulkner,
1732. 12p. ; 4⁰.
Foxon P916; Griffith 277.
11632.bb.55.

t005706

POPE, Alexander, the Poet
Of the characters of women: an epistle to a lady. By Mr.
Pope. - London: printed by J. Wright, for Lawton
Gilliver, 1735. (2), 16, (2)p. ; 2⁰.
With a half-title and a final leaf of advertisements.
Foxon P917; Griffith 360,1.
1484.m.7(10) : The half-title is misbound immediately after the
titlepage.
162.n.25
Ashley 4939 : A variant, with misprint Flettstreet in the
imprint.
Ashley 4940 : A made-up copy, wanting the final leaf of
advertisements.
644.m.14(4) : Imperfect; wanting the half-title.

t005707

POPE, Alexander, the Poet
Of the characters of women: an epistle to a lady. By Mr.
Pope.. - London(i.e. Edinburgh): printed by J. Wright,
for Lawton Gilliver, 1735. 15, (1)p. ; 8⁰.
The imprint is false; Printed by Ruddiman on the
evidence of the ornaments (Foxon).
Foxon P918; Griffith 362.
993.e.51(5)

t005708

POPE, Alexander, the Poet
(Of the knowledge and characters of men). An epistle to
the Right Honourable Richard Lord Visct. Cobham. By Mr.
Pope. - London: printed for Lawton Gilliver, 1733. (4),
13, (3)p. ; 2⁰.
Half-title: Of the knowledge and characters of men ....
With a final leaf of advertisements.
Foxon P920; Griffith 329.
C.59.h.9(6)
Ashley 4936
644.m.14(6) : Imperfect; wanting the final leaf of
advertisements.
162.n.23 : Imperfect; wanting the half-title and the final leaf
of advertisements.

t005709

POPE, Alexander, the Poet
        Of the knowledge and characters of men. An epistle to
        the Right Honourable Richard Lord Viscount Cobham.. -
        London (i.e.Edinburgh): printed (by Robert Fleming) in
        the year, 1734. 12p. ; 8⁰.
        Anonymous. By Alexander Pope. The imprint is false;
        Printed by Fleming on the evidence of the ornaments
        (Foxon).
        Foxon P921; Griffith 330.
11630.bbb.42(10)

                                                        t005710

POPE, Alexander, the Poet
        (Of the knowledge and characters of men). An epistle to
        the Right Honourable Richard Lord Viscount Cobham. By
        Mr. Pope.. - Dublin: London: printed. And re-printed in
        Dublin, by George Faulkner, 1734. 20p. ; 8⁰.
        With a half-title.
        Foxon P922; not in Griffith.
11631.aa.47(6)
C.136.aa.1(14)

                                                        t005711

POPE, Alexander, the Poet
        Of the use of riches, an epistle to the Right Honorable
        Allen Lord Bathurst. By Mr. Pope. - London: printed by
        J. Wright, for Lawton Gilliver, 1732(1733). (2), 20p. ;
        2⁰.
        Most copies read ypon in p. 13, line 13, for yon; the
        error is noted in the erratum on p. 20 (Foxon).
        Foxon P923,4; Griffith 280-2.
1484.m.7(12)
1485.f.7 : A variant, with corrected reading yon on p. 13, line
13 (Griffith 281).
162.n.20
C.59.h.9(4)
Ashley 5205

                                                        t005712

POPE, Alexander, the Poet
        Of the use of riches, an epistle to the Right Honourable
        Allen Lord Bathurst. By Mr. Pope.. - The second edition.
        - London: printed by J. Wright, for Lawton Gilliver,
        1733. 22, (2)p. ; 2⁰.
        14 books advertised on the recto of the final leaf.
        Foxon P925; Griffith 324.
1485.dd.7
12273.m.1(2) : A made-up copy, containing the titlepage only of
the second edition; the text is of the first edition.
                                                        t005713

POPE, Alexander, the Poet
        Of the use of riches, an epistle to the Right Honourable
        Allen Lord Bathurst. By Mr. Pope.. - The second edition.
        - London: printed by J. Wright, for Lawton Gilliver,
        1733. 22, (2)p. ; 2⁰.
        16 books advertised on the recto of the final leaf.
        Todds B edition.
        Foxon P926; Griffith 323.
11657.m.24

                                                        t005714

POPE, Alexander, the Poet
        Of the use of riches, an epistle to the Right Honourable
        Allen Lord Bathurst. By Mr. Pope. - London(i.e.
        Edinburgh): printed by J. Wright, for Lawton Gilliver,
        1732(1733). 24p. ; 8⁰.
        The imprint is false; Printed by Ruddiman on the
        evidence of the ornaments (Foxon). Publication date
        from Foxon.
        Foxon P927; Griffith 283.
11630.bbb.42(6)

                                                        t005715

POPE, Alexander, the Poet
        Of the use of riches, an epistle to the Right Honourable
        Allen Lord Bathurst. By Mr. Pope.. - Dublin: printed by
        S. Powell, for George Risk, George Ewing, and William
        Smith, 1733. (4), 20p. ; 8⁰.
        With a half-title.
        Foxon P929; Griffith 326.
C.136.aa.1(5)

                                                        t005716

POPE, Alexander, the Poet
        Of the use of riches. An epistle to the Right Honourable
        Allen Lord Bathurst. By Mr. Pope.. - Dublin: printed at
        London: Dublin, re-printed by and for George Faulkner,
        1733. 22p. ; 8⁰.
        Foxon P930; Griffith 327.
11630.aaa.45(5)

                                                        t005717

POPE, Alexander, the Poet
        Of the use of riches. An epistle to the Right Honourable
        Allen Lord Bathurst. By Mr. Pope. - Dublin: London:
        printed. Dublin, re-printed, by and for George Faulkner,
        1733. 22, (2)p. ; 8⁰.
        With a final leaf of advertisements.
        Foxon P931; not in Griffith.
11631.aa.47(4)

                                                        t005718

POPE, Alexander, the Poet
        One thousand seven hundred and thirty eight. A dialogue
        something like Horace. By Mr. Pope. - London: printed
        for T. Cooper, (1738). (2), 10, (2)p. ; 2⁰.
        With a half-title and a final leaf of advertisements.
        (Price ONE SHILLING.) on titlepage. Publication date
        from Griffith.
        Foxon P932; Griffith 484.
162.n.21
Ashley 5229
644.m.14(13) : Imperfect; wanting the half-title.
643.l.28(24) : Imperfect; wanting the half-title.
                                                        t005719

POPE, Alexander, the Poet
        One thousand seven hundred and thirty eight. A dialogue
        something like Horace. By Mr. Pope.. - London: printed
        for T. Cooper, (1738). (4), 10, (2)p. ; 2⁰.
        A reimpression; (Price One Shilling) on titlepage; sig.
        D under her. With a half-title, and a final leaf of
        advertisements.
        Foxon P933; Griffith 485.
11630.h.41
Ashley 5230
                                                        t005720

POPE, Alexander, the Poet
        One thousand seven hundred and thirty eight. A dialogue
        something like Horace. By Mr. Pope.. - London: printed
        for T. Cooper, 1738. (4), 10, (2)p. ; 2⁰.
        (Price 1s.) on titlepage; reset throughout. With a
        half-title and a final leaf of advertisements.
        Foxon P935; Griffith 498.
Ashley 5231
                                                        t005721

POPE, Alexander, the Poet
        One thousand seven hundred and thirty eight. A dialogue
        something like Horace. By Mr. Pope. - London(i.e.
        Edinburgh): printed for T. Cooper, 1738. 12p. ; 8⁰.
        The imprint is false; Printed by Ruddiman on the
        evidence of the ornaments (Foxon).
        Foxon P936; Griffith 487.
C.175.a.13
                                                        t005722

POPE, Alexander, the Poet
        One thousand seven hundred and thirty-eight. A dialogue
        something like Horace. By Mr. Pope.. - Dublin:
        re-printed by Geo. Faulkner, 1738. 12p. ; 8⁰.
        Foxon P937; Griffith 488.
11602.bb.33(6)
C.136.aa.1(12)
                                                        t005723

POPE, Alexander, the Poet
        One thousand seven hundred and thirty eight. Dialogue
        II. By Mr. Pope.. - London: printed for R. Dodsley,
        1738. 16p. ; 2º.
        Last line on p. 10 has misprint Fools for Tools.
        Foxon P938; Griffith 494.
1476.dd.29
Ashley 5232
644.m.14(13) : A variant, with corrected reading Tools in the
last line of p. 10.
162.n.22 : A variant, with corrected reading Tools in the last
line of p. 10.

                                                    t005724

POPE, Alexander, the Poet
        One thousand seven hundred and thirty eight. Dialogue
        II. By Mr. Pope.. - Dublin: printed by R. Reilly. For G.
        Risk, G. Ewing, W. Smith, and G. Faulkner, 1738. 16p. ;
        8º.
        Foxon P940; Griffith 496.
1488.bb.28
C.136.aa.1(13)

                                                    t005725

POPE, Alexander, the Poet
        The rape of the lock. An heroi-comical poem. In five
        cantos. Written by Mr. Pope.. - London: printed for
        Bernard Lintott, 1714. (8), 48p., plates ; 8º.
        Titlepage in red and black. First published in
        Miscellaneous poems and translations, 1712, in two
        cantos.
        Foxon P941; Griffith 29.
C.70.bb.1(1)
C.59.ff.13(1) : Imperfect; wanting the plate to Canto 3.
Ashley 1297

                                                    t005726

POPE, Alexander, the Poet
        The rape of the lock. An heroi-comical poem. In five
        cantos. Written by Mr. Pope.. - London: printed for
        Bernard Lintott, 1714. (8), 48p., plates ; 8º. .
        Titlepage in red and black. On large and fine paper.
        Foxon P942; Griffith 30.
C.116.e.31

                                                    t005727

POPE, Alexander, the Poet
        The rape of the lock. An heroi-comical poem. In five
        cantos. Written by Mr. Pope.. - The second edition. -
        London: printed for Bernard Lintott, 1714. (8), 48p.,
        plates ; 8º.
        Titlepage in red and black.
        Foxon P943; Griffith 34.
11659.aaa.90

                                                    t005728

POPE, Alexander, the Poet
      The rape of the lock. An heroi-comical poem. In five
      cantos. Written by Mr. Pope.. - The third edition. -
      London: printed for Bernard Lintott, 1714. (10), 52,
      (2)p. : ill. ; 8º
      With a final leaf of advertisements.
      Foxon P944; Griffith 35.
11631.bbb.39(2)

                                                t005729

POPE, Alexander, the Poet
      The rape of the lock. An heroi-comical poem. In five
      cantos. Written by Mr. Pope.. - The fourth edition
      corrected. - London: printed for Bernard Lintott, 1715.
      (10), 52, (2)p. : ill. ; 8º
      With a final leaf of advertisements.
      Foxon P946; Griffith 43.
12274.h.10

                                              t005730

POPE, Alexander, the Poet
      The rape of the lock. An heroi-comical poem. In five
      cantos. Written by Mr. Pope.. - The fifth edition. -
      London(i.e. The Hague?): printed for T. Johnson, 1716.
      30, (2)p. ; 8º
      In: The works of Mr. Alexander Pope, printed by Johnson
      for B. L., 1718. With a final leaf of advertisements.
      Foxon P947; Griffith 62.
12271.e.12

                                            t005731

POPE, Alexander, the Poet
      The rape of the lock: an heroi-comical poem. In five
      cantos. Written by Mr. Pope.. - The fifth edition
      corrected. - London: printed for Bernard Lintot, 1718.
      (10), 53, (1)p. : ill. ; 8º
      Foxon P948; Griffith 100.
12274.h.3(1)

                                            t005732

POPE, Alexander, the Poet
      The rape of the lock: an heroi-comical poem. In five
      cantos. Written by Mr. Pope.. - The sixth edition
      corrected. - London: printed for Bernard Lintot, 1723.
      (10), 53, (1)p. : ill. ; 8º
      Foxon P949; Griffith 140.
1164.b.5(1)

                                            t005733

POPE, Alexander, the Poet
      The rape of the lock. An heroi-comical poem. Written by
      Mr. Alexander Pope.. - Dublin: printed for J. Thompson,
      1729. 32p. ; 8⁰.
      Foxon P950; not in Griffith.
11630.aaa.45(3)

                                                      t005734

POPE, Alexander, the Poet
      The rape of the lock, an heroi-comical poem, by A. Pope.
      Adorned with plates.. - London: printed by T. Bensley;
      for F. J. du Roveray; and sold by J. and A. Arch; and J.
      Wright, 1798. xxix, (1), 79, (1)p., plates ; 8⁰.
      With a half-title.
1163.b.40

                                                        t005736

POPE, Alexander, the Poet
      The rape of the lock: an heroi-comical poem. By A. Pope,
      Esq. Adorned with plates designed by Stodhart, R.A.. -
      London: printed by Daniel Elzevir; and sold by William
      West; and T. J. Hookham, -1799. (2), 75, (1)p., plates :
      port. ; 16⁰.
      At foot of titlepage: Price seven shillings and sixpence
      with coloured plates; and five shillings plain.
Cup.550.aa.59

                                                        t005735

POPE, Alexander, the Poet
      A Roman Catholick version of the first psalm, for the
      use of a young lady. By Mr. Pope.. - London: printed for
      R. Burleigh, 1716. 2p. ; 1/2⁰.
      Drop-head title.
      Foxon P953; Griffith 58.
Ashley 5202

                                                        t005737

POPE, Alexander, the Poet
      The second epistle of the second book of Horace,
      imitated by Mr. Pope.. - London: printed for R. Dodsley,
      1737. 19, (1)p. ; 2⁰.
      Footnote on p. 12 misnumbered 16 (for 15); p. 4, line 16
      reading Godfry. The fine paper issue was apparently
      intended to accompany Coopers 1737 edition of the first
      epistle, issued with the general title The second book
      of the epistles of Horace (Foxon P882).
      Foxon P955,6; Griffith 447.
Ashley 4941
644.m.14(11)

                                                        t005738

POPE, Alexander, the Poet
        The second epistle of the second book of Horace,
        imitated by Mr. Pope.. - London: printed for R. Dodsley,
        1737. 19, (1)p. ; 2°
        Pp. 3-12 reset, the remainder reimpressed (Foxon); p. 4,
        line 16 reading Godfrey.
        Foxon P957.
1489.d.51
                                                              t005739

POPE, Alexander, the Poet
        The second epistle of the second book of Horace.
        Imitated by Mr. Pope. To Colonel *****. - (Edinburgh?):
        printed in the year, 1737. 19, (1)p. ; 8°
        Probably printed in Edinburgh.
        Foxon P958; Griffith 448.
1509/88
                                                              t005740

POPE, Alexander, the Poet
        The second satire of the second book of Horace
        paraphrased. By Mr. Pope.. - London(i.e. Edinburgh):
        printed for L. G., 1734. 20p. ; 8°
        The imprint is false; Printed by Ruddiman on the
        evidence of the ornaments (Foxon). Parallel Latin and
        English texts.
        Foxon P962; Griffith 344.
993.e.51(3)
                                                              t005741

POPE, Alexander, the Poet
        The second satire of the second book of Horace
        praprhased (sic). By the author of the first.. - London:
        printed by J. Wright for Lawton Gilliver, 1735(1734?).
        (2), 18p. ; 2°
        The author of the first = Alexander Pope. Publication
        date from Foxon. Parallel Latin and English texts.
        Foxon P964; Griffith 410.
1484.m.7(8)
                                                              t005742

POPE, Alexander, the Poet
        Several copies of verses on occasion of Mr. Gullivers
        travels. Never before printed.. - London: printed for
        Benj. Motte, 1727. 30p. ; 8°
        Usually attributed to Pope, perhaps in collaboration
        with Gay and Arbuthnot. With a half-title. Four poems
        only. Also issued as part of the second edition of
        Gullivers travels.
        Foxon S356; Griffith 187; Teerink 1224.
992.h.7(6)
                                                              t005743

POPE, Alexander, the Poet
    Several copies of verses on occasion of Mr. Gullivers
    travels. Never before printed.. - London: printed for
    Benj. Motte, 1727. 17, 14-30p. ; 8⁰.
    Another issue of Mottes edition, with an additional
    poem, on sig. *2, inserted between B4 and C1. Usually
    attributed to Pope, perhaps in collaboration with Gay
    and Arbuthnot. With a half-title. Also issued as part
    of the second edition of Gullivers travels.
    Foxon S357; Griffith 188; Teerink 1224.
Ashley 1302

                                                               t005744

POPE, Alexander, the Poet
    (Several copies of verses on occasion of Mr. Gullivers
    travels). Poems occasiond by reading the travels of
    Captain Lemuel Gulliver, explanatory and commendatory..
    - Dublin: printed by and for J. Hyde, 1727. 16p. ; 8⁰.
    Usually attributed to Pope, perhaps in collaboration
    with Gay and Arbuthnot. Four poems only.
    Foxon S358; Griffith 189; Teerink 1224.
12274.e.1(8)

                                                               t005745

POPE, Alexander, the Poet
    (Several copies of verses on occasion of Mr. Gullivers
    travels). Poems occasioned by reading the travels of
    Captain Lemuel Gulliver, explanatory and commendatory.
    .... - (Dublin?), (1727). 1 sheet ; 1/2⁰.
    Usually attributed to Pope, perhaps in collaboration
    with Gay and Arbuthnot. Four poems only.
    Foxon S359; Teerink 1224; not in Griffith.
1872.a.1(11)

                                                               t005746

POPE, Alexander, the Poet
    The sixth epistle of the first book of Horace imitated.
    By Mr. Pope.. - London: printed for L. Gilliver,
    1737(1738). (4), 15, (1)p. ; 2⁰.
    With a half-title. Publication date from Griffith.
    Parallel Latin and English texts.
    Foxon P965; Griffith 476.
644.m.14(9)
Ashley 5225

                                                               t005747

POPE, Alexander, the Poet
Sober advice from Horace, to the young gentlemen about
town. As deliverd in his second sermon. Imitated in the
manner of Mr. Pope. Together with the original text, as
restored by the Revd. R. Bentley ... And some remarks on
the version.. - London: printed for T. Boreman; sold by
the booksellers of London and Westminster, (1734). (3),
10, 10, (1)p. ; 2º
By Alexander Pope. Parallel Latin and English texts;
duplicate pagination. P. 5, line 3 reads amiss.
Foxon P968; Griffith 347.
840.m.1(18)
643.m.16(13)
162.n.43
Ashley 5223
t005748

POPE, Alexander, the Poet
Sober advice from Horace, to the young gentlemen about
town. As deliverd in his second sermon. Imitated in the
manner of Mr. Pope. Together with the original text, as
restored by the Revd. R. Bentley, ... And some remarks
on the version. - London: printed for T. Boreman; and
sold by the booksellers of London and Westminster,
(1735?). (3), 10, 10, (1)p. ; 2º
By Alexander Pope. Parallel Latin and English texts;
duplicate pagination. P. 5, line 3 reads amise; sheets
A-C are reset, the rest reimpressed (Foxon). Also
issued as part of made-up sets of the Works, possibly in
1739.
Foxon P969; Griffith 356.
Ashley 5222
t005749

POPE, Alexander, the Poet
Sober advice from Horace, to the young gentlemen about
town. As deliverd in his second sermon. Imitated in the
manner of Mr. Pope. Together with the original text, as
restored by the Revd. R. Bentley, ... And some remarks
on the version. - Dublin: London: printed. And, Dublin
re-printed by George Faulkner, 1735. (3), 10, 10, (1)p.
; 8º
By Alexander Pope. Parallel Latin and English texts;
duplicate pagination.
Foxon P971; not in Griffith.
T.902(10)
t005750

POPE, Alexander, the Poet
(Sober advice from Horace). A sermon against adultery:
being sober advice from Horace, to the young gentlemen
about town. As deliverd in his second sermon. Imitated
in the manner of Mr. Pope. Together with the original
text, as restored by the Revd R. Bentley, ... And some
remarks on the version.. - London: printed for T.
Cooper; and sold by the booksellers of London and
Westminster, (1738). (3), 10, 10, (1)p. ; 2º.
By Alexander Pope. A reissue of the (1735?) folio
edition of Sober advice from Horace, with a cancel
titlepage.
Foxon P973; Griffith 489.
11602.i.20(2)
Ashley 4938

t005751

POPE, Alexander, the Poet
Sober advice from Horace, to the young gentlemen about
town. As delivered in his second sermon. Imitated in the
manner of Mr. Pope. Together with the original text, as
restored by the Rev. R. Bentley, ... And some remarks on
the version. Likewise two letters and epigrams, not
inserted in the late editions of Mr. Popes works.. -
London: printed for T. Sewell, 1755. 24p. ; 8º.
By Alexander Pope. Parallel Latin and English texts.
Horizontal chain lines.
1487.b.4

t005752

POPE, Alexander, the Poet
The temple of fame: a vision. By Mr. Pope.. - London:
printed for Bernard Lintott, 1715. 52, (4)p. ; 8º.
With a half-title, and a 4-page proposal for Urrys
edition of Chaucer.
Foxon P974; Griffith 36.
C.59.ff.13(2)
Ashley 3768

t005753

POPE, Alexander, the Poet
The temple of fame: a vision. By Mr. Pope.. - The second
edition. - London: printed for Bernard Lintott, 1715.
52, (4)p., plate ; 8º.
With a half-title, and a 4-page catalogue of Books
printed for Bernard Lintott. The frontispiece, found in
the majority of copies, may be a later addition.
Foxon P975; Griffith 45.
12274.h.8

t005754

POPE, Alexander, the Poet
   (Temple of fame. Latin and English). Mr. Popes Temple of
   fame. And his Messiah, a sacred eclogue, in imitation of
   Virgils Pollio: translated into Latin. With the English
   prefixd to each poem. With a latin dedication to His
   Grace the Duke of Newcastle. By Usher Gahagan. Done
   since his confinement in one of the cells in Newgate.. -
   London: printed for B. Dickinson, 1748. vii. (1),
   62(i.e. 75), (1)p. ; 8⁰.
   Parallel English and Latin texts.   Pp. 65, 73-5 are
   misnumbered 52, 59, 58 and 62.
   Foxon G4; Griffith 634.
11602.ee.1(5)
                                                    t005755

POPE, Alexander, the Poet
   To the ingenious Mr. Moore, author of the celebrated
   worm-powder. By Mr. Pope.. - London: printed for E.
   Curll, 1716. 2p. ; 1/2⁰.
   Foxon P978; Griffith 53.
12273.m.1(6)
Ashley 5201
                                                    t005756

POPE, Alexander, the Poet
   The universal prayer. By the author of the Essay on
   man.. - London: printed for R. Dodsley, 1738. 7, (1)p. ;
   2⁰.
   The author of the Essay on man = Alexander Pope.
   Reading Incence in last line.
   Foxon P982; Griffith 492.
C.57.g.7(5)
C.131.h.1(4***)
                                                    t005757

POPE, Alexander, the Poet
   The universal prayer. By the author of the Essay on
   man.. - London: printed for R. Dodsley, 1738. 7, (1)p. ;
   2⁰.
   The author of the Essay on man = Alexander Pope. A
   different edition from the preceding, reading Incense in
   last line. Also issued as part of made-up sets of the
   Works, possibly in 1739.
   cf. Foxon P982.
Ashley 5233
                                                    t005758

POPE, Alexander, the Poet
   (Universal prayer. Latin and English). Alexandri Popii,
   sive universi generis humani, supplicatio latine reddita
   a Johanne Sayer, A.M.. - Londini: impensis W. Owen,
   1756. 15, (1)p. ; 4⁰.
   Translated by John Sayer. Parallel English and Latin
   texts.
11410.e.9
                                                    t005759

POPE, Alexander, the Poet
    (Verses on the grotto at Twickenham. Polyglot). Verses
    on the grotto at Twickenham. By Mr. Pope. Attempted in
    Latin and Greek. To which is added Horti Popiani: ode
    sapphica. Also The cave of Pope. A prophecy.. - London:
    printed for R. Dodsley; and sold by M. Cooper, 1743.
    16p. ; 4º.
    The Latin translations are by Robert Dodsley. No. IV,
    in Greek, is signed, W.H. ex aula S. Mari, Oxon.. No.
    VI, The cave of Pope, is by Dodsley. With the English
    text.
    Foxon D390; Griffith 576.
11656.r.7(10)

                                                    t005760

POPE, Alexander, the Poet
    Verses upon the late D-ss of M-. By Mr. P-------.. -
    London: printed for W. Webb, 1746. 5, (1)p. ; 2º.
    Mr. P------ = Alexander Pope. A suppressed passage from
    Popes Of the characters of women, probably referring to
    Katherine, Duchess of Buckingham rather than to Sarah,
    Duchess of Marlborough. Spacing of 14 and 10 mm.
    between V, E, R on p. 3 (Foxon).
    Foxon P985; cf. Griffith 613.
Ashley 4946

                                                    t005761

POPE, Alexander, the Poet
    Verses upon the late D-ss of M-. By Mr. P-------.. -
    London: printed for W. Webb, 1746. 5, (1)p. ; 2º.
    Mr. P------ = Alexander Pope. A suppressed passage from
    Popes Of the characters of women, probably referring to
    Katherine, Duchess of Buckingham, rather than to Sarah,
    Duchess of Marlborough. A different impression from the
    preceding: Spacing of 11 and 13.5 mm. between V, E, R on
    p. 3 (Foxon).
    Foxon P986; cf. Griffith 613.
11631.h.15

                                                    t005762

POPE, Alexander, the Poet
    Windsor-Forest. To the Right Honourable George Lord
    Lansdown. By Mr. Pope.. - London: printed for Bernard
    Lintott, 1713. (2), 18p. ; 2º.
    Foxon P987,8; Griffith 9.
643.l.26(6)
Ashley 4918
C.131.h.1(1) : On fine paper.

                                                    t005763

POPE, Alexander, the Poet
        Windsor-Forest. To the Right Honourable George Lord
        Lansdown. By Mr. Pope. To which is added, The rape of
        the locke: .... - Dublin: printed by S. P. (Stephen
        Powell) for G. Grierson, 1713. 48p. ; 12⁰.
        Includes also Sir Robert Howards The duel of the stags.
        The text of The rape of the locke is the two-canto
        version.
        Foxon P990; Griffith Add. 28a.
1488.de.46(4)
1606/1451(3) : Cropped at head, affecting some of the page
numbers.
                                                t005764

POPE, Alexander, the Poet
        Windsor-Forest. To the Right Honourable George Lord
        Lansdown. By Mr. Pope.. - The fourth edition. - London:
        printed for Bernard Lintot, 1720. 58, (6)p. : ill. ; 8⁰.
        Possibly issued in 1719. Includes also Popes Messiah.
        The last three leaves contain advertisements.
        Foxon P991; Griffith 125.
991.h.25(2) : Imperfect; wanting the three leaves of
advertisements.
                                                t005765

POPE, Alexander, the Poet
        Vinsorium nemus: carmen. Authore A. Pope. Latine
        reddidit G. Paterson, in academia A. Pollok, ... -
        Londini: typis Dav. Wilson, & T. Durham, 1758. viii, 26,
        (2)p. ; 4⁰.
        The recto of the final leaf contains errata.
1346.i.61 : MS. emendations and corrections.
                                                t005766

_____

POPE, Alexander, the Poet
        Are these things so? The previous question, from an
        Englishman in his grotto, to a great man at court. By
        Alexander Pope, Esq;. - Dublin: London: printed, and
        Dublin reprinted, in the year, 1740. 16p. ; 8⁰.
        The attribution to Pope is false; in fact by James
        Miller. Editions without attribution on the titlepage
        are entered under Miller. Sig. A2 under my.
        Foxon M241; Griffith 520.
11633.bbb.40
                                                t005767

POPE, Alexander, the Poet
    Are these things so? The previous question, from an
    Englishman in his grotto, to a great man at court. By
    Alexander Pope, Esq;. - Dublin: London: printed, and
    Dublin re-printed in the year, 1740. 16p. ; 8º.
    The attribution to Pope is false; in fact by James
    Miller. Sig. A2 unsigned.
    Foxon M243.
1488.bb.30

                                                    t005768

POPE, Alexander, the Poet
    Are these things so? The previous question, from an
    English-man in his grotto. To a great man at court. By
    Alexander Pope, Esq; To which is added, the answer, Yes
    , they are!. - Dublin: London: printed, and Dublin
    re-printed in the year, 1740. 10p. ; 8º.
    The attribution to Pope is false; in fact by James
    Miller. Without the answer Yes, they are; p. 10
    concludes Finis. Probably issued with one of the Dublin
    editions of Yes, they are.
    Foxon M245.
1486.s.8

                                                    t005769

POPE, Alexander, the Poet
    Court poems. Viz; I. The basset-table. An eclogue. II.
    The drawing-room. III. The toilet. A copy of verses to
    the ingenious Mr. Moore, author of the celebrated
    worm-powder. All four by Mr. Pope. To which is added W.
    T. to fair Clio.. - Dublin: reprinted by S. Powell; for
    G. Risk, 1716. 24p. ; 12º.
    The greatest share in the authorship of these verses is
    that of Lady Mary Wortley Montagu. Only the verses To
    ... Mr. Moore are by Pope. W. T. = William Tunstall.
    Griffith 64; Foxon, p. 476.
1162.f.34

                                                    t005771

POPE, Alexander, the Poet
    (Court poems. 1717.040). Popes miscellany. Viz. I. The
    basset-table. II. The drawing-room. III. The toilet. IV.
    The looking-glass. V. The worms. VI. The first psalm.
    Translated for the use of a young lady. .... - The
    second edition. - London: printed for R. Burleigh (or
    rather, Edmund Curll), 1717. (4), 22, (2)p. ; 12º.
    Only The worms and The first psalm are by Pope. A
    second part was also published in 1717; copies were
    reissued in Court Poems, 1719. With a final leaf of
    advertisements.
    Griffith 90; Foxon, p. 476.
1346.d.33(4)
12274.e.5(1) : MS. notes by F. Grant.

                                                    t005773

POPE, Alexander, the Poet
(Court poems. 1717.050). Popes miscellany. The second
part. Containing, I. The Hyde-Park ramble. II. The
parsons-daughter. III. The court-ballad. IV. Court
epigrams. To which is added, The Westminster ballad: ...
By Mr. Joseph Gay.. - London: printed for R. Burleigh
(or rather, Edmund Curll), 1717. (2), 24p. ; 12º.
Only The court-ballad and Court-epigrams are by Pope.
Joseph Gay is a pseudonym for John Durant Breval. Also
found as part II of Court poems, 1719, and of Court
poems, 1726.
Griffith 89; Foxon, p. 476.
12274.e.5(2)

t005774

POPE, Alexander, the Poet
Court poems. In two parts. By Mr. Pope, &c.. - London:
printed for E. Curll, 1726. (2), 34; 24p. ; 12º.
A number of the pieces in part I, and two of the pieces
in part II are by Pope. Part I is also found in
Miscellanea. The second volume., 1727. Part II is made
up of remaindered sheets from Popes miscellany. The
second part., 1717. P. 3 in the first part is
misnumbered p. 1. Sig. B2 is misprinted A2.
Pt. I - Griffith 176; pt. II = Griffith 89; Foxon, p.
476.
1347.d.53 : Pp. 25-34 of pt. I are misbound after p. 24 of pt.
II.

t005775

POPE, Alexander, the Poet
An imitation of the sixth satire of the second book of
Horace. ... The first part done in the year 1714, by Dr.
Swift. The latter part now first added, and never before
printed.. - London: printed for B. Motte and C.
Bathurst, and J. and P. Knapton, 1738. (4), 23, (1)p. ;
2º.
Most of the additions to this edition are by Alexander
Pope. Parallel Latin and English texts.
Foxon S860; Griffith 479; Teerink 757.
643.m.14(12)

t005776

POPE, Alexander, the Poet
Miscellaneous poems and translations. By several hands..
- London: printed for Bernard Lintott, 1712. (8), 320,
(3), 356-76, (8)p., plate ; 8º.
Contains a number of poems by Alexander Pope, including
the first printing of The rape of the locke, in two
cantos. The whole probably edited by Pope. With a
half-title; the last four leaves contain advertisements.
 The pagination leaps, without loss. Pp. 110, 194 are
misnumbered 101 and 491.
Griffith 6; Case 260(1)(a).
C.71.e.26

t005777

POPE, Alexander, the Poet
Miscellaneous poems and translaticns. By several hands.
Particularly The first bock of Statius his Thebais
translated ... By Mr. Pope.. - The second edition. -
London: printed for Bernard Lintott, and William Lewis,
1714. (8), 322, (2), 321-376, (10), 377-424p., plate ; 8⁰.
A reissue of the edition of 1712, with a new titlepage
and half-title, and with additional material, mostly by
Pope.   The whole probably edited by Pcpe.
Griffith 32; Case 260(1)(b).
C.125.d.29 : In this copy the original titlepage and half-title
have been left uncancelled, and are bound, with the two leaves
of contents, before the half-title for the second edition.
Without the errata leaf found in some copies. Imperfect;
wanting the titlepage to The rape of the locke.
Ashley 3766

t005778

POPE, Alexander, the Poet
Miscellaneous poems and translaticns, by several hands.
Particularly, I. Windsor-Forest, ... By Mr. Pope.. - The
third edition. - London: printed for Bernard Lintot,
1720. 2v. : ill., port. ; 12⁰.
Vol. 2 contains only cne piece by Pope; the whole
probably edited by him.
Griffith 124; Case 260(1)(c) & (2)(b).
12274.e.9 : Imperfect; wanting vol. 2 and the frontispiece to
vol. 1.

t005779

POPE, Alexander, the Poet
Miscellaneous poems and translations, by several hands.
Particularly, I. Windsor-Forest, ... By Mr. Pope. - The
fourth edition. - London: printed for Bernard Lintot,
1722. 2v. : ill., port. ; 12⁰.
The whole probably edited by Pope. Titlepage in red and
black.
Griffith 135; Case 260(1)(d).
Cup.402.i.17
12274.e.10 : Imperfect; wanting vol. 2.

t005780

POPE, Alexander, the Poet
(Miscellaneous poems and translations.1712. 1726).
Miscellany poems. Vol. I. By Mr Pope. - The fifth
edition. - London: printed for Bernard Lintot, 1726-27.
2v., plate : port. ; 12⁰.
The whole probably edited by Pope.
Griffith 164; not in Case.
11609.aaa.33,34

t005781

POPE, Alexander, the Poet
(Miscellaneous poems and translations.1712. 1727).
Miscellany poems. Vol. I. By Mr. Pope.. - The fifth
edition. - London: printed for Bernard Lintot, 1727.
2v., plate : port. ; 12º
The whole probably edited by Pope. Vol. 1 is a reissue
of the edition of 1726 with a new titlepage.
Griffith 192; Case 260(1)(e).
12274.f.2 : Imperfect; wanting vol. 2.

t005782

POPE, Alexander, the Poet
Miscellanies in verse and prose, by Mr. Pope; found
amongst his papers after his death, and now first
publishd by Mr. Warburton.. - Dublin: printed for
William Ranson, 1748. 75, (1)p. ; 12º
The attribution to Pope is false.
994.d.23

t005783

POPE, Alexander, the Poet
     (Letters.1735). Letters of Mr. Pope, and several eminent persons
     from the year 1705, to 1711. ... - Dublin: re-printed by G.
     Faulkner. Sold by him, by R. Gunne, and by J. Smith and W. Bruce,
     1735. 2v. ; 12°.
     The titlepage to vol. 1 is a cancel; that to vol. 2 bears the
     imprint "Dublin: printed by M. Rhames, for R. Gunne, J. Smith and
     W. Bruce, and G. Faulkner".

1568/5458.

POPE, Alexander, the Poet
     (Of false taste). An epistle to the Right Honourable Richard Earl
     od Burlington. Occasion'd by his publishing Palladio's designs of
     the baths, arches, theatres, &c. of ancient Rome. By Mr. Pope. -
     London: printed for L. Gilliver, 1731 (1732). 14, (2)p. ; 2°.
     Half-title: "Of false taste, ..."; twelve books advertised on
     recto of final leaf. - "A reimpression" (Foxon). - Todd's edition.
     - Publication date from Foxon.
     Foxon P911; Griffith 265.
1565/37.

POPE, Alexander, the Poet
     One thousand seven hundred and thirty eight. A dialogue something
     like Horace. By Mr. Pope. - London: printed for T. Cooper, (1738).
     (4), 10, (2)p. ; 2°.
     A re-impression of the preceding, with the titlepage partly reset;
     sig. D under "behind". - With a half-title, and a final leaf of
     advertisements.
     Foxon P934; Griffith 486.
1565/36.

(Another copy) Essay on man. Epistles 1-4. (1733-34). Foxon P822, 833,
     839, 845; Griffith 294, 300, 313, 331. C. 143.g.4(4-7).

(Another copy) First satire of the second book of Horace, imitated. 1733.
     Foxon P886; Griffith 288. C.143.g.4(8).

(Another copy) (Of false taste). An epistle to the Right Honourable
     Richard Earl of Burlington. 1731. Foxon P908; Griffith 259.
     C.143.g.4(1).

(Another copy) (Of the knowledge and characters of men). An epistle to the
     Right Honourable Richard Lord Visct. Cobham. 1733. Foxon P920;
     Griffith 329. C.143.g.4(3).

(Another copy) Of the use of riches. (1733). Foxon P923,4; Griffith 280-2.
     C.143.g.4(2).

- - - - (Works. 1776). The works of Alexander Pope, Esq. 1776.
     Format: 12°. 12274.e.4.

- - - - (Poems). The poetical works, ... Glasgow: printed by Andrew Foulis,
     1785. 3v. ; 2°.
     Footnote refers to copy at 75.i.2-3, not 1505/352 as stated.

- - - - Rape of the lock. 1799.
     Footnote: With 'plain' plates. - Imperfect; wanting the half-title.
     Cup.550.aa.59.